BORN TO TRAVEL

By

Drew Carruthers

Grosvenor House
Publishing Limited

All rights reserved
Copyright © Drew Carruthers, 2022

The right of Drew Carruthers to be identified as the author of this
work has been asserted in accordance with Section 78
of the Copyright, Designs and Patents Act 1988

The book cover is copyright to Drew Carruthers

This book is published by
Grosvenor House Publishing Ltd
Link House
140 The Broadway, Tolworth, Surrey, KT6 7HT.
www.grosvenorhousepublishing.co.uk

This book is sold subject to the conditions that it shall not, by way of
trade or otherwise, be lent, resold, hired out or otherwise circulated
without the author's or publisher's prior consent in any form of binding or
cover other than that in which it is published and
without a similar condition including this condition being imposed
on the subsequent purchaser.

A CIP record for this book
is available from the British Library

ISBN 978-1-83975-815-7

TABLE OF CONTENTS

Chapter 1-The Early Days	1
Chapter 2-The Road to Kuwait	22
Chapter 3-Scorpions Don't Play Chess	38
Chapter 4-A New Broom Sweeps Clean	51
Chapter 5-A Miracle in the Desert	63
Chapter 6-Relics and Guns	75
Chapter 7-A Wimpey Wins the Day	87
Chapter 8-Lessons Learned	97
Chapter 9-A New Washing Machine	109
Chapter 10-The Game Hunter	121
Chapter 11-Caves and Cockroaches	135
Chapter 12-We Don't Throw Stones Anymore	150
Chapter 13-Smell the scene	165
Chapter 14-Wonders of the Desert	173
Chapter 15-Modern Day Pirates	192
Chapter 16-It's 5 o'clock somewhere	206
Chapter 17-He Might Have Been Shot	231

Chapter 18-Cruising Down the River Li	249
Chapter 19-Keeping Warm in Tiananmen Square	263
Chapter 20-Keep Your Camera Handy	274
Chapter 21-Fish Can Fly	289
Chapter 22-Too Young to Retire	294
Chapter 23-Bond and Bombs	308
Epilogue	328

PREFACE

On the 14th February 1957, I was fifteen years, five months, and six days old. That day, I joined the Royal Air Force (RAF) as a 'boy entrant'. They taught me discipline, to follow orders and to believe the words of my superiors. In 1942, the Second World War raged throughout Europe. I recall the conflict because people who lived in those times cannot forget it. My father believed there would be no more war, but history proved him wrong. They drummed it into me. "We are in a new war, the 'Cold War'. Russia is our enemy." They made me proud to be a British citizen, and I wanted this new enemy to be destroyed. Two months after I took the Queen's shilling for which I swore an oath to protect her subjects, Britain dropped an atom bomb near Christmas Island in the Indian Ocean. I cheered as I watched the film showing the mushroom of smoke ascending into the air. I wanted to blow up the people who didn't agree with my government's views. At fifteen years old, I had little knowledge of sex, far less of knowing why I would want to blow up hundreds of thousands of human beings.

For fourteen years, I did my duty and made the world a better place. At least, that is what I thought. I followed the rules and never questioned if what I was doing was right or wrong. My government had promised me a long and rewarding career, but they lied to me and cut my career short because they did not want to pay my pension. When I left the military in 1972, the British people were seeking freedom from oppression, but to get it they had to sell their souls to trade unions and anarchists. I experienced more brainwashing and found it difficult to adjust to civilian life. In 1977, I left my job and set off to work in Kuwait.

For most of my life, I worked in countries other than my own and saw how different cultures lived and did things differently from what I was used to. During that time, I met world leaders, sheikhs, government ministers, rich people and people similar to myself. One time, I tried to teach the wife of a governor to toss rice in a basket. Another time, I made a 'no smoking' pact with the chief of police and head of the secret police in southern China. During that time, I formed new opinions.

My book is about working and living in the Middle East deserts, the jungles of Borneo and the Special Economic Zones (SEZs) in China. It is about people and beauty. It will make you think again about how you perceive these countries, their leaders and the people they rule. My travels changed my perception of the world. Possibly, my book will change yours.

CHAPTER 1

THE EARLY DAYS

In today's world, a child might travel to several countries by the time they are fifteen years old. In the world I grew up in, the furthest a child travelled was to Blackpool or, going the other way, to Edinburgh Zoo. As a youth, I travelled once to Northern Ireland to play football. A chance to see the world came when I reached fifteen years old. I journeyed to Glasgow to sign up as a boy entrant in the Royal Air Force. By the time I reached sixteen, I had visited every country in Britain. I visited cities, but my heart loved the countryside and country people.

In the fifties, Britain was recovering from the Second World War and was facing new threats from Russia and China. By joining the RAF, it meant opportunities for me, as I could volunteer for overseas postings, which would give me a chance to travel the world.

Films gave me an idea of where I wanted to go and as soon as I was old enough, I applied for a posting to Hong Kong. My uncle was posted there when he was in the army, but for reasons unknown to me, it was cancelled and he never got to see it. I decided I should go there to find out what he had missed. When confirmation of my posting came through, I jumped for joy and waited patiently for the date of departure to arrive. A few weeks after my nineteenth birthday, I said my goodbyes and waited on the station platform for the train to take me to RAF Lyneham from where I would fly. The train stopped, and I opened the door, but before I could get my kitbag inside I heard someone shout my name. An orderly rushed down the embankment and screamed, "Don't get on the train, it's cancelled, you're not going to Hong Kong!"

The news shocked me, and my friends were surprised to see me back at work. A few nights later, at the cinema, the love of my life, who I had sadly left behind, sat with another man's arm around her shoulders. I was devastated.

Days later, I reported to the administration office and was given another departure card and the following day. I waited again for the train to take me to RAF Lyneham to board a flight to Malta. What a let-down, I wanted Hong Kong! I'd been let down a second time, first seeing my girlfriend with someone else and now I was off to Malta and not Hong Kong. I felt that I just wanted to get away from the disappointments. Would it be as inspiring as my dream destination? I was in no mood to think about it.

It was breakfast time as we touched down at Luqa airport. Tired, hungry and ignored by the orderlies, who gave priority to married families, I sat and waited. After an hour, a corporal, accompanied by a man in civilian clothes, approached me. The corporal introduced the man. "This is Mr Vella, he will take you to Takali, your new base."

Only toast and cold porridge were available for breakfast because, by the time I reached the mess, they had cleared the hot food away. It had been four hours since I had eaten so when friendly Mr Vella invited me to his house for lunch and to meet his wife, I readily agreed.

I liked Mrs Vella, a rounded woman with a cheery smile. Her much smaller husband took a bottle of brandy from the cupboard and filled two glasses. By the time Mrs Vella served the rabbit stew accompanied by a large plate of dark and very crusty bread, my eyes were closing from lack of sleep and brandy. I had eaten many a rabbit as a child, but they were roasted or boiled. This one had been put in a casserole dish and covered by a spicy tomato sauce, which I enjoyed.

After Mr Vella had consumed most of the bottle of brandy, he became talkative and described Takali. It was good that I was posted there because this was where the VIP flight was based. Top brass from the three military services and the North Atlantic Treaty Organization (NATO) flew from there to destinations around the Mediterranean. He moved on to pubs and clubs. "If you want a cheap drink, go to the Labour Club, on the right-hand side, halfway down the walking street," he advised.

Mrs Vella interrupted, "If you want to meet a nice girl, then you should go there, but stay away from the street further down, drunken sailors and bad girls go there."

Mr Vella had the last word. "It's called 'The Gut' and comes to life when the fleet is in port."

I thanked Mrs Vella for my lunch and set off for Takali with a slightly intoxicated Mr Vella at the wheel. He drove slowly, arriving just in time for me to get bedding from the quartermaster and collect my arrival card from the administration office. Every airman had to visit places like the payroll department, security, their workplace, and sign for such things as bedding. When all the important sections had signed your arrival card, you knew you would get paid at the end of the month. My first impression of the base was that it was small compared to my previous home. What did not impress me was the corrugated tin hut I would share with seven other airmen, but they made me welcome. Military police were based here and occupied several huts near to mine. I had no time for the police because they gave me a hard time when I was a boy entrant.

My boss was Chief Hank Jansen. He never raised his voice and had a laid-back attitude, because of this he was highly respected. As there were less than 300 airmen on the base, I got to know almost everyone in a short time. The military police were okay people, and I played football regularly with them.

Malta's economy depended on the 10,000 military personnel based there. Daily life revolved around sports, bars, and the deserted beaches scattered throughout the island. Getting around required transport, and the island had an excellent bus service. The road to Rabat passed close to the base and a regular blue bus passed that way, ending its circuit at the central bus station in Valletta. From there, I could catch a green bus to stops in Sliema and St. Paul's Bay. Each destination had its bus colour.

As soon as June arrived, I headed with my mates to the Sliema front, or Golden Bay, to swim and meet girls. Work interested me, but I wanted a good time as well. In the summer months, work finished at 1pm, so there was plenty of spare time to play football and enjoy myself.

The highlight of my week was the Saturday night dance at the Phoenicia Hotel. I thought this hotel was posh because I was used to chairs or benches set around dancehall walls, and if you asked a girl up to dance, she never refused. Girls here were accompanied by their parents or a chaperone. I considered myself to be a gentleman, so the first time I wanted to ask a girl to dance, I decided to ask her parent's permission. With a light swagger, I approached and stood in front of her father. I think I used the wrong words. "Can I please hit the dance floor with your gorgeous daughter?"

"No," was his firm reply.

Later, I saw her get up and dance with another lad, I guessed her father took me for a drunken sailor because of my swaggering approach.

Despite the strict rules, I still enjoyed myself. Sex before marriage was frowned upon in this culture and era, but that did not mean that the young women were housebound. My friends and I met a fantastic group of girls but they were subjected to a 10pm curfew on a weeknight and 11pm on Saturday. On Sundays they were allowed out after they had been to church. Without their parents' knowledge, most Saturday nights we met them in Paul Vela's bar and Sunday afternoons we met at Golden Bay.

One of my closest friend's – Lamps – hobby was to photograph feet. He did not stick photographs of girl's faces or movie stars on the inside of his locker, it was plastered in feet. What a weird thing to do! He had plenty of opportunities for his photography on the golden sands. As a group, we had a good time at weekends, but kissing a girl at the beach on a Sunday – there was no chance. Carmen, a dark-haired, black-eyed beauty and my favourite girl, let me walk her home once. I never forgot that goodnight kiss, the only one I got – or was it?

For young single men, one big problem existed. If a girl agreed to sex, you couldn't go to the barber's shop and buy protection the way you could in the UK. Lamps had heard that the quartermaster gave out French letters, and they were free, but he never dared to ask. Putting on a brave face, I stepped through the door into the store. The quartermaster was reading a book and two airmen were stacking items on shelves. The quartermaster looked at me. "Can I help you?"

I whispered, "Sergeant, can I have some 'French letters' please?"

He straightened up, and I knew he recognised me. "The correct term is 'condom' and no, you can't have any, because you are not married. They are issued to married couples only."

He spoke loud enough for others to hear, and I heard sniggering. I wanted to hit him for embarrassing me, but I knew better than to do anything silly. I never understood why they gave free condoms to families, but not to single servicemen.

One afternoon, I was sunbathing on the rocks at Sliema beach and I took hold of a girl's hand. Someone tapped me on the shoulder and when I looked up, a man shoved a police card in my face and told me, "No touching." This puzzled me, as the previous night, I visited The Gut and saw a show where a woman performed sex acts. There was never any trouble down The Gut because of a police officer called 'Tiny'. No one messed with Tiny, who, at seven feet tall, could pick up a sailor in each hand and crack their heads together. Despite this mammoth of a man, the troops had an amazing, exciting and unforgettable time there.

With so many restrictions on my love life, I satisfied my frustrations on the football field. The games were always competitive because of the large numbers of military personnel on the island. Takali may have been a small base, but we were top of the league. Maltese international footballers joined the Maltese Air Force and were based there so, with quality players, including myself, an ex-schoolboy international goalkeeper, we did not lose many games. The best football pitch to play on after the national one in Sliema was the one at Corradino Military Prison. Consequently, many of the games were played there. The prison was run by the army and the formidable guards, with their slashed peak caps covering their nearly bald heads, and necks that rippled with muscles, were not to be upset. I hated being disciplined and ducked down as the bus passed through the gate in case one of them didn't like the way I looked at them and dragged me out of the bus.

Professional teams came to Malta to relax, train and prepare for top tournaments, and they wanted practice matches. I was honoured to play for the combined services team in matches against some of the best players in the world. The most memorable was against Benfica, who beat us, but I had the acclaim of letting in two goals scored by Eusébio, the number one player in the world in that decade.

Most of us have good days and bad days. Playing football was a good day and military exercises were always bad days. I hated exercises because I never knew what day they would start or end and that interfered with my social life. The authorities only ever gave out the bare facts. During one exercise, the commander gave me a password to memorise, then a regiment corporal placed a black hood over my head and drove me to an isolated spot. When he removed my hood, I recognised where I was as it was near the Blue Grotto, where I had been previously. The aim was to make my way back to base without being captured by the enemy, which was the army. If I got captured, I must only give my name and service number, but not the code word, 'Red Apple'.

My survival time, before being captured by a fully armed troop in battle dress, lasted for twenty minutes.

One of my captors shoved the butt of his gun into my belly and barked, "What is the code?"

This guy was not huge, but his mates were, but it didn't bother me because I knew the rules of the game. The enemy must not use physical torture to extract information. No man, even one with corporal stripes, had the power to get the code out of me. I gave my name, rank and number.

"Tell me the code!" the little runt bawled.

I laughed in his face.

A soldier handed the runt a baseball bat, but I knew the rules: 'no physical harm'. I laughed out loud.

The runt bawled, "Last chance, give me the code!

He was getting desperate. "Go to hell," I screamed back, "it's time to go home!"

One part of their weaponry was puzzling me. I couldn't think of a reason they would carry an empty galvanised bucket. I soon found out when one of them put it over my head.

"For the last time, the code!" the runt screamed.

"No," I screamed back.

The sound deafened me, stars jumped around inside the bucket and my head. As the second strike of the bat hit the bucket, I was blinded and was sure death would come at any moment. I cried out, "The apple is green."

Someone removed the bucket from my head and the little runt thanked me for the information and drove me back to base.

My commander congratulated me for not giving the correct code, which was 'Red Apple', and not 'The apple is green'. My lying had worked and gained me praise from the higher echelon of command. A perk for the pain I had suffered.

Soon after this exercise, Hank asked me if I liked entertainment. Was this going to be a reward for not divulging the code?

I suspected his question had an alternative motive, as I understood from others that friendly questions could have a hidden agenda. You never volunteered in the military because there was always a catch and I fell for it by telling him the truth. "I love entertainment."

"Good, there will be a celebration soon, and I want to put on a good show. You can be in charge of organising the party."

"Thanks, Chief." I cursed under my breath. My boss was sneaky.

Two weeks later, the Malta to Gozo ferry sailed out of Valletta harbour. On board were 500 military personnel, their wives, girlfriends and several dignitaries. The ferry cruised around the island with passengers enjoying the sunset. This was followed by a buffet meal and dancing to a real orchestra. A fantastic time was had by all, and I organised it. Chief Hank was pleased.

Another good night out happened on my twentieth birthday. I don't know how Chief Hank knew, but he let the secret out in front of some friends. That night, at an impromptu party, twenty of us congregated in a lounge at the Xara Palace Hotel within the walls of the silent city of Mdina. With no draught beer available, we were on bottles of Blue or Cisk. As the table filled with empty bottles, Don cleared them by stacking empties into two fireplaces in the room, instead of taking them back to the bar. We followed his example and before long, the fireplaces were full of empty bottles. The hotel manager came to wish me a happy birthday and asked us to keep the noise down. Xavier, who knew us from earlier visits, was a good sport who kept control, preventing us from getting too carried away. His parting words were, "And no stealing the ashtrays."

The noise became louder as we drank more than we should have. Adam asked for silence and said, "We can't go back with just ashtrays in our pockets. We have to show Xavier that we can take anything we want and not be caught."

That generated suggestions ranging from stealing a pair of knickers from a guest bedroom to kidnapping one of the gorgeous girls from reception. Unbelievably, our befuddled, soused brains fixed our minds on absconding with the piano.

I'm not sure how we managed it, but we wheeled it through the silent city, arousing nobody. Our usual shortcut down the goat track passed through vineyards and that would be problematic so we wheeled it two miles along the main road back to base. We needed to create a diversion to get it past the main gate, this was no problem with Alex in our group. He rushed up to the guardroom window and screamed, "I am going to be sick!"

As one guard opened the door to see what was going on, Alex crashed through it and while the snoops were occupied, we opened the gate and wheeled our prize through. Poor Alex spent a night in the cells, but he didn't mind, he still got a good night's sleep. As it was my birthday, I had the job of informing Xavier that we had stolen his prized piano. He was not pleased and in colourful language, demanded its immediate return.

A mate from transport arranged for a covered truck and, fortunately, as we passed the guard room with the piano on board, we were waved on and the guard opened the gate. I was so glad he waved us through because if he had asked questions, I would have been put on a charge and my previous good deeds would be obliterated by a big black mark. Our favourite hotel manager forgave us when he saw the piano was not damaged. I bet our escapade joined his repertoire of stories that he would relate many times to his customers for many years to come.

Luck played a part when Chief Hank once more asked for a volunteer and I stepped forward. My astonished buddies gawped in disbelief at me. 'You never volunteer' was an unwritten rule. I would not regret this action. He asked for an assistant to help the current crew chief during flights around the Mediterranean. What he wanted was someone to serve tea and coffee to the VIPs on board. It was the right decision because I flew several times to Italy, Libya and Egypt, and learned much from Lenny, the crew chief. One time we flew to Idris in Libya just to bring back Christmas trees. I don't know where they sourced the trees as Idris is in the desert.

On arrival at a destination, the passengers, usually generals, were whisked off in official cars and I never saw them until they arrived back for the return flight. One time we had two male passengers dressed in civilian clothes on board. After we landed at Idris airport, Lenny and I were first off to supervise the ground crew, who were connecting the external power supply and waiting for me to open the cargo hold door. Only this time, there was no cargo. As the passengers alighted, they stood in a line and waited as three Landrovers, one flying a pennant, approached the aircraft. Two of the vehicles stopped, while the one with the pennant drove up close. A Libyan army officer got out and placed his cap, with a scrambled egg peak, on his head and came forward. Lenny whispered, "That's Colonel Gaddafi."

I hadn't heard that name before Lenny mentioned it. Everyone now knows the name of this infamous character. I was oblivious to his importance.

None of the VIPs came to attention as they shook his hand. I presumed it was because the colonel was of lower rank. Before shaking his hand, Lenny stood straight and brought his heels together and I did the same. Only now do I realise I met and shook the hand of the man who would become the Libyan leader. We flew back to Takali after whatever business was discussed on that important day.

The RAF allowed airmen to stay in an overseas post for a maximum of three years. They only gave me two and a half in Malta. Perhaps the authorities were worried in case I got the girls on the island pregnant. There was no chance of that because culture and opportunity were against any amorous inclinations. At the end of my tour, I flew back to a cold winter.

My next posting to the Norfolk Fens was different to the sea and sunshine of the Mediterranean. There they either have fog, rain or snow and most of the time, all three. Those responsible for my career move wanted me to experience the cold war and posted me to a V bomber base. My first job was to do prefight checks on Valiant bombers. They are not small, but in a dense fog, they were difficult to find.

For a young junior technician, my job offered plenty of challenges, and I had to learn quickly. I received good training on how to deal with nuclear accidents and how the bomb release mechanisms worked. Bombs were transported back and forth from the bomb dump on a trailer towed by a tractor. A favourite trick of mine was to ride on the bomb just like someone riding a horse. I never considered the power under my backside, as I rode across the airfield with my legs straddled across an atom bomb.

Airfields with V bombers had to be operational twenty-four hours a day, even on the snowiest days in winter. Teams took turns to clear the runway with a snow-flow, a massive plough driven by a jet engine with a fuel bowser behind it. My job required me to stand on a platform between the bowser and the engine. I was given a two-way radio to communicate with the bowser driver and operate the engine controls according to his instructions. That is the closest I came to flying a plane. When my stint finished, this frozen airman swigged down a warming large tot of rum, normally only given to naval personnel.

My worst nightmare happened when the snow started just after midnight. I was ordered to wake up those that didn't turn out for snow duty. Unable to wake one of them, I knocked hard on his door but there was no reply. I banged more and shouted until I woke up the neighbours. An upstairs window opened, and I looked up, but not in time to avoid the basin of water. I can't repeat the words of the female whose tousled head was poking through the window. The sergeant who lived in the house was in my section at work, so I made up a story that explained why I was soaked and for his non-arrival for snow duty. I downed two tots of rum that night. The following day, my promotion to corporal came through and that made me happy. The sergeant congratulated me on my promotion and his wife forgave me for swearing. I forgave her for throwing the water over me.

As well as getting doused in water by an irate wife, there were two things I didn't like about my job. These were exercises and being on QRA (Quick Reaction Alert). The exercises meant preparing the V bombers to take off and land at another airfield. I suppose they did that in case of war and wanted to keep the location of the bombers secret. When the siren sounded, you knew that for a few hours there would be no relaxation. Aircraft under maintenance or repair were hastily but carefully reassembled and made ready to fly. When all the serviceable bombers were in the air, we were informed where they would land. It could have been anywhere in the world, but usually, it was Cranwell, home to the Royal Air Force College (RAFC) that trained new officers and aircrew. It was where brown grass was painted green and probably still is.

After my first visit to Cranwell, I realised that as a Bomber Command unit, we were not liked. I guess we were not posh enough. The officers there despised a lack of discipline. They didn't like us because it was known that in winter we wore flannelette pyjama bottoms tucked into our socks beneath our coveralls, to keep warm. We were a scruffy, proud outfit, and we stuck together. It was a fact; we were the best at everything.

My most memorable time on a visit to Cranwell was the time the commanding officer kicked our unit off the station. When the bombers returned to Cranwell, we had to do the after-flight checks, fix any faults and get them ready to take off at a moment's notice. We were lucky if we finished before 2200 hours. One night, we were lucky and finished early. After readying the bombers for their next flight, we headed to Sleaford for a well-earned relaxing pint and that night we caused trouble.

Sleaford is a busy market town whose skyline is dominated by the 144-foot stone spire of St. Denys' Church. It has an ancient heritage and notable historic buildings, including the remains of a twelfth-century castle where the ailing King John is supposed to have been taken after his accident in the Wash estuary. We weren't interested in historical sites and facts and I can't remember anything about King John, but I remember the good pubs and a superb Chinese restaurant.

The night out started well but went from bad to worse after the second pub. We lost more games of darts to a Sleaford team than we won. With the losers buying the round, it was expensive and we quickly got intoxicated. At closing time, we were all starving and wanted to devour a tasty Chinese meal. The restaurant was busy, so we knew to be on our best behaviour and not give them any cause to ask us to leave. Ron spoke to the waiter in a slurred voice. "Sorry, but we have spent all our cash, can we have a meal and come back tomorrow to square the bill?"

"You must pay after your meal," the waiter insisted. I had a brilliant idea. I took out my 1250 ID card and held it in front of him.

"You see this, it has my name, rank and number. If we don't come back, you can report us."

"I will talk to my boss."

The boss looked to be a nice guy until he insisted, "If you cannot pay, you will not be served, so why do you come here?"

Ron answered him. "We are visitors to the airbase up the road and have enjoyed a night out in your lovely town, but we did not bring enough money with us and we are hungry."

"How much do you have?" We scraped together all we had and laid it on the table. He checked it. "You can have eggs and chips and two large bottles of beer to share, but no credit."

We agreed and sat down at the table. After two eggs and a decent sized plate of chips, plus more beer, we left the restaurant and burst into song as we stumbled back to the base. Minutes later, Cliff called out that he needed a piss and disappeared along a bushy path. A few moments later, a police car pulled up. Two officers got out, one of them was twice the size of the other. I considered whether to run or stay. I decided it might be better to listen to the bigger of the two. "Complaints have been received about you lot. Your antics in the restaurant and the noise you're making that you consider to be singing is not acceptable in this town."

No one had time to answer, Cliff exited from the track and called out, "That's better, nothing beats a good piss?"

The officer approached him, "Is that right, where did you have your piss?"

"Oh, it's all right, Officer, I didn't piss in public. I pissed up there against a big wall."

The officer was getting red in the face as he blurted the words out, "That wall you pissed against is the side of my church and you have desecrated it."

We were all very apologetic because we wanted to avoid a night in the cells. If that happened, we'd be in more trouble.

The bigger officer calmed down. "Right, you see that sign there? That's where the town ends and I don't care what you do after that. Just get the hell out of here."

That was a big relief, and I knew we were in the clear until Ron pleaded, "Can I have a lift back to Cranwell?"

His answer must have been heard a mile away. The words were garbled, but they included a swear word followed by off and what sounded like you and then maybe idiot. We didn't escape the wrath from the RAF either, we were banned and sent back to where we were permanently based. We were unpopular with the Sleaford police and the commanding officer at Cranwell.

The Cold War interrupted my life every four to six weeks. They called it QRA (Quick Reaction Alert). Four aircraft loaded with atom bombs were parked somewhere near the start of the runway. When the alarm bells rang, we rushed to take our positions just in case the world had been plunged into nuclear war. On other V bomber stations, the aircraft roared down the runway with smoke billowing out the back until the message came over the plane's radio. "We are not at war. Return and stand down."

Our bombers could not start engines because of some agreement with the Americans. We had their bombs, and they made sure we didn't steal or sabotage them. American security guards with big dogs accompanied us everywhere. I even had a guard sitting with me as I straddled across a bomb. His dog raced behind us as we transported it from the bomb dump to the aircraft. If I needed to do checks in the cockpit, he tied his dog to a rail and placed a hand on his gun and followed me up the steps. I heard a rumour that on one shift a guard went crazy and fired his gun into a bomb. Surely this was not true?

When we were waiting for action, I spent a whole week playing bridge and being bored. People on QRA became proficient bridge players. I never gambled, but some did and by the end of one shift, one guy had bet and lost his car. Airmen were forbidden to own a house, which was lucky for him as he would have gambled and lost that.

I enjoyed working on Valiant bombers in the UK, but I wanted to be in the sun. Once again, I requested a posting to Hong Kong, but I got Cyprus instead. This time I got a three-year posting to Akrotiri. They gave me a good job maintaining and testing the equipment removed from the aircraft for maintenance or repair. Many types of aircraft passed through on exercise or were based there, so I gained a wealth of experience and further promotion.

The first troubles between the Greek and Turkish Cypriot communities occurred three years after the republic gained its independence. This was during my posting. Limassol was under lockdown and the United Nations 7000-strong peacekeeping force erected barriers on the streets to separate the two quarters. Families of RAF personnel needed armed escorts to go into town to shop, but that didn't deter me from going to the Turkish quarter without an escort. A group of us found a taxi driver prepared to drive us to Ali's, where you were served the best kebab and Kokinelli wine in town. Someone told me that this wine came from the dregs left in the barrels of good wine. You made sure never to drink all the wine in the bottle in case you swallowed rust. Someone had described it to me as Cypriot red wine that could be used for cleaning carburettors and paint stripping and should never be mixed with beer. We mixed it and the night ended with several of us dancing, with an upturned glass of water on our heads, to the music of Zorba the Greek.

Bars and beaches were my entertainment. Lady's Mile beach had no security restrictions, it was the place where families flocked at weekends. You were allowed to drive to one of the other beaches on the island, despite the restrictions but few people did.

Cyprus, to me, was not as good as Malta because of the political situation, and I can't say I was sorry to leave the island. It was even more restrictive in some ways than Malta.

After serving twelve years' man service, I applied to extend my service to twenty-two years so that I would get a pension at a young age. I was turned down and my choice was to extend to fifteen years or leave. Other airmen, like myself, accepted the extension, but many others left the service. I thought and still think that the government did this to avoid paying a pension to us. After two years, I became disenchanted with my job and my morale had reached a low point, so I applied and bought myself out of the RAF for £300. My gratuity for my service years came to £300, which I suppose meant that I paid nothing for my release. I left after thirteen years and one hundred and twenty days with no pension and feeling cheated. I have never forgiven the government for what I thought was a 'dirty trick'.

Soon after my demob, I secured a job as a calibration engineer at a company based in Edinburgh and I stuck this employment for a year. I left because I was inside a factory all day with no natural light and I was always in the bad books of our union representative. I did things to improve safety that were considered to be someone else's responsibility. My union rep did not like that. In my second job, I went back to working for the government at a training establishment near Dundee. I liked this job but after three years, I was made redundant. Unemployment in Britain had reached 1.5 million, and I was just a number in this pile. It was time to move on and leave these shores behind me.

CHAPTER 2

THE ROAD TO KUWAIT

Relaxed on the couch, I spotted a small advert at the bottom of a page in *The Sun* newspaper. The advert read, *Wanted for a three-year single status contract in Kuwait, Engineers, and Senior Electrical Foremen. Petrochemical and overseas experience essential. Excellent conditions plus three weeks home leave every six months.*

I never heard of this country and looked in an atlas to find where it was. After searching, I found it, a small country bordered by Iraq to the north and Saudi Arabia to the south. I didn't excel in geography at school, I only wanted to play football and never listened to my teachers.

Not much wiser, I dialled the number listed in the advert and a moment later I heard a man's voice. "Rex Chapman here, can I help you?"

"My name is Andrew Carruthers. I want to apply for the job in Kuwait advertised in *The Sun* newspaper."

After a brief pause, Rex began questioning me. "Have you worked in the Middle East?"

"No, but I served in Malta, Cyprus, and Libya with the RAF."

"Have you worked on petrochemical plants?"

"No."

The questions continued, and I answered no to all of them.

"I'm sorry, but you don't meet the criteria for any of the positions but I am only the agent so why not send me your CV anyway and I will pass it on to the client. They may take a different view, but don't build your hopes up."

He read out the address and I wrote it down and thanked him before replacing the receiver. For the next hour, I mulled over the pros and cons the job could offer. I fancied the job, and despite there being no chance of getting it, I posted my CV. A week later, Rex telephoned and gave me details of my interview in London, I was surprised and excited.

The overnight train from Edinburgh to London arrived at 7am. I had never been to London to see the attractions and wanted to do some sightseeing and this interview would be a good opportunity for that. In films, I saw images of Buckingham Palace and the Tower of London and they were the priority. Unsure which direction to take and how long I needed to do the tourist stuff, I decided to take a taxi direct to the office and look for tourist attractions on the way or see them later.

During the fifteen-minute taxi ride to Peckham, I did not spot any famous buildings or monuments and I arrived too early and found the office closed.

My opportunity to visit London and find Buckingham Palace misfired. The surrounding buildings in Peckham looked like any other town I visited, except the streets were buzzing with activity. To kill time, I wandered around the streets close to the office. A throng of colour blazed from the shops open for business; unfamiliar fruit and vegetables, various clothes styles, handbags and trainers filled the shelves and displays. African pop music blasted from market stalls and vendors gave out free samples to encourage me and other customers to buy more. I passed Victorian and Georgian buildings then came to a sprawling patch of green that looked strange surrounded by so many buildings. The hour chimed on a church clock therefore I turned round to head back to the office.

A locked office door still prevented me from entering, so I found a coffee shop from where I could keep an eye on the door. A man, dressed in clothes that looked similar to what people wore in Libya, approached to take my order. "You can have a Pakistani breakfast or eggs on toast."

"Eggs on toast, please."

I enjoyed my breakfast and small talk with Abbas, the café owner. He enlightened me about the tourist sights. I paid for my food with Scottish notes and he wanted to exchange all of my Bank of Scotland notes for English ones. He told me about Peckham and that many Nigerian people arrived there in the past five years. He said that they livened up the place with their music and festive ways.

Back at the office, I found the outside door open, so I knocked on the inner door and entered. A grey-haired man with a moustache and glasses and the same height as me, rose from his chair to greet me. I guessed his age to be around fifty-five and from my experience, he looked like an ex-military man. He introduced himself. "My name is Tom Tweedie. I'm the general manager of National Engineering Services (NES), we employ a multinational task force of around 800 people working on a maintenance contract for the Kuwait Oil Company." A knock on the door interrupted him. "Come in," he called.

A young woman dressed in a white top and a tight-fitting chequered skirt entered the room. She carried a tray holding a huge coffee pot, cups, milk, sugar and a plate of biscuits. She placed the tray down and handed me thirty pounds. "This is your expenses to cover the train fare and meals."

"Thank you very much." I signed the paper she gave me, then she left.

Mr Tweedie took hold of a cup and saucer and picked up the coffeepot. "Would you care for a coffee and a biscuit?"

"Just coffee, thanks, I ate breakfast after I arrived in Peckham." I wanted a cigarette to calm my nerves, but I decided against lighting up in case he did not smoke.

He started the questions.

"Tell me about your maintenance experience on motors and switchgear?"

"I worked on both in the RAF, but they are small to fit into an aeroplane."

He cupped his hands together and looked straight at me. "They work the same for a motor this big or, he held his arms wide, as for one this big. Am I right?"

"I suppose so."

"You were a sergeant in the RAF, you must be an experienced man manager?"

"Yes, I am."

The questions intensified, then silence followed while he poured himself another coffee.

"Would you like a coffee now?"

I was desperate for a drink. "Yes, please."

After sipping his coffee and eating another biscuit, he continued. "Do you know what 'flash' is?"

"A flash results from an explosion."

He smiled. "No, not that, what I mean is, Kuwait is a dry state, no alcohol may be sold or drank anywhere in the country. Flash is pure alcohol made in a still. You will be in charge of the workshop and therefore responsible for still-making. Can you manage that?"

The mention of stills confused me. Why mention stills if they prohibited alcohol? I took a sip of coffee and gave him my answer. "Yes, I can."

He looked pleased. "How soon can you travel?"

Emotion welled up inside me at the job offer. "In two weeks."

Then he gave me a piece of paper with the conditions written on it. I would get twice my current salary plus a company car. This job exceeded all my expectations. We shook hands, and I left for my return journey to Scotland. Did I miss seeing the tourist sights of London? This loss of cultural experience did not bother me, but the bit about the stills did! If I said no to making them, would I have been offered the job?

Days after my medical, I travelled to Heathrow Airport to meet up with four other engineers. Keith was the oldest, Ted looked like he was Spanish, Dennis was nervous and Steve looked the youngest, despite his beard. Chit-chat followed and eased any tension or worry that any of us had. After an hour, I boarded a Boeing 747, on course for adventure and my chance of a lifetime.

Steve sat in the seat next to me. During our conversation, I discovered that to gain employment in Kuwait, you needed to be twenty-six years old. Despite this, they hired him when he was twenty-five. His experience with Imperial Chemicals in the North East made him favourable. Throughout the flight, he talked about his girlfriend, music and cars, all of which he was an expert on.

We landed after midnight and exited through the rear door. As Steve stepped out to disembark, he stopped and panicked. "The engines are still running, the air is too hot!" I think everyone on the flight heard him.

I tried to calm him. "The engines are not running, that's the normal temperature of the air."

He remained agitated, and I remembered the announcement after we landed. "Welcome to Kuwait, where the time is twelve minutes past midnight and the outside temperature is thirty-five degrees centigrade with a light breeze."

I tried to reassure him. "The engines are not running. Look, the turbine blades are not rotating."

He became calmer. "Gosh, no one told me about the heat. I did not realise it would be so hot."

We reached arrivals where a well-built male, clad in a white cotton kurta on top of a pyjama suit, displayed our names on a card. He introduced himself as Mohammed.

Keith commented, "This guy must have influence, passengers are the only ones allowed in this area of an airport."

Mohammed arranged our entry permits and immigration stamped our passports with no questions. When we arrived at customs, we all opened our bags and suitcases so the customs officer could check for contraband. After quick scrutiny, he put a chalk mark on each piece, and we headed for the exit. Would our future dealings with the authorities be as swift and trouble-free as this without our Mr Fix-It? I didn't think so.

Ted and Steve loaded our luggage into a Dodge Estate car, which reminded me of a Morris Traveller, only much bigger. A taxi carried our excess luggage and followed behind. An hour later, we arrived and checked in to the Gazelle Beach Club. Mohammed gave us instructions to meet after breakfast and, after welcoming us to his country again, and wishing us a restful sleep, he left.

My head and muscles ached from the journey and the box unit air conditioner in my room made loud squeaky noises, so I turned the controller off, opened the window then slid into bed. I would be awake again in a few hours.

The heat, rather than the alarm clock, woke me and I showered and dressed then walked to the breakfast room to join the others at our reserved table. Dennis did not show up for breakfast, and Keith volunteered to check on him. When he returned he said, "Dennis has a touch of malaria and won't be able to join us."

I knew about this disease; you caught it in the jungle, not the desert. In case the others noticed my lack of overseas experience, I kept silent. After breakfast finished we headed for the reception to meet Mohammed, who greeted us and asked, "Where is Dennis?"

Keith answered, "He is unwell."

Mohammed did not create a fuss, he requested we give him our passports, and we set off in the Dodge for the police station. The heat from the leather seats burned my bottom, and I made sure I didn't touch any metal parts. Police stations are not one of my favourite places to visit. Foreign police often treat visitors with little respect, but not this time. We were ushered into an air-conditioned room and they helped us fill in the forms, which were written in Arabic. I signed my name where the official pointed to on the page, not knowing what I signed for.

The hot air outside made me breathless, and I hurried to get into the air-conditioned car. Our next stop puzzled me as we pulled up outside the hospital. I asked Mohammed, "Do we need another medical?"

"No, unnecessary, but because Kuwait does not have a large blood bank, they ask foreigners to donate a pint. The other reason is that, if you cooperate to this request, it will make it easy to get residence and work permits."

I did not mind donating blood to help others and the tea and biscuits afterwards reminded me of donating blood back home. I arrived at the Ministry of Social Affairs and Labour with a ball of cotton wool on my arm, evidence of my donation. Long queues of individuals dressed like Mohammed stood in lines in front of a dozen hatches. We did not line up because Mohammed led us into a cool office. Again, I signed in the box where the official indicated. Twenty minutes later, I arrived back at the car, holding my temporary work and residence permits, leaving the long lines of other applicants still waiting to get theirs. Having someone to guide us certainly helped with the procedures.

The Dodge cruised onwards to Ahmadi and bumped into a dusty, junk-littered yard with a wooden building near the back. Outside were two Chevrolet Caprice cars and a top-of-the-range Cadillac. Inside, I could hear the air-conditioning units running at full blast. The building comprised a large open plan layout and three closed offices labelled Boardroom, General Manager and Managing Director. It felt like a winter's day inside. A male receptionist escorted us to the boardroom.

A minute later, Mr Tweedie entered and shook hands with each one of us. The others called him 'Tom', so I did the same. Two men placed trays of soft drinks, coffee, and cakes smothered in honey in front of us. The cakes made my mouth water and, despite the flies, I helped myself to one plus a canned drink.

Tom gave us what he considered dire news. We would need to stay at the Gazelle Club for a few more days. This pleased me because I got free food and a spacious en suite bedroom so I was happy to stay there. Before I finished my refreshment, a plump, black gentleman dressed in Arabic business dress and wearing a pair of expensive brown open-toed sandals entered the room, holding a string of prayer beads in his right hand. Mr Tweedie rose from his chair and introduced him as Wahab El Agamy, the owner and director of National Engineering Services. Keith stood too and the rest of us followed his example.

The newcomer said, in good English, "Sit, gentleman, please. Welcome to Kuwait. If any of you need anything or any help, inform Tom or me so we can help you settle in." He chatted for a few minutes about Kuwait and the contract before leaving. Luckily for him, and me, he did not shake my hand because it was a sticky mess from the honey.

On the way out, Tom introduced us to Ahmed Al Nouri and Ian Wilson, other members of our team.

Before he left, Steve asked Mohammed, "Can you give me my passport back please?"

Keith interjected, "You can't have it, the company keeps it until you leave the country. That is the law."

Steve looked apprehensive but kept quiet.

The choice was difficult but obvious, the rule threatened our freedom and compelled us to trust our passports to strangers. Mohammed drove us back to the Gazelle Club and left us to relax. Because of all the running around in the stifling heat, I felt tired and wanted to sleep, so I skipped dinner.

As the sun rose, I showered, dressed and browsed through my residence and work permits then set off for the dining room. I ate a typical English breakfast, but with beef bacon and chipolata sausages because pork is a banned food in Kuwait. Full of food and energy, I went to reception to wait for Mohammed. I liked him because he always arrived at the agreed time. He had a high standard of English and he never waffled but stuck to the facts. I admired the man and asked myself if I could learn Arabic as he had learned Arabic and English. Mohammed outlined the day, and we all piled into the Dodge to set off on the busy highway to Mina Al Ahmadi Oil Refinery.

At the security gate, Mohammed handed the guard a piece of paper and after close scrutiny of its contents and the people in the vehicle, he opened the barrier. Within minutes, we pulled up outside the large open steel doors of a workshop with offices at the side. We sat in the car and waited until a tall, slim, fair-haired fellow came out of the open entrance to greet us. Mohammed said, "That is Mr Rory Harrison your contract manager."

We got out to greet him. Mohammed left us at this point and drove off in the same direction we arrived. As he approached the group, Mr Harrison held out his hand. "Nice to meet you again, Keith."

"You too, Rory."

We introduced ourselves, and he shook everyone's hand. As we followed him through the workshop, the workers stared at the new arrivals. We sat down in the meeting room, but Rory remained standing. "Welcome to the Kuwait Oil Company, everyone. After refreshments, we'll go to the main office and you will meet our general superintendent. Anyone got questions?"

No one asked a question, so Rory gave us information that covered the contract and what would be expected from us. A short, stocky Arab man entered the room and apologised for interrupting. "Sorry, Rory, I need to leave and won't be back today. I wanted to say hello to the new people before I leave."

"Guys, meet Ammar, he is the KOC engineer in charge of the refinery and workshops. Steve, Andrew, you report to him."

I stood up to introduce myself, as did Steve. While we shook hands, someone tapped on the door and two men entered. The tall one with dark wavy hair and a moustache smiled as he entered, the other smaller man with sun-bleached blonde hair said, "Sorry to interrupt, Rory, but we heard that the new men arrived, so we wanted to welcome them." They gave their names as Alan and Steve and Rory explained they were two of the oil company engineers to whom the others would report. Then, another engineer came to join the welcoming party.

I felt relieved when he spoke his name. It was Sid and not Ted or Andrew, or more confusing, another Alan or Steve!

Rory looked at his watch. "Time to go for your interviews with the superintendent." We walked to the offices where a receptionist showed us into a waiting room with oil industry magazines on the table for visitors to read while they waited.

Each person spent around five minutes in the interview. When Dennis came out, his hands were shaking, he was so nervous.

My turn came last. "You must be Andrew, please sit." As I sat, I scrutinised him. I decided he was an ex-military man because he was smart, cleanly shaven and spoke in a tone of voice that sounded like an order and not a request. My nerves steadied until I heard him say, "Andrew, I'm afraid I've got some bad news for you!"

"It's not serious, I hope."

"No, but you will not get any handover for the workshop, you will take over from today." The news came as a complete shock. "Let me explain. Your predecessor died a few weeks ago, and I didn't replace him because NES won the new contract."

"Fair enough."

He paused, "When I reviewed the recommendations from my engineers, they recommended we should not offer you a job, because you lacked petrochemical experience."

Why the hell am I here? That is what I wanted to say, but I kept my mouth shut.

"I agreed with them, but because of your military experience, I gave you a chance. I decided that if you do not shape up in two months, you will be sent home."

I swallowed and interrupted him. "I won't disappoint you."

"Good, I have confidence in ex-military people."

I thought that was it but he spoke again. "That workshop is a mess; I will give you two months to get it cleaned up. I want to see a workshop that has no junk and is clean, do we understand each other?"

"Yes, I understand."

"Right, Andrew, I will keep a check on your progress."

I joined the others and Steve spoke first. "How did it go?"

"I got a bit of a surprise, I am not getting a handover. I'm in charge of the workshops from today." Steve now looked shocked, he did not want to be thrown in at the deep end like me.

Following three days of hard slog, the end of the week came and it was my first opportunity to get outside to relax. Not having transport, I joined the others to check what facilities the club could offer. Activities included water-skiing, tennis, an outdoor basketball court and an Olympic-size swimming pool. Steve said, "This looks inviting. I'm going to buy a costume and go in for a dip."

Keith didn't want to swim and he left with Ted to go back to their rooms. We headed for the club shop and selected our costumes from the display. The shop assistant insisted, "I can sell you costumes, but you cannot use the pool."

"Why not?"

He answered, in a sarcastic tone, "Only families and single ladies can use the pool, you can use the stretch of beach reserved for unaccompanied men."

We bought our costumes and walked to the beach, passing some horse jumps and a stable where two horses stood with their heads sticking over the door. The sand burned my feet, but when I entered the water my body felt relaxed and warm. I enjoyed my swim and decided this would be a nice way to spend my weekends.

The government forbid alcohol, but during my first weekend at the Gazelle Club, I saw bottles of wine and spirits placed under the table out of sight. Another learning experience for me to consider. As I sat with the others at dinner, guests dressed in evening wear arrived. Ted said, "Looks like a party, I wonder if we are invited?"

"I doubt that," I said. People were dressed in suits and dresses beyond my budget. We watched and carried on eating. Steve and Ted ordered baked Alaska, whereas Keith and I ordered the chocalomot dessert. Both choices I considered to be weekend treats. The food was overpriced, but our company was paying the bill, so it didn't matter. As I headed back to my room, gentle dance music came from the ballroom. I peered through a window and could see people waltzing on the dance floor. I wished I could join the dancers because the night was still young. It took me a long time to doze off that night because of the sounds of enjoyment.

With all these rules in place, you needed to watch your step and be aware of how they did things here. I needed to be careful or I could get into trouble. I could talk to other guests, providing they were men. Women only spoke to their husbands and children. It would take me a few months to work out a way to enjoy myself and have a good time.

CHAPTER 3

SCORPIONS DON'T PLAY CHESS

When Rory introduced me to Younis, the workshop foreman, and told me I would share the office with him, I did not like that, but decided not to complain because I needed his cooperation to keep my job. He started as a fitter twenty years ago and had been the foreman for the past ten years. I needed to be careful, so I let him take the lead. The standard question came first. "Do you want tea or coffee?"

"Coffee please, no milk, no sugar."

Younis looked puzzled. "Do you not want sugar or milk?"

I had committed my first sin in Kuwait.

He called the tea boy over. "Bring coffee for Mr Cruder, without milk, or sugar."

The tea boy also looked puzzled. "Yes, Sir."

From that day, Younis always called me 'Mr Cruder'.

After Younis explained our responsibilities to the other areas of the plant, he gave me a guided tour. He introduced me to the thirty plus workers, who were sitting on wooden blocks on the floor or standing at benches, working on motors in various stages of repair. All the motors were larger than any machines I worked on. Two weighed around three tons and another, around seven tons, sat underneath an overhead crane, ready for lifting after repair, for transfer back to the worksite. A lean but sturdy man, of about six feet tall, operated the crane. Younis introduced him as Khan the chargehand. In one corner of the workshop stood a porcelain sink containing several dirty mugs. Next to that, on a wooden shelf, sat a tea urn and a small refrigerator. A filthy open cupboard revealed packs of tea bags and a jar of coffee. I shuddered because I had already accepted a drink from these facilities. All of my workers came from the Indian subcontinent, most of them from Pakistan. Scrap machines of all descriptions littered the place, I could see why Peter Thomson wanted a thorough, organised clean up.

Younis placed all the current records on my desk. "Mr Cruder, I am going to the power station to check on a job. You can familiarise yourself with our records system."

Not long after his departure, Steve came in, accompanied by the engineer he would be replacing. They wanted my opinion on a problem they had in the refinery. I decided not to wait for Younis to return and followed them. I needed to show that I could be decisive and the boss. I had never worked in a refinery, but saw straight away the motor needed a welding repair. Common sense told me the job needed to be done in the workshop to avoid an explosion. Bob didn't want to remove the motor and insisted, "We can get a hot work permit."

I had never heard of this term, but Steve saved my embarrassment, he said, "It will be safer to take the motor to the workshop." For his age, Steve was decisive, and that is what I needed to be.

Younis returned and accepted the job without complaint, but he could have been hiding his feelings and was annoyed that I never consulted him.

Dennis did not turn up again for work and Keith remarked, "He's not up to the job and will have returned home." Maybe he chose to leave, or the company decided for him. Whatever, I never met Dennis again.

Two days later, I collected my Toyota Corolla from the hiring company. I dreaded driving on the right, or what I called the wrong side of the road.

Keith revealed the driving code for Kuwait. If I hit a car driven by a Kuwaiti, I would go to jail because they considered me to be an infidel and I should not be there. I needed to drive and did so at every opportunity to familiarise myself with left-hand drive vehicles. After a month, I became confident and found driving on the right side easier than the left.

Our working week started Saturday and finished on Wednesday. The weekend started on Thursday with Friday the official day for prayer for the Islamic religion. Tom invited the group to his house for lunch. His house lay midway between the coast road and a new highway that ran between Kuwait City and the Saudi border. A high wall with an arch surrounded his compound. I drove through the arch and parked outside a house with no overhanging roof to keep the walls cool. A circular brick well, with a barrel-shaped bucket attached to a rope and pulley, stood at one end of the compound. The place looked like a scene from a cowboy movie because of the heat and wisps of tumbleweed rolling across the ground.

The inside of the house had a rich look, with overhead fans and air conditioners running full-on. Unfortunately, they were ineffective against the sun beating on the roof. For a woman in her late forties, Edith, Tom's wife, had a style of her own, somewhere between that of a thirty-year-old and someone in their forties. She wore a tight floral dress with a matching headband and sandals and displayed no airs or graces. Her pleasant features and welcoming personality brightened up my morning and made me at ease straight away.

Tom said, "Who wants a beer?" A shock after what he told me at the interview.

"Yes, please!" came the replies.

"Lager or bitter?"

We gave our choices of two lagers and two bitters.

Halfway down my first beer, Edith called from the kitchen, "Everyone to the table." Once we were all sitting, she commented, "I hope you like lamb. Beef here is tough and tasteless, but the lamb is exceptional."

The dinner table conversation centred around plans for future development. Tom told us they aimed to convert the outside buildings to a standard acceptable to house senior foremen and engineers.

After lunch finished, I wanted to go to bed and not outside in the heat, but Tom wanted to show us around the compound and our future accommodation. What I saw shocked me. Five uninhabited two-man Portakabins stood close to some buildings under conversion. Tom told us that the cabins were not connected to electricity or plumbing and needed air conditioners to be installed. "We haven't been able to complete the work. Our problem is labour, we haven't enough manpower as we're just too busy with the new contract," he complained.

Keith interrupted, "No problem, we can finish the job. I can get labourers, and we can get the electricity and plumbing connected in a week."

What? Who? He used the royal 'we' and this undertaking did not appeal to me, but, too late, Keith committed us to the task. How would he get the men? I was the only one in charge and possibly able to persuade my men to do the work if I paid them overtime. However, I liked the Gazelle Club and would prefer to stay there. Obviously, not my choice to make.

Two weeks later, after much organisation and hard slog doing my bit, I moved into a Portakabin. I even had to clean it myself before I could get into bed. Memories flooded my mind, back to the time I had served in Libya during my service in the RAF when I became homesick. Conditions there had been bad, I had shared a hut with thirty-nine others and the room stank of sweat. I sat outside to clear my head and tears flowed down my cheeks. I kept telling myself to get a grip, but I just wanted to go home. I lit a cigarette, stuck my head between my legs and tried to think of a thousand excuses to get me home. When I raised my head and looked across the dunes, a camel train zigzagged across the waves of sand and a vivid red sunset glowed in the background. I stood up to watch it. I had seen nothing like that before, not even at the cinema. Gritting my teeth, I ground the cigarette butt in the sand, my homesickness cured. Would it be as bad, or worse, here? I signed a contract that I could not break. I had no say in the matter, no way out. I would experience new things here, some would be good, some bad. If I quit, I could miss the opportunity of a lifetime.

Now we needed to organise our new desert life. The five of us got together to decide on the menu for the week. Timmy, our cook, who came from Goa, bought the food and cooked it. He looked to be in his sixties, but his skills as a cook pleased us all.

A replacement for Dennis arrived, a Scotsman named Sandy, he was accompanied by his wife and two primary school-age children. They moved into the last available Portakabin. I would not have subjected my family to such a life.

Life continued with its difficulties, Kuwait TV only transmitted programmes in Arabic and with little to do after work and few places to go for entertainment, I became bored. We found a way around the no alcohol problem. Contacts kept Keith and Ian supplied with beer and flash, but we needed activities to kill time. I did not play chess but liked to watch Steve and Keith play; they allowed me to talk while they concentrated on the game. We always met at Keith's place because he had the beer and Steve brought his music. As usual, Steve's conversation concentrated on music and how much he missed his girlfriend. He recited the names of singers, the albums and even which track played. I never worked out whether he preferred music or his girlfriend. After a while, I got fed up listening to him. "Steve, you need to experience some real life. When you go home, spend some time in London and visit the nightclubs in Soho."

He looked alarmed, as if I upset him.

I apologised, "Sorry, I should not have said that."

Keith whispered, "Stay quiet, and don't move."

Steve looked pale as he stared at the floor. I followed his gaze and looked down. Between his sandals, a big black scorpion, at least three inches long, lay on the floor, unmoving but very much alive. These scorpions are deadly, and a sting from one of them means a slow death! He mumbled, "Shit, what do I do now?"

Keith leaned over and picked up the fly swot. "Stay still and don't panic,"

"That will not kill it," I whispered.

The air smelled more of sweat than beer.

The hit stunned the scorpion, and it tried to recover, but too late, I picked up one of Keith's safety boots and smashed the sole down on its body. The deadly insect stood no chance.

To celebrate our success and Steve's death reprieve, Keith opened another beer and filled our glasses. As he tried to overcome his brush with death, Steve returned to my question and stuttered, "London sound's a great idea." We polished off the remaining beer, spilling some from the glasses that shook in our hands.

The deadline for the workshop clean-up approached, but to survive in Kuwait, we needed alcohol so the priority became making a still. My team included electricians, fitters, welders, and a machinist; all experts with steel and copper. Younis produced a drawing and I knew his men had made stills for other people. It had to be built after normal working hours so no one would ask questions that would be difficult to answer. If we did it in the open, then many people would end up in jail. I authorised the overtime for the construction of an illegal piece of essential equipment.

The finished product included a fifty-litre vessel to hold the mash, electric heaters with thermostats, a reflux column, condensers and built-in safety valves, a professional job of high quality. To get it through the security gate without being arrested would be risky, and my responsibility. I handed the work order to the security guard, hoping he would not question it. He took the paper, glanced under the cover and waved us through. Khan came with his men to lift it off the truck and finish the onsite installation.

Keith volunteered to be the chief brewer. He made sure that we all understood the process and the safety precautions. Any stupid mistakes during distilling would blow up the compound and its residents. The rules included, no syphoning off your private stock, or sample drinking. A nurse at the hospital would test the finished product for safety and purity and no one was allowed to drink it until that happened.

We bought the ingredients – three sacks of sugar and bread yeast. Our nurse, who tested the sample, worked in the hospital laboratories and supplied us with two-and-a-half litre demijohns, the bottles came from the outgoing people and Ian's friends and Timmy took care of the process while we were at work. We took turns to call in to make sure the still remained stable and to check that Timmy was not helping himself to the finished product. The first mash produced eight litres of ninety-eight per cent pure alcohol. After cutting with pure water, it gave us 20 bottles of the best vodka in Kuwait.

Two weeks before taking over, we held a party in honour of the staff about to leave. A still cool night made it a perfect evening to socialise and dance the night away.

The strict laws that prohibited alcohol, meant my social life centred around the darts league at the Ahmadi Desert Motoring Club (ADMC). Every week over one hundred people met there to play darts, dominoes and bridge. With darts, you needed beer, after all, this is a pub game. Most players carried a cooler of beer in the boot of their car. To avoid complications with the police, you must arrive by 7:30pm and the cooler must be empty before leaving the premises. Naturally, most drops of this homemade brew got consumed before the inside of the cooler was washed. The bar closed at 10pm and everyone left by 10:30pm. Besides darts nights at the ADMC, another darts league took place in people's homes. The criterion was that every host supplied homemade beer, wine and snacks so no one needed to carry beer to the venue. Players took the competition seriously because each individual tried to win the accolade of 'Best Male' or 'Best Female' player in that season. These nights were good fun.

Inexperienced in matters of finance, I soon discovered I made a colossal mistake signing a contract that was paid in local currency. At the start, I received a very good salary of 500 Kuwait dinars a month, equivalent to £1000, but I did not consider how the exchange rate could affect my take-home pay. The value of the pound doubled and my salary was reduced by half. With high unemployment in Britain, I had to continue in this job. It would be very difficult to find another one. I needed the pound to crash so my life would return to what I had visualised at the interview.

In 1975, the Kuwait Government took control of the Kuwait Oil Company from British Petroleum (BP). Most of the BP staff left Kuwait, but a few of the long-service expatriate employees stayed on because of the value of a low pound to the dinar exchange rate. They stayed on to boost their severance pay paid in Kuwait dinars. A statutory law entitled all employees to a month's salary for every year of employment and that increased to two months depending on how many years total you were employed. If the exchange rate was in favour of the dinar they stood to make a fortune, but they suffered the same fate as me. The rapid increase in the pound's value eroded any severance and bonus payments due.

Once I gained confidence, I drove to Kuwait City. I set off along the coast road through Salmiya and parked just a short distance from the centre. I made sure I arrived after 4pm to avoid the hottest part of the day. What had once been a beautiful old city had been destroyed and replaced with skyscrapers housing banks, officialdom and businesses. The traditional old streets lined with gold and electronic shops had gone and had been replaced by classy establishments. That meant only one thing, everything inside these monuments to shopping would be more expensive.

Shoppers came out at sunset when the cool, dry air made the heat bearable to shop. I strolled around for an hour, gawking through windows and dodging people in the streets. I found difficulty comprehending my surroundings. Some people wore western-style clothes, but most men wore white dishdashas and women dressed in long black robes with their faces totally covered.

Thirst overcame me, I needed a drink. I wanted to avoid the exorbitant prices in the café so I stopped at a street vendor where many people resembling a rugby scrum tried to get served. As the vendor passed bottles of Pepsi and cartons of cold water and tea to the customers, a man in a suit shouted over the others and received his drinks. I said to him, "How do I get one of these?"

He shouted to the vendor, and I got served. I almost finished the bottle in a single gulp. The nice man stood near me, talking to a woman wearing a veil. I turned to the man and thanked him and she stepped backwards while we talked. When we finished talking, I headed for the shops that he recommended and did some shopping before returning to the farm in the desert.

Once more, I saw ladies in chic, expensive dresses, but not at the Gazelle Club, this time at Dousra. Up to now, Tom only visited us if he wanted to ask for our help. This time, he wanted to invite two of us to his house as important people would be there and he wanted us to help to entertain them. We needed to wear a necktie and be polite. Our replies disappointed him.

Keith said, "I don't want to go."

Ted remarked, "I don't have one."

Ian added, "I have several you can borrow one."

Tom concluded, "Right, Ian and Andrew, 8pm, sharp."

Ian said, "Andrew, stop eating, save your appetite for later. I assume food will be available, Tom?"

His face looked like that of a drill instructor.

Later, I called on Steve. "Can I have a splurge of your aftershave? You never can tell who I might meet tonight."

"Help yourself."

When we stepped outside, Ian joined us. He looked smarter than me, but I smelled better.

As I looked across to Tom's residence, I made out that some men wore jackets, but most just wore trousers with a long-sleeved shirt and necktie. The ladies looked gorgeous in their long dresses. My inferior outfit made me regret agreeing to the invitation. I didn't want to go but I had to, so I followed Ian across the waste ground. Tom opened the door and greeted us with a stern, "You're late."

Edith rescued us from her grumpy husband and told us to get inside and mingle with the other guests.

I wanted to enjoy Edith's cakes and scones first, but she took our arms and led us away from the table. She introduced us to several guests. I recall meeting the head teacher of the oil company-sponsored school and a wing commander, who was possibly a British spy. The principal guest, the British Ambassador, arrived soon after us and left before us; the protocol for such a visit. The people I spoke to were polite, but by the end of the evening, it was clear they preferred to talk to people whose spouses accompanied them. The air force man and his wife stayed late, and I got to know them better. Ian and I left the party after everyone else left so we could help Edith clear up. We returned to our beds, carrying a supply of Edith's home cooking and a six-pack of Tom's real beer. I enjoyed my introduction to Kuwait society.

CHAPTER 4
A NEW BROOM SWEEPS CLEAN

As soon as we took over, I knew that one of us would be on call to attend to any emergency. Nobody wanted to be the first one. Unfortunately, I drew the short straw. My first call-out came while I was having dinner on Sunday night. The pier, where the LPG tankers load their highly explosive cargo, experienced a power supply failure. When I arrived, I parked my car on waste ground next to a white Rolls Royce, then signed in at the security gate. A hot wind blew in my face as I strode up the wooden slatted pier towards the control room. One area was in darkness, but there was light enough to see the workers idly standing or crouching down, waiting for something to happen. I had never been on an operational pier before, but I knew it sounded too quiet. As I approached the group, there was an eerie silence. I greeted the foreman. "Hi, Sadiq."

"Hello, Mr Andrew, the main circuit breaker burned out and the panel shut down, stopping the pumps. I have sent the driver to pick up a new breaker."

Sadiq, a surly, tall, thin man with a pockmarked face, was difficult to work with. He often came to the workshops and created problems. This fault would be easy to fix if there was an available replacement.

"Any other problems?" I asked.

"The control room supervisor is angry,"

"Why is he angry?"

"He is always angry."

"Should I talk to him?"

"Yes, Mr Andrew, you need to do that, but be careful, don't make him angrier."

I smiled. "I will try not to."

The humidity had made me sweat profusely so, when I opened the door, a welcome gush of cold air rushed out of the room and hit me full on. Two men dressed in trousers and shirts sat at a table with mugs of tea in their hands. "Good evening, gentlemen, I am the duty engineer."

Both eyed me dubiously as I approached the table. One of them sat up straight and spoke in a raised voice, "When can we load?"

"The driver is on his way to pick up a replacement. Power should be back on within an hour. Sorry, that's the best I can do."

"The tanker cannot load its cargo and so far it has cost $20,000 in penalties. It will cost double if you don't get the power back on soon."

Nobody had explained to me about penalty clauses. I needed to convince him the shutdown was not our fault. A chance came with a break in his speech.

"It is a very simple problem caused by poor design!" I said.

"What's wrong with the design? I have worked here for ten years and the pumps have always worked."

I chose my words carefully. "KOC plan to replace this panel with one that has two bus bars. If one pump shuts down, you will still be able to use the other two."

He looked puzzled, I think he recognised my bullshit. "You're from the new company, correct?"

"Yes, I'm the workshop senior foreman."

"Do you know Mr Sid?"

"I have met him, he told me about the planned changes to the panel."

"He is a good man. I am Abdullah, and he is Rashid. What's your name?"

"My name is Andrew."

"Do you want a drink, Andrew?"

"Yes, please." I sensed he was cooling down.

Abdullah took a key from the drawer and unlocked one of the two refrigerators standing against the back wall. When he opened the door of one of them, I was amazed by the contents.

"Do you want one of these?"

"Yes, please."

He handed me a can of Tennent's lager, which sported a photograph of a lady in a swimsuit on the side of the can. After I finished it, I said to Abdullah, "I will go check on progress."

"No need, Sadiq will finish it." He gave me another can with a different lady on the side.

An hour later, the lights on the panel were on, and the noisy pumps had started up. Abdullah was in a jovial mood. "Don't worry about the penalty. I have put in my report that we experienced problems because of poor weather."

At shift change, I tottered back along the pier to the security gate with Abdullah and Rashid. Abdullah got into the Rolls Royce, Rashid into a Chevrolet Caprice and me into my Toyota. No more call-outs occurred that week. My bullshit had paid dividends with a welcome bonus of real beer.

Building relationships and attending events whilst still sticking to the strict codes that were prevalent in Kuwait society was essential to survive here. Ian hatched a plan to put this theory into action. He invited some friends to a social night at Dousra, and this included the nurse who tested our flash. To boost the female side of the celebration, she was asked to bring along her colleagues. She helped us to provide an important element: safe alcohol. Without her expertise in product control safety, the party would have lacked sparkle. Over forty people attended and Timmy laid on a delicious, mouth-watering buffet meal. Two teachers brought wine and others contributed what they were able to make or buy. The party was a success. From now on, I would not be short of friends or invitations to dinner and darts. One teacher, called Linda, suggested we help each other out by exchanging flash and beer for wine. This was the start of a very beneficial arrangement.

Two weekends after the party, I was in my room listening to a Lena Martell tape when someone hammered on my room door. It was Timmy, panicking. "Mr Andrew, police are here, they are in the dining room."

"Timmy, you stay in the kitchen, I'll handle this."

He shot off into the kitchen and closed the door quietly behind him. I knew Ian was in his room but did not know the whereabouts of the others. Three Toyota cars, plus a large American-style jeep, with two uniformed police seated in the rear, were parked outside.

I entered the dining room and found two men standing at the bar. The tall, slim one wore a dishdasha, ghutra, and egal. The other man was older, of stocky build, and wore a uniform with three stripes on the arms. The one in the dishdasha was the Kuwaiti and the boss. He was eyeing the bar and glasses on the shelves, plus the large refrigerator in the corner. "Good afternoon, gentlemen, welcome to Dousra Farm."

The one in charge answered, "Good afternoon."

I smiled and tried to look relaxed as I moved behind the bar and asked our guests, "Would you like some refreshment?" I opened the fridge so they could see it only contained soft drinks. We kept alcohol in our rooms or locked in a store outside.

"Just water."

I took a large bottle from the fridge, two of the best glasses from a shelf and wiped them clean before pouring the water.

"Thank you. How many people live here?" the boss asked.

"Our manager lives in the farmhouse with his family. Four engineers live in the Portakabins and four live in the rooms here. One engineer has his wife and family visiting from the UK."

"Do you enjoy living here?"

"Yes, I like it very much. The desert is so peaceful at night."

"You must be very careful living here. People come around shooting birds. It can be dangerous; they are not always very good shots."

"Thanks, I will tell everyone to be careful."

The boss continued, "Bedouins come to rest and use the water from the well. If they come again, you must let them come inside to rest and drink water. That is the law of the desert."

I was relieved at his relaxed attitude. "Thank you, I will not forget and will pass your information to the others."

He took a card from his pocket, holding it between the fingers of both hands for me to take it. "If you have any problems, you can call me."

I accepted the card the same way that he offered it. "Thank you very much for visiting us, I will call you if we need your help."

My body sighed in relief as they turned, glanced around again and left. The two police officers were still sitting in the truck. Thankfully, they had not been nosing around the outbuildings. We just had a lucky escape from being front-page news in the newspapers.

The laws of the desert are common sense. The police officer's instructions were very clear, if Bedouins visited the farm, they should not be refused permission to get water. I would never have done that anyway, I was brought up to respect anyone who knocked on our door and wanted help. Returning from work one day, we had unexpected guests near the well. There were two large tents pitched inside our walls, the Bedouins had arrived. At dinner, my colleagues displayed concern over the close proximity of these desert nomads, except Keith who was an experienced desert worker. He told us a story from his earlier years when he got caught in a sandstorm and Bedouins rescued him and took him to their camp where he fell asleep. When he woke, he faced two men pointing dangerous old guns at his head. They were wary of this stranger, however, following desert rules, they gave him water, food and helped him to get back to safety.

We were curious about the visitors in our backyard so Ian and I sat outside to look for activity, but there wasn't any. Only the faint glow from an oil lamp lit up the darkness. We soon got fed up and went back to the dining room for a game of darts.

Darkness fell around 7pm all year round and I took my coffee and sat outside to relax and continue spying on our neighbours. There was still no activity and this was annoying me because I wanted to see and possibly meet a genuine Bedouin family. A light came on, but not a paraffin lamp, a real electric light bulb and two men emerged from the tent and sat down at a fold-up table underneath the shaded extension. I called Ian to come out to see. I was keen to find out where they were getting the electricity.

After he joined me, I pointed to the light bulb and queried, "Where do you think they're getting their electricity? I can't hear a generator."

"Me neither. Let's find out."

Our electricity supply came from a panel inside the compound. Someone had connected a cable into one of the spare circuits and ran it across to the tent. I knew we had to share the water, but electricity?

Ian was concerned. "We need to visit them."

"We can't just go over there, we need to take a present and definitely not beer."

We raided Timmy's fridge, filling a bag with cookies and soft drinks. I contributed an unopened carton of cigarettes. Cautiously, we drew closer, holding the sack high, so they would see it. The flaps on the tents were closed, but a light flickered through the gaps. Ian's Arabic was better than mine, so he did the introductions. The older one accepted the gifts and invited us to sit, and the younger one barked out an order for tea.

A woman brought tea and dates, and we sat for the next hour relaxing together in the cool evening, using broken Arabic and sign language to chat. We thanked them for their hospitality and slept with no worries. No one mentioned the electric light bulb, it would be an unnecessary complication. Two days later, they left.

Bedouins who live in Kuwait or just pass through are animal herders. They migrate into the desert in the winter months and move back toward the cultivated land in the dry summer months. Bedouin society is tribal and male-controlled. The government tries hard to preserve Bedouin culture and also tries to introduce them to the benefits of modernisation. Camels, sheep and goats remain an important part of their life. The new 'Desert Camel', a pickup truck with wide tyres has also become a necessity. In several instances, the military and police forces have incorporated them into their organisations, and others have found employment in the construction and petroleum industry.

My next encounter with a Bedouin happened at the storage tank farm. Younis telephoned to tell me the crane had arrived. I knew little about cranes, but I needed to be there in case of an accident, and they wanted me there as someone (me!) had to take the blame should an accident happen. I parked the car and walked over to Younis. "What's wrong, Younis, you look unhappy?"

He looked towards the control room and a man sitting against the outside wall. "It is the Bedouin crane driver, Mr Cruder, I don't like him. He will only work if he wants to."

I failed to understand this, the crane driver was employed by the company to lift motors onto trucks. I wanted to find out why he didn't want to do this. "Younis, you wait in the control room and I will talk to him." The crane operator sat cross-legged in the shade. I approached and greeted him. "As-salām alaykum, ismee Andrew." I indicated I wanted to sit next to him and he did not object so I sat close to him. For the next two minutes, neither of us spoke. Another minute passed and he picked up his flask and poured tea into a mug, then into the cup supplied with the flask.

He held out the mug and said, "Chai." I recognised this as tea. This was desert etiquette in practice. I had learnt a lot about the politics of Arab behaviour and knew to be patient and not to be forceful. I thanked him for the tea and remained silent as I sipped it.

As soon as I finished, he took my cup, washed it with the remaining tea, placed his cup back on the flask and stood up. I walked with him silently over to the crane. After a successful lift, he shook my hand and we exchanged names. His name sounded like Omar, so that is what I called him. He always cooperated with me after that day, but I always drank tea with him before starting the job.

A test to our friendship came a few months later. Omar had to lift a three-ton motor off a truck so my men could get it into the workshop. He checked the load and slings and started the lift. The problem came after he lifted the motor from the bed of the truck. It tilted, and he panicked, causing the motor to drop and smash the truck floor. I watched helplessly as he attempted to lift it again. As it got higher, it swayed more dangerously, and the crane rocked backwards and forwards. The motor crashed into the front of the adjacent workshop and the side of the wall crumpled before he could lower the motor to the ground. Onlookers gathered to watch the spectacle. Ammar joined them, followed later by the new general superintendent.

Younis, who saw the whole thing, said, "They will blame us."

"They will blame me," I replied.

As the onlookers dispersed, Ammar turned to me. "Andrew, let's go to my office."

Ammar was direct. "Someone could have been killed."

"Did you find out what went wrong?" I expected him to add, *it was lack of supervision,* but he didn't. "The crane driver has admitted that the sling slipped, and when the motor swayed, he lost control."

His remark stunned me, Bedouins are a law unto themselves. Omar need not have taken the blame. If he said 'I don't know', I would have been blamed, sacked and on the next plane home.

"What happens now?"

"We will repair the workshop, check the crane and slings, and that will be the end. The general superintendent is satisfied and no further action is required."

I thanked him and conveyed the news to Younis, who looked pleased. "Mr Cruder, the Bedouin has respect for you."

Later, we needed the crane during a rainy spell, but it was not available. I asked Younis, "Why not, don't crane drivers work in the rain?"

He chuckled. "Not the Bedouin, he has gone home to check on his goats and sheep."

I chuckled. "Good for him,"

Rainfall in Kuwait is less than 100 millimetres (4 inches) per year. It occurs from November to April, as very heavy showers that cause floods.

A new engineer called Kenny arrived, our first engineer to work on the new three-train gas plant. His job was to familiarise himself with the plant and oversee the commissioning engineers. He moved into the last of the decorated rooms at Dousra.

Winter approached fast, and the desert cooled. The air conditioners had no heaters so my room never got warm. I bought an electric heater from the souk, and the others did the same. Before long, the heaters overloaded the electrical circuits and they tripped out. It was so cold overnight that, in the morning, ice formed on pools of water, and the windshield on my Toyota was frosted over.

Seven months after my arrival to Kuwait, my first field break came. After the British Airways flight landed at Heathrow, I waited three hours for an internal flight home. To pass time, I found the bar, which I expected would be empty so early in the morning, and the restaurant to be busy, but both were full of customers. I ordered a beer, then talked to a group of expatriates. I found out that this was the place to come if I needed to find out which companies were hiring ex-pats. Useful to know for any future employment, should I need it.

CHAPTER 5
A MIRACLE IN THE DESERT

Tom asked if I wanted a weekend job at Wafra Power Station. I needed Younis plus four men to do the job, which was to remove the rotor from a gas turbine generator and transport it to Ahmadi workshops for modification. Conditions at Wafra are harsh, so Tom agreed to pay me a hundred Kuwait dinars, Younis, fifty, and each worker, twenty-five. We all agreed to the payment.

We left early enough to reach the power station by mid-morning. Sandstorms often made the road to Wafra impassable, but today we were lucky. As the power station came into view, the truck stopped and the men got out. I stopped my Toyota behind them to check why they had stopped. As I approached, Joaquim, who came from Sri Lanka, was being teased by the others. About half a mile away, I could see a Bedouin camp, and Younis was heading towards it. I thought he wanted to urinate, but, even for his modesty, he was going a long way. I called out, "Younis, why go so far, we won't look when you pee."

He turned and came back towards me and shouted, "I am going to the Bedouin camp."

"Why? There's no time for a visit, we have a job to do."

"Joaquim has too many girlfriends and needs to settle down and marry, so I will buy him a wife."

Hearing these words and fearing that Younis was not joking, Joaquim took off across the desert in the opposite direction. Laughing at this response, Younis shouted, "Don't worry, Mr Cruder, he will join us soon. He is young and will get hungry." I was apprehensive and worried for his safety, but thankfully he appeared when food was served.

We arrived at our destination and the shift supervisor signed the permit to start work. After the isolations were completed, we removed the covers from the turbine and eased the lifting frame into position. It wouldn't go in. The power station was built in the fifties and there had never been a reason since to remove a rotor.

Younis was disappointed the lifting frame was not suitable for the task. "It has to fit, if it doesn't, we'll need a crane. What can we do?"

The supervisor confirmed a crane would not be available until Saturday. We sat on the wall outside to relax and decide whether to stop two nights here or go back home. Neither of us wanted to stay, but we did not want to go back either.

I ditched the dregs from my coffee cup and pondered over the decision. As I stared into the desert, sand appeared to shimmer and blow.

"Younis, is that a mirage?" I had seen mirages on the cinema screen, but never in actual life.

Younis stood. "It is the wind causing the sand to swirl around in the air."

It was a sensible answer, but it moved too fast. "It can't be a sandstorm. It looks like a big truck."

We waited until it got closer.

"It's a crane, Mr Cruder."

"It is a miracle," I replied.

He looked at me. "Sent by Allah, Mr Cruder."

The driver refused to lift the rotor, but changed his mind when I offered to pay him fifty dinars. For another ten, he agreed we could follow him back to Ahmadi in case of a mishap.

It was getting dark when we loaded the rotor onto the truck and the supervisor suggested it was unnecessary for me to follow the crane, I could take a shortcut home. Trucks running between the power station and the gathering centre made the track safe for cars to drive on. After that, there was a road suitable for small vehicles which stretched all the way to Ahmadi, a shorter route. Satisfied that it would save time, I thanked everyone and set off.

It was dark when I reached the gathering station. The moon shone high in the night sky, stars twinkled and oil flares lit up the desert as I turned on to what I thought was the road. After twenty minutes, I became disorientated and knew I was not on the correct road. I had driven into a wadi, a dried-up river bed. Stupidly, I forgot to fill a canteen from the water bottle in the Dodge truck and as a result, I felt panic and fear.

Terrible things came to mind, what if I get stuck? I would need water and once the only bottle I had was emptied, there was no water except for that in the radiator. I was thinking out loud. "I bet this car will break down any minute."

Desert people often follow dried-up river beds or spend the night in them. Because of flash floods, more people in the desert die from drowning than from dehydration. I was in a wadi and my body shook as I pictured what might happen. My vision was blurred, but I saw a flickering light behind me. I stopped the car to check, but kept the engine running to make sure the petrol in the carburettor didn't vaporise. I hadn't imagined it, but the lights looked to be far away. The hope of rescue made me settle down and think rationally, but suddenly the lights disappeared. My body shook again as I got back in the car. My hands trembled as I flashed the lights, worked the brake pedal so the stoplights would flicker, and pressed hard on the horn. The light was still there and came closer. I relaxed for a moment, but I panicked again. What if they don't see me? What if they decide not to help? They might be bandits and rob and kill me. Even if the authorities found my car, they might assume I wandered off and got buried in the sand. These frightening scenarios flashed into my brain.

The truck approached and stopped twenty feet from the wadi. Two men got out, both of them wore white dishdashas making them look like large ghosts. One carried an ancient rifle and looked like he meant business. Beads of sweat ran from my forehead, down my cheeks and onto my chest and back. As I raised my hand to wipe the sweat from my brow, it knocked my sunglasses to the floor. Fear had made me forget I was wearing them. As the figures approached, I called to them, "Please help me."

Their reply sounded friendly, and the gun was a shepherd's crook. My nerves steadied as they tied a rope to the axle and towed me to the tarmac road. I thanked them in Arabic for my rescue and my life. I followed their truck to Ahmadi and thanked them again. I never told Younis or Tom what happened.

In the summer months, most Kuwaitis rested in the afternoon or avoided going outside. I worked in the open air no matter how hot it got. One day, Kenny commented, "It's hot enough to fry eggs on the bonnet of my car." The following day, he proved it!

In contrast, the days in the winter months became hot but bearable, however, at night, the temperature fell, and I had to cover myself with several blankets to keep warm. One night, I didn't need to huddle in my blankets, I sweated in bed and found it hard to get to sleep. I checked, and the heater was off, so it couldn't be that, but the air was clammy. The clock on the wall read 4:10am. I got out of bed and put on my tracksuit bottoms and top, grabbed a can of orange crush from the refrigerator and sat outside on the veranda. The air was muggy, and stars twinkled in the sky, the silence made the night peaceful. A door squeaked and Ted joined me. "What's wrong, can't you sleep?"

"No. Sorry, did I wake you?"

He looked wide awake. "No, I can't sleep either. The air tonight feels strange."

Another squeak of a door revealed Steve, who sat down next to Ted and we chatted for a while. Then it happened! As the sun rose above the horizon, Steve hollered, "Look at that sunrise."

As my eyes squinted to look, my hand reached out, as if to touch it, as a colossal, brilliant, orange ball came into view.

Ted shouted, "It's on fire!"

Summer had arrived. The strange temperature during the night that had caused our insomnia was the signal for the season to change.

In winter or summer, part of my job description was to develop Kuwaitis. An oil-rich country does not have to push its citizens to work. There are poor Bedouins, but no poor Kuwaitis.

Abdullah needed to develop as an engineer. I got on very well with him, in fact, I liked him. One day he asked me for an empty barrel. Somebody had told him empty barrels made the best barbecues. In barely an hour, my men satisfied his wish. They split a barrel in half, added legs and even put hooks to hold the skewers while the meat cooked. When Abdullah came to collect it, he thanked us for our efforts. I stepped in to help the men lift it onto his pickup, and he caught my arm and pulled me back. "Andrew, let them pick it up, you are their boss, you don't have to do that." Lesson learned, supervisors are not meant to lift. This time, the student had taught the teacher. Once the barrel was secured on the truck, I thought he would leave, but he stayed. "Andrew, do you like football?"

"Yes, I play in the Ahmadi league."

"Good, tomorrow we will go to watch Kuwait play Australia." Was this his way of saying thank you for the barbecue?

He arrived on time to pick me up, honking the horn atop of the range Chevrolet. I got in and greeted him. "Good afternoon, Abdullah, I like your car."

"A present from my future wife."

I knew him well enough to jest. "She must love you, few women would buy a man a car like this just to get married."

He chuckled. "Andrew, this is Kuwait."

I was thinking, *he probably does not know what she looks like.* This would be an arranged marriage.

A sizeable crowd lined up outside the stadium, waiting for their turn to enter. Somehow, Abdullah weaved his way through the people and stopped the car outside the entrance. I tried to see the car park and this was not it. He removed two plastic bags and handed me the one that contained chilled drinks and opened the door to get out. On the way in, he spoke to an usher and handed him the car key. Now I understood, important Kuwaitis can park anywhere and get somebody to park their car.

The stadium seats were concrete, but before I sat down someone handed me a cushion. We sat in the family area and watched the rest of the stadium fill up with male supporters. Once the game started, Abdullah opened the bag of goodies. As I looked inside, the stadium erupted with cheering. Everyone stood up and cheered, except me. I had missed the only goal of the game.

I did not see Abdullah again for almost three months. His arranged marriage took place, and I left on field break to the UK. The next time we met, I inquired if he liked married life. He emphatically said, "I love it."

I asked him, "Have you bought a house for you and your wife?"

"No need, my wife has moved in with my family."

"How many people live in your house?"

"My father and mother, my grandfather, my two brothers, their wives, and four children, and my two younger sisters."

"Who is the boss?"

"My mother, of course," he answered without hesitation.

"What happens if you disagree or fall out with your wife?"

He had a mischievous look in his eye. "I go to the club."

I had heard about secret Kuwaiti clubs, and Abdullah just confirmed it. Unfortunately, we were interrupted by a phone call and I never found out what he did in the club.

The highway that led to the refinery made it easy to drive to work, but hold-ups still happened. At 6:30am the road could be a nightmare. I needed to concentrate, but one time I failed. The traffic ahead stopped, but I didn't. The rear end of a big American saloon loomed in front of my eyes. I braked, but it was too late. There was a thud and crunch of metal on metal and the tinkling of broken glass rung in my ears as my body shot forward and the seatbelt locked. The front of my car crumpled and, for a moment, I heard no sound. Seconds passed before my shocked brain registered the fact that I would go to jail until they decided who was to blame. The only person at fault was me. I had to think fast, my knee hurt but that could wait. Only one action might prevent me from going to jail, so I took it. I laid down as close to the floor as possible and pretended to be dead.

Traffic stopped and someone tried to open the door and, after several attempts, it opened. Voices all around me were shouting in Arabic, possibly discussing if I was dead and what they should do. Someone with muscular arms pulled me from the wreck. I tried not to react and let them get on with it, at least they laid me down gently. Someone pumped my chest, and I agonised in case they gave me the 'kiss of life'.

I heard a voice I recognised, it was Fathallah calling, "Andrew, don't worry we will get you to the hospital soon."

What a relief. I made a slight movement so he would know that life still existed in my inert body and he lowered his head close to my ear to reassure me. I whispered, "I am fine, just get me out of here." He reacted as if he had seen a ghost, but recovered quickly and sprang into action. At six feet two, and muscular, he brushed the onlookers out of the way and put me into his car. Within minutes, we were on our way to the refinery. I don't know if anyone called the police or an ambulance, but it did not matter. For now, I was safe.

Soon after we arrived at the office, Younis showed concern for my wellbeing and ordered tea with lots of sugar. "Mr Cruder, you must have this, it will make you better." We didn't have an appointed first-aider, but someone who I didn't recognise bandaged my knee. The incident was far from over, but I had a recovery time of two hours before Fathallah drove me to the police station.

As I stepped through the door, a young man rushed across the room towards me. He looked like he was about to strangle me, but he begged my forgiveness and kept saying, "I am sorry, I thought I killed you!"

I didn't want to say too much in case I said the wrong thing. I could only think of, "No, I drove too close and when you stopped, I ran into the back of your car."

He insisted the opposite. "No. no. It was my fault; I must have been asleep, then woke up and braked too fast. I am sorry."

The police sergeant came over to check my injuries and offer tea. He handed me two forms. "Sign these please."

By now I recognised the Arabic writing for signature. I signed my name and handed them back.

He returned one to me. "Give this to the car company and they will remove and repair your car."

I escaped going to jail and the hiring company removed my car. They removed it, but didn't repair it; they gave me a new one.

Ramadan is difficult for those that have to work in the scorching sun. The basic rules of Ramadan are strict. Muslims have to fast and abstain from bad habits and sins, such as smoking, swearing and fighting, as well as eating and drinking. Hard rules to follow, particularly in blistering heat.

These rules tested not only my men, but me as well. My first test came on a job that involved open-air work, physical effort and patience. Younis suggested they start the work after the first prayer and I agreed. When they arrived, I was waiting for them and Younis looked at me, puzzled – why had I arrived before the men started work? I greeted them. "Good morning, everyone. Let's get the job finished and we can all go back to bed."

No one remarked I need not be there, and neither would they let me do any manual work. It was worse for me, just standing there, exposed to the heat. Twice Younis wanted me to rest, but I refused. By midday, we finished and headed home to rest. The first thing I did was to drink a gallon of water and light up a cigarette. It may not have been necessary, and stupid of me to arrive on the job before the workers, but I know my men respected me for it.

Another difference between my workers and me was I got my flight home twice a year paid for. Younis got one paid flight every three years. His disposition and moods had changed recently, and I didn't know what caused the change. Through my careful questions, he explained,

"Mr Cruder, I am happy because my family will come and stay with me for the winter months to avoid the freezing temperatures back home. This makes me happy." As the time for their arrival came closer, his excitement grew and I wanted to help. "Will you hire a taxi to bring your wife from the airport?"

"No, taxis are expensive. I will use my truck."

"Younis, get Khan to drive your truck and you take my car. You cannot drive your wife from the airport in a truck."

Our company made a rule that we must hang our keys on the keyboard when not using the car. At breakfast, a week before his family was due, Timmy handed me a note.

Dear Mr Cruder,

I am sorry; I make a mistake.

My family not coming next week.

They will arrive today.

Sorry I got the wrong date.

I will return your car tomorrow.

I was pleased he had taken up my offer.

CHAPTER 6
RELICS AND GUNS

My field break coincided with Ian's and he suggested we fly to Syria and have a one-night stopover in Damascus. The idea appealed to me, so I agreed. The office gave us cash to buy tickets, and we booked on a Syrian Arab Airlines flight. They were the cheapest airline to fly with. The money saved from the flight would pay for the hotel and a night out. If we caught the early flight, we would have almost two days there because our onward flight to London left after midnight the following day.

Our flight took off on time and arrived at Damascus airport just before 10am. Entry requirements did not enter my mind until I presented my passport at immigration. The official held out his hand. "Your visa please"

I took out my Kuwait residence and work permits and placed them in front of him. The officer checked my passport for Israel stamps, if he had found one then I would be refused entry to the country. I had never visited Israel. He stamped the passport and handed it back to me.

We took a taxi to the centre of Damascus and arrived at our hotel just before lunch. The building looked run down, but there were signs that in the past, it was a classy place to stay. The coppery red velvet drapes and oak furniture showed wear, fading and scratches, but still presented an air of elegance. The manager, dressed in a light grey suit, white shirt and necktie, greeted us. Sweat ran down his cheeks as he explained hotels do not send a list of guests to the authorities. Guests must report in person to the police station. He showed us on a map where to go and it was not far.

The police station was a hut not much bigger than a sentry box and held one officer who looked like Stan Laurel. I showed him my passport which he examined, then registered my details in the book, and Ian did the same. Stan smiled. "Welcome to Damascus."

We thanked him and headed back to the hotel.

We passed what looked like a travel agent, so we stopped and entered. A man dressed in a white shirt and casual trousers and a tall, dark-haired woman dressed in a Syrian airlines uniform greeted us. I explained we wanted a guided tour of the city and we needed it now as we were here for just one night.

The woman did the talking. "I am 'Amira' and he is 'Asher', our guide. What currency do you have?"

"Kuwait dinars, American dollars, and English pounds. I also have some Syrian pounds."

"If you pay in Kuwait dinar, it will be ten for a four-hour tour." I took ten from my wallet and handed her the note.

Our first stop was the Umayyad Mosque (or masjid), also known as the Grand Mosque. Asher related the history of the mosque. It is one of the largest and oldest mosques in the world and the fourth holiest place in the Muslim world. Priceless Persian carpets cover the floor. There were many similarities between the Muslim religion and the Christian religion. In a domed mausoleum stood a gold casket. Asher knew its history, this casket held the head of John the Baptist, known to Muslims as the Prophet Yahya.

I said, "How do you know his head is in there?"

"It is there because Muslims believe it is there."

I wanted to know where he was from. "Where in Syria are you from, Asher?"

"I am not from Syria; I am from Israel. I came here many years ago and now have Syrian citizenship."

Ian was keen to get on with the tour. "Where to now, Asher? I like Damascus."

"You have seen a famous mosque, now you will pass through one of the most famous streets in the world. We will take refreshments there."

We sauntered through the narrow streets of the old city until we arrived at Bab Sharqi, better known as 'Straight Street' (or in Latin, 'Via Recta'). We entered through the arches of the Roman gate of the Sun.

There were so many shops. which sold a variety of textiles, cotton, domestic articles, spices, and imported goods. Artisans worked, not with modern electrical tools, but tools like their ancestors must have used from ancient times, making furniture, household utensils, clothes, and shoes.

My favourite was a children's shoe shop. The shoes were all carefully handmade and so beautiful. Our guide painted such a vivid picture of the history of Damascus I could visualise what it was like all those years ago.

When we stopped for refreshment, a woman brought Arabian coffee plus a glass of water, cheese pasties, small dishes of spiced meats, olives and flatbread. We finished with a big plate of delicious watermelon.

Shortly after we set off again, we came to the House of Judas and Asher related the history again. This is where Saul of Tarsus became blind as punishment for hunting and killing Christians. After he saw the error of his ways, he regained his sight and converted to the Christian faith. After his conversion, Saul changed his name to Paul.

"Now you will visit the most famous church in Damascus."

The original church was long gone, but in its place stood a small chapel. "This is the site of the Church of Saint Paul, who made his escape by being lowered in a basket from a window." He continued with a running commentary on our surroundings as we walked to the next point of interest.

The next important site was the National Museum, Syria's largest museum. It exhibited history from over eleven millennia and displayed various important artefacts, relics, and major finds. Most came from Mari,

Ebla, and Ugarit, three of Syria's most important ancient archaeological sites. Asher told us, "The mosque, church or government pay to have artefacts moved to the museum."

The ruins in Libya, Malta and Cyprus were worth seeing, but they were not as remarkable as these.

We stopped at one shrine where a biblical story was painted on one wall. It identified the story of Moses and the Ten Commandments. Carbon dating confirmed its date as 1000 years BC. From that day, I have believed that Moses existed, and he saw God.

Rooms covering two floors held their own exhibitions showing the afterlife, commerce, conflict, the craft industry, hydrological engineering and religion. The exhibits were all labelled in Arabic and English. It would take more than a month to study it all.

On one floor were marble exhibits, roped off so nobody could touch them. One looked like a tomb, ten feet long and six feet high. Carved on the sides were images of animals and people. I looked but found no information to describe the content or use of this artefact. I wanted to get a closer look and stepped over the rope to examine it. I knew I was in the wrong and put my hand out to touch it. A loud shout that meant 'stop' in Arabic echoed around the room, scaring me. I turned to see who it was and faced a Syrian soldier who pointed a rifle at my chest. I put my hands up level with my head and stepped back over the rope. As I did, a man dressed in a light-coloured suit and necktie came towards us, shouting to the soldier, who lowered his firearm. He apologised profusely. "I am sorry, but we do not permit you to cross over the ropes. These are very important, priceless exhibits. I am the curator of the museum, please come with me." He escorted us to his office and on the way I realised that the soldier would have shot me if I touched the exhibit.

The curator filled three paper cups with water from the cooler and placed them at the edge of the table. "Sit, please, and drink water."

Ian and I sat while Asher stood behind us. He did not defend my behaviour and that made me anxious. After the soldier left, the curator introduced himself. "My name is Abdul Hamid. I am sorry our soldier frightened you."

"Sorry, Abdul, but there is no information and I was inquisitive to know what is inside."

"Don't worry. Where are you from?"

"Scotland, but I work in Kuwait."

My fear disappeared as the conversation drifted into small talk. I was keen to learn about the exhibit. "Abdul, can I ask you a question, please?"

"Of course." He seemed keen to please us.

"What is inside the marble exhibit?"

His reply surprised me. "It is a tomb, discovered in 1942 and moved to the museum."

"Whose tomb is it?"

"We don't know."

"Why not open it and see?"

"We can't, not yet. We have done many tests and have more to do. If you return in fifty years, I might tell you who, or what is inside."

I smiled. "I will try to return then."

Abdul returned the smile. "Thank you for your visit to our museum. Now you may enjoy the rest of the exhibitions, but we close at 6pm."

I made our apologies and thanked him for his understanding. Despite my stupidity, I enjoyed my day. Asher invited us to his home to meet his family and have dinner. I apologised, "I am very sorry, Asher, but Ian and I have been in Kuwait for over six months. If you don't mind, we would like to experience Damascus nightlife."

Asher laughed and added, "I understand, come with me and I will introduce you to a good place."

We passed our hotel and came to an open entrance with shops on either side. An illuminated sign was above steps that led down to open double doors. At the top of the staircase, a man wearing a colourful shirt distributed leaflets that advertised the club at the bottom of the stairs. Asher spoke to him, then we followed him. Inside was a mixture of round and square tables with enough seating for 200 people. There was a solid tiled bar with fabricated stools to sit on. Shelves were stacked with a wide range of spirits in bottles, none were on optics. At least fifty men and women were in the club, eating dinner and drinking alcohol or soft drinks. A decent-sized stage with outstanding quality speakers stood in one corner. Close by, an entrance led to the toilets. I liked the non-intimidating atmosphere. Asher spoke to the man then turned towards us. "This man will make sure you have the best table to see the show that starts at 10pm."

We thanked them both.

At 7:15pm, I handed Asher a ten dinar tip, which he appreciated very much. We returned to the hotel where Ian suggested we get showered and go straight out to explore.

Damascus looked different in the dark. The city did not look run-down as much as it did in daylight. People shopped and ate in full restaurants. I felt safe. Just one beggar approached us and thanked me for the coins I dropped into his tin. For a city that suffered so much in the past, people appeared to be happy.

After our stroll, we headed to the club and by 9pm, we were seated at a table with a splendid view of the stage. The beer tasted nice, and we ate typical Arabian food. The main dish of braised lamb in a spicy sauce came in a clay pot. Rice, vegetables, and nuts came with it. It was delicious.

At 10pm, the lights dimmed, and the doorman took to the stage to act as compere. He took the mic from its stand and announced the programme in Arabic. Glancing towards our table, he repeated it in English.

"We have a fantastic show for you tonight." Everyone applauded.

For the first act, a man in tight trousers and a green shirt sat on a stool and tapped a drum placed across his legs, while a lady performed a belly dance. I didn't look at the man because the belly dancer mesmerised me. She wore a long, green, layered skirt, colourful, revealing bra and a hip belt from which dangled different sized coins, which jingled as she rotated her hips and belly. Her necklace was made from silver discs and she wore matching earrings. A headpiece, colourful armbands and a hip scarf made her a woman of beauty. Her movements were elegant and hypnotising as she moved the upper and lower parts of her body to the sounds of the drum. Her performance ended too soon.

A male Filipino guitar player accompanied by two female singers came on stage for the second act and entertained the crowd with the latest love songs and instrumentals. They left the stage to loud clapping and shouts of approval. For the final act, a tall woman with brown hair, dressed in a cowgirl outfit and carrying a bullwhip came on stage and sang country and western. Her songs were easy to listen to, and her skills with the bullwhip were captivating. As her enthusiasm grew, she cracked the whip harder and put her foot on a chair, but she missed and tumbled to the floor as the chair shot across the stage. No one cared, they wanted more.

The short break in Damascus had certainly been memorable. While I looked out of the window as the flight took off, I promised myself that one day I would be back. I had to establish what was in that tomb. Maybe I'd even visit the same nightclub.

On my return to Kuwait, Tom had left, and an Iraqi called Salam El-Saad had taken over as general manager. A month later, Rory and Ian left. Nouri, another Iraqi became the new contract manager. I kept asking myself how these changes would affect me, or would I be the next to go? Two weeks later, Nouri instructed me to report at 9am to the Ahmadi office, the general manager wanted to talk to me. At dinner, I found out the same instructions had been relayed to others. Ted was pessimistic. "This is it, then, the end of our time in Kuwait. I'm sure we're going to be sacked and replaced with Indian or Polish engineers."

The next day, Nouri led the way to the boardroom and minutes later, a sturdy, clean-shaven man dressed in a smart suit and necktie entered and we stood up. I expected him to smile, but he didn't. I thought, *that's it, they will finish us.*

Mr Saad spoke in a quiet, authoritative voice. "Sit, gentlemen, please." I sat, fearing the content of this meeting. He opened by saying, "You have been working for the company for a year now. It is time for a pay review. You can have a pay rise of twenty-five dinars and no more." I heard everyone sigh with relief. We smiled and thanked him. He continued, "Our accommodation needs have changed and we plan to close Dousra Farm and move everyone out." He and his family had moved into Tom's house, and I suspected we were moving out because he didn't like westerners being so close to his family. "We have a lease on one apartment in Fahaheel and two people can move in right away. So, who wants to move?"

Keith replied first. "Not me."

Ted second. "Not me, I have to go back to the UK for an eye operation."

Steve third. "I want to, but I go on field break on Thursday."

"No problem, Steve, you can either move into the villa we are going to lease or into an apartment later. Andrew, perhaps you and Kenny would like to share an apartment?"

I jumped at the chance. "Yes, please, I will tell him tonight."

"Settled, then."

He explained the changes that were being made. They needed engineers and senior foremen for the new gas plant, and other projects were in the pipeline. The future looked good for our long-term employment.

Over a coffee, before we returned to our respective worksites, we discussed our prospects. Steve's comment was more down to earth and very important to our social life. Where would we move the still to if Dousra closed? This was a problem to solve immediately.

Keith volunteered. "I'm the best man to stay in Dousra as I'm the chief brewer. It'll probably take time to get leases for accommodation for us and the new people for the gas plant, so I'll be there longer. That'll give us time to work out where to move the still to." Problem solved!

My new home with Kenny was an apartment in the Dabbous block in Fahaheel. It was where our friends lived; a couple called Val and Mike and two of the apartments were where the teachers from the oil company school resided. We would be closer to work and a Wimpy Bar, electronics and gold shops. There were no decent restaurants, but there was the possibility of home entertainment with friends close by. Fast food and spit roast chickens from the souk would be an advantage for meals after a long day at work. Life in this desert country was improving.

CHAPTER 7
A WIMPY WINS THE DAY

It pleased Linda when Kenny and I moved to the same block of apartments. Exchanging wine for our beer inside the block meant she did not have to carry alcohol in her car, which was a very real danger for anyone and particularly a female. A few weeks after we moved in, the holy month of Ramadan began and that meant no flash because it was too dangerous to use the still during this period. Schools closed for the summer holidays and Fahaheel became a ghost town. Most expatriates with young children returned home for the holidays and a few older students who attended boarding school came back to join their parents. The two caretakers, Taj and Suleiman, treated Kenny and me with suspicion. They had never had two single men living in their block. Mike told us it was against the law for single men to live in a family block, but added it was unlikely anyone would report us because expatriates lived there. We were careful and kept a low profile. Taj and Suleiman needed to get to know us and trust us. The police were much stricter during Ramadan too.

The teachers returned a few days before the school term began. My wine supply was low, so I telephoned

Linda because her beer stocks were depleted. You never stored beer for a long time as it went off or had the tendency to burst out of the bottles during the summer heat. Nobody wants to return to find their wardrobe or cupboard full of sticky, stinking broken glass. We agreed on the swop. I carried a box of beer and my darts were in my back pocket. There were two sets of stairs and two lifts in the block. This meant going to the ground floor in one and then changing to the other lift to go up again to her apartment. As I came out of the lift, Taj spotted me. "Hello, Mr Andrew, you are good, yes?"

"Yes, Taj. I am good."

Since we moved in, Kenny and I kept the caretakers happy. We gave them a Ramadan bonus and tips each week. It was normal for them to help residents with heavy shopping and parcels. He took the box from me and followed me into the second lift and pressed the button for the third floor. I was curious when Taj walked to Linda's apartment door and pressed the bell. I knew the caretakers were the eyes and ears of the Dabbous block, but how did he know which bell to press? At well over six feet tall, ladies would describe Taj as a handsome man. When Linda opened the door, he greeted her politely. "Mr Andrew to see you, madam. Where do you want me to put the box?" Linda looked a bit surprised when she saw Taj and me together at her door.

"In the kitchen, please, Taj."

"Hi, Linda, good to see you. Welcome back." She stepped aside to allow Taj to pass, and I entered behind him and gave her a welcome-back hug. I whispered, "Two of the bottles are cold."

Taj remained still. "Anything else, madam?"

"No thanks, Taj." Once he had gone, we looked at each. "That was weird, I hope you're giving them both good tips. Do you want a cuppa?"

It was a treat to have tea and real English biscuits. I was polite and ate only two biscuits before playing darts and drinking beer.

On our third game of 501, I heard a door open and turned my head. From the bedroom came a very attractive woman in her late twenties, who was around five-foot, six inches tall. Her hazel eyes made her face glow and her short fair hair framed a round friendly face. She looked athletic and beautiful. Wearing a blue-flowered dress, open sandals and without a touch of make-up, she was beautiful, even with a huge cold sore on her top lip that stood out like a sore thumb. She stood still because Linda started her throw.

"Sixty," Linda called and turned to face the newcomer. "Gilly, this is Andrew who lives in the apartment on the other side of your bedroom wall. Andrew, this is my new flatmate, Gilly."

I shook her hand and welcomed her to Kuwait.

The Kuwait Oil Company's family and recreation club was the envy of every club in Kuwait. The big attraction was the sports facilities, with squash courts and a very nice pool. They invited single women to become members, but no other outsiders. This was one reason I had not met many women. I hoped Gilly played darts, so I might see her again in a social setting. She didn't stay and chat as she had a lot to do to organise for her new teaching post.

Almost a month later, I visited the apartment, and that's when I saw her again. She joined Linda and me for a game of 'Killer'. I got the impression that she liked darts. She wanted to know which beach we went to. I thought, *my luck's in, here's my opportunity.* "Gilly, if you'd like to go to a good beach, we can go at the weekend."

Linda assured her, "You'll like it there. It's a long journey, but worth it. People take their barbecues and it's fun."

Being polite, I asked Linda to join us, but she declined. "Sorry, I've already planned to go on a natural history field trip this weekend."

My prayers were answered when Gilly said, "I would love to go."

The day out to the beach I had looked forward to all week started out well, but we never reached our destination. After a half-hour, disaster struck. Smoke billowed out from the car bonnet, so I pulled over to check. One of the radiator hoses had burst. We were going nowhere in this car, and it would have to be picked up by the leasing company. I made the car safe and removed our bags and barbecue from the boot.

Gilly looked perturbed and anxious. She was in the middle of nowhere with few cars on the road, with a virtual stranger – me. It would have been so much easier if it was the present, a twentieth century mobile would have got us out of this quandary in no time, unless there was no signal. As it was the 1970s, I hoped help would come along soon. Twenty sweaty minutes later, I could see that Gilly was getting increasingly worried. A distant dust cloud was the sign of our rescue and I flagged down the vehicle. We squeezed into a big American-style taxi with four other Arabs dressed in dirty dishdashas. They smoked continually, so the windows were half-open to let out the cigarette smoke and the smell from whatever was in their bags. We rode back to Fahaheel in silence.

The taxi driver dropped us close to our apartment block. As we entered, the only thing that I could say was, "Sorry, Gilly, do you want to go another weekend?"

She looked disinterested, as if she would consider it, but not with me. However, I was surprised by her reply. "Sure, why not, I don't blame you for the problem with the car. It was an experience, in particular, our taxi companions. I wasn't keen on their aftershave."

That's when I had an idea. "Gilly, it hasn't turned out well today. It's still early and if you like, I'll go back to my apartment and cook you some barbecue and bring it over. We can have a game of darts, drink beer and eat. How about it?"

It took her a few moments to answer. "Okay, I will make some salad."

I dumped the barbecue and bags, then two minutes later entered the Wimpy bar carrying a large wooden tray. I ordered the best barbecue on the menu. They wrapped it in tinfoil and laid it out on the tray. I added a real bottle of white wine to accompany the meal and make up for the disastrous afternoon. When she opened her door and smelt, then saw the food, she said, "This is amazing." I had turned the day around. The food was delicious, and she was amazed by the real French wine. She teased me about our escapade in the desert and next she beat me at darts.

There were over 20,000 men in Kuwait on bachelor status, but from that moment, I led the race for her affections. Many interesting and fun outings followed this bad, then successful, beginning.

A desert is a dangerous place, but a fascinating place to visit. I had heard of an oasis that held water from November until March. Gilly had already ventured into the desert with members of the Natural History Society so I asked her if she would like to come with me to find it, and she agreed.

We set off on the ring road and turned on to the highway at Jahra, then drove towards Saudi Arabia, leaving civilisation behind. My car was behaving perfectly this time. After an hour, bushes and trees appeared. I knew we had arrived because I spotted a dirt track that led to a small island surrounded by a sea of sand. I parked between the trees and stepped out into a cool breeze. On the opposite side to us, a small boy of about ten years old sat on a fallen tree. It looked like a scene from an old bible movie. He wore shepherd's clothes and held a crook in his hand. Goats grazed on the dry grass and fallen leaves.

The boy watched us unload the car and lay out the picnic. I waved and he waved back. I told Gilly about the rules of the desert and she suggested sharing our picnic. She put a chicken sandwich, some Australian ginger nut biscuits, fruit and a cold drink into a plastic bag. Circumventing the lake so as not to frighten the goats, I greeted the boy in Arabic. He responded, but he would not leave his herd to join us. He accepted the food and drink before I backtracked to our picnic.

Before eating, we stretched our legs and investigated our surroundings. Near to the water we found many plants. The desert can be beautiful and colourful after rain or near water, and we admired the beauty of the delicate flowers, a memory to treasure. The walk made us hungry. When we finished, I put all the rubbish in a bag and showed it to our neighbour, the goatherd. He copied my actions and placed his rubbish into the bag. To conserve and preserve the beauty of this area, I returned to him to collect it. I handed him another drink and returned to the car. As we drove away, we waved, and he waved back. I felt good, and I think Gilly did.

On our way home, we passed a rather large man sitting with two women dressed in abayas and niqabs. They had four children with them. Remembering our disastrous escapade and how we had felt waiting in the heat, we thought their transport may have broken down and they might need food and drink. I pulled up a little way after them and suggested that we join them.

"Yes, let's join them, they look hot and hungry and I don't see any sign of food or drinks. We've plenty of soft drinks and some leftover food."

I approached the group, carrying the food and drinks, and greeted the man. Using hand signals and broken

Arabic, I asked if we could join them. He welcomed us and we chatted and finished what was left of the picnic. None of us could understand what we were talking about, but we smiled and nodded our heads a lot. I am sure they were pleased we joined them. Khalil shook my hand and everyone, including his two wives, waved goodbye. It felt good to show friendship and more desert etiquette to the indigenous population. This is how different nations get to know and begin understanding each other and our different cultures.

As the car approached civilization, we drove down a wide stretch of road that looked as if it could be an emergency runway, we were very close to the airport. Fifty or more white painted villas appeared on the horizon and I would have driven straight past, but Bedouin people were living in tents pitched in the square, and the animals were in the houses. The Kuwait government could build modern accommodation for the Bedouin, but they would only accept and use the things from modern life that suited their way of life. They could not be forced to be brought into the twentieth century and follow new rules and culture.

Late afternoon, we split up to take separate lifts to our respective apartments. Just as she was about to get in the lift, she put her hand on my arm. "I enjoyed my day today. Can we do it again sometime?"

I felt excited. "Of course we can. I look forward to it."

News spread fast, and tickets rapidly sold out for an international darts match between Kuwait and Great Britain. The Gazelle Club put on an eye-watering buffet and free soft drinks to accompany the event. Naturally, there was no alcohol, but those Brits and other Europeans, who were lucky enough to purchase tickets, placed their coolers and bottles under the table out of sight. It would be a glorious night. The match rules were simple, it would be the best of five games for singles and the same for doubles. You could put your name down to play against a professional in an hour of fun after the match and the buffet finished. If there were enough people sober enough to throw darts, a game of killer would end the event.

Great Britain's team lined up to a tremendous reception. They were John Lowe, Bobby George and Eric Bristow from England, and Jocky Wilson from Scotland.

The organisers had erected a competition, and two practice boards on a raised platform for the benefit of spectators. I sat with Gilly, Linda and Kenny and a group of others I knew. Kenny supplied the best quality flash and Linda, her professionally labelled bottles of homemade wine.

The Kuwait players came from the house dart's league. Chong, who I had met several times, captained our team. After the welcome ceremony and introduction of the players, Chong took his place in front of the competition board. John Lowe, the British team captain, joined him. By luck or not, Chong's first three darts scored one-hundred and eighty. This caused an uproar. I think it shocked John too as he only scored sixty. The match continued with our guests enjoying tastes of home-brewed beer and tales from the desert in between playing serious games of darts, which resulted in Great Britain winning the match by five games to nil.

After the competition ended, a Middle Eastern-style buffet was served. When the tables were cleared, a raffle was drawn. The top prize was two airline tickets to Cyprus. I didn't win a prize, not even the bottle of whisky, another much sought-after prize. Gilly was much luckier, her prize was a giant stuffed lion she named Leo. She had fun taking Leo back to the UK after her first year in Kuwait. She squashed Leo into her sports bag and, on arrival at Heathrow, was stopped by customs, who asked her what was inside the bag. Her reply was, "You'll never believe this. It's a lion. I won it in a raffle." The dumbfounded officer made her unpack it to check it out for contraband. It was X-rayed and passed back to her. Out of sight of the officers, she cursed them. She couldn't squeeze Leo back into her bag and struggled on the underground with a heavy suitcase, an empty sports bag and a cuddly toy stuffed under one arm.

For the finale, the ladies' team took on the guests. The guests found their ability to hit treble twenty had diminished to such a point the ladies won most of the games. Alcohol in Kuwait is very strong. The night came to a close, the music stopped, and the organiser thanked us all for coming and reminded everyone to rinse out the bottles we had brought and dump any beer left in the coolers. Everyone enjoyed the function, especially the GB team.

CHAPTER 8
LESSONS LEARNED

Kuwait is a semi-desert area. The land comprises sand and gravel with occasional outcrops of rock. The conditions are common to all deserts, high temperatures, a lack of water, and high salt content in the soil. Despite these adverse conditions, it has a rich biodiversity of 374 plants comprising dwarf perennial bushes, annual grasses and herbs. This includes 256 annuals, 83 herbaceous perennials, 34 shrubs and one tree. (Shamal Az Zour Al Aoula KSC). I am not sure where the tree is. It must have been well protected and I wonder what happened to it in the Gulf War.

Mutla Ridge is where people go to relax in winter. Once you get there, in one direction you can see to Kuwait city, in the other direction is Iraq. To continue our adventures together, I invited Gilly to accompany me to Mutla. On the way, we stopped at the harbour where artisans build traditional old sailing ships called dhows. It was a sunny day and the temperature was perfect, just like a blazing hot day we can experience in a UK summer. In the past, dhows were used for coastal trade, fishing and pearl-diving. No modern tools or metal are used to build them. I loved to watch the men with sun-dried features as they filled the air with smoke from thick hand-rolled cigarettes, which smelled like camel dung, working at carving the planking and ribs for the boat. They used dowel drills to make holes through which they hammered the wooden plugs to fix planking to the ribs. Each drill had diamond-shaped points to produce the range of holes needed. Gilly bought a drill, with help from my bargaining skills. She explained it would be an artefact to use in her teaching career. We were lucky to witness such skills.

My technicians did jobs that needed skills to perform them. I appreciated people like Younis who, on one occasion, cut a seized bearing from a shaft using a welding torch, rags, and icy water. When the inner race split, it left no marks on the shaft. I don't think my skills matched his.

On my return from work one afternoon, I saw Gilly with Linda and Taj gathered around a small white car. Gilly had bought it from an expatriate who was going home. Feeling proud of her purchase, she had filled a bucket with water as she intended to give it a good clean, inside and out, just like she would do at home in Yorkshire. It was not to be. Taj appeared as if by magic, explaining that it was not right for 'madam' to do manual work. This was true, it would be frowned upon. The other reason being it was the caretaker's perk job to do such tasks. He could make a decent monthly profit from all the apartment dwellers' cars. After arranging a monthly deal, she left Taj to finish what she had started. I watched all these negotiations then went over to offer to check out her car. I would run it up on the ramp at the ADMC and make sure it was roadworthy. On the way, she chatted about the car, she told me she bought it because she wanted her independence. She was getting a lift to work, but had to leave when her lift left. With her car, she could see more of Kuwait and go places without having to bother anybody.

I was worried because she wouldn't need me anymore.

I drove the compact Mitsubishi Lancer onto the ramp and checked it over. I was cheeky and interested to know how much she paid for it. She told me and I praised her. "You got a bargain there."

"I'm from Yorkshire, what would you expect? Would you mind stopping at the supermarket, I need to buy some food."

"Not at all."

The outside temperature must have been close to freezing as I pushed open the door at White's supermarket. Gilly hurried around the shop, searching for what she wanted. I felt happy and relaxed as I followed her, but tensed when, ten feet away, I spotted Akar. Earlier, Nouri asked me to find a job for him, and I gave him a job as the tea boy. The other workers did not accept him, and I stepped in to help. He was a nice. cheerful young man, who had difficulty settling in because he was an outsider from Egypt.

What happened next embarrassed me. Wearing a heavy army greatcoat and a beret, he came over. To my horror, he jumped to attention and saluted me, attracting the attention of other shoppers. I wanted to hide.

Gilly looked shocked and then amused. "You're popular, aren't you?"

I shook his hand, but I wanted to kill him. Word of my embarrassing moment spread like wildfire, and my friends made fun of me for a few days, but I soon got over it.

The hostility towards Akar did not stop, so I asked Younis to explain the reason. I suspected racial discrimination. "Mr Cruder, he is a tea boy, and he is paid more than the other labourers."

Wages were Nouri's responsibility, but I knew the labourers were poorly paid. I requested Nouri to pay the labourers more to remove the hostility, and he agreed. Problem solved!

I returned to the office and told him the good news. "Younis, I have promoted the four labourers so they will get a pay increase. Will that keep them happy?"

"Yes, Mr Cruder, it will."

The following day, the labourers helped the fitters, but did not tidy up or sweep the floor. I asked Younis, "Why aren't they clearing up?"

He laughed. "Mr Cruder, yesterday you promoted them, now they think they are semi-skilled workers and not labourers."

"So, Younis, do I need to hire four new labourers?"

"I think so, Mr Cruder."

I grabbed a three-foot broom and swept the floor.

Khan rushed over and called out, "Mr Andrew, you can't do that."

"Sorry, Khan, there is no one else qualified to do it."

Khan yelled in his language and the labourers jumped up and grabbed the other brooms. He pleaded, "Please stop, Mr Andrew!"

Another lesson was learned, but, this time, my workers learned it.

The harmony lasted a few months until I made a big mistake. One morning, the driver telephoned the office. He explained that the shop had no yellow label tea bags, and he needed to go to another shop to buy them. He wanted permission to claim the cost back, as we only had an account with the shop he was at. Younis was out, and I was annoyed he called me. "Don't they have any other tea bags?

"Yes, Mr Andrew, they have red label."

This was the moment my drastic error was made. I didn't give him time to finish his explanation and cut him off. "Okay, get the red label and I will give you a refund."

"Yes, Mr Andrew."

I should have been more patient. He was a driver and would not question my decision.

When Younis returned, I saw Khan complain to him and then Younis quizzed the driver. I knew better than to go out and ask if there was a problem. He returned to the office and repeated the gist of the conversation. "Mr Cruder, the men are refusing to work."

I was stunned. "What's the problem, Younis?"

He looked serious. "Mr Cruder, we have the wrong tea bags."

"What's wrong with the tea bags, tea is tea, isn't it?"

He told me firmly, "No, Mr Cruder. Here we only drink the yellow label. You told the driver to buy the red label. The men are angry."

Tea could have been the start of an expensive time for my company and the reason for my dismissal. I apologised. "Sorry, Younis, as you know, I drink coffee, I did not think. Send the driver to get the correct tea bags."

He was happy. "Yes, Mr Cruder, right away."

I waited a day, then asked the men to stop work and gather round. I apologised. "I am sorry for my mistake; I know nothing about tea; you need to teach me." There were smiles all round. My theory was: There are times to be tough and there are times to grovel.

That night, I relaxed by listening to music. When the telephone rang, I just heard it. I removed my earphones before answering. It was Gilly, she sounded to be in a panic. "Andrew, are you busy, my car won't start and I need a lift to the Kuwait Little Theatre and I am already late." I readily offered, I wanted to please her.

On the way, I asked her, "What's on at the theatre?"

"Nothing, I am going to be in *Oklahoma!* It will be one of the biggest productions that the KLT has ever done." She sounded excited.

"What part do you have?"

"I am a dancer in the 'dream ballet'."

"How many nights do you have to practise?"

"Every night."

"Would you like me to wait for you?"

"No need, there are plenty of people there that will give me a lift."

"I'll check your car tomorrow after work and see if I can fix it."

"Thanks. You're a star." She dropped her car key in the drinks holder. As I pulled up close to a side door, I heard loud music. "Oh, heck, I'm too late," she groaned.

"Let me check."

We got out, and I pushed the side door open just enough to peep inside. People sat on benches, singing their hearts out.

I heard a female voice call out, "Come inside and sit down."

Before I could say anything, Gilly pushed me inside and the door closed, so there was no escape. A lady gave us song sheets and by the end of rehearsal, I was signed up. I was in the show as a cowboy in Oklahoma.

Before setting off for work, I checked her car. It was a simple problem, the battery was flat. I removed it and took it to work for charging. Once I fitted it back, her car started on the first attempt. I left the key with Taj and asked him to clean the car, then return her key. Later, she telephoned me. She sounded grateful. "Thank you for fixing my car, I owe you a meal. Are you going to rehearsal tonight?"

"Yes, would you like a lift?"

"No, but we can go together, I'll drive."

"All right, but remember, I get free petrol." She giggled. Petrol in this oil-rich country was almost free.

"I'll call you when I am about to leave and meet you downstairs. Bye."

I did not expect rehearsals to be so tough. Patti, one of Gill's teacher colleagues, choreographed the show, and she believed in perfection. The men were not just expected to be cowboys, they had to be stuntmen and dancers too. It was a hard slog for us, trying to meet her standards, but it was fun.

After three weeks of rehearsals, several of the husband and wife teams assumed Gilly and I were a couple. There was a public holiday so we would get a day off from rehearsal. A cast member suggested our group go to the Sheraton for dinner and ten of us agreed.

The buffet at the Sheraton excelled itself that night and the homemade wine was perfect. A starry night, cooler temperature, music, good company around a poolside table made Gilly sigh and she gazed around the pool area. "It's like a scene from a James Bond movie! Any moment now, someone will dive from the highest board to escape the villain!" It was a glorious night and everyone wanted the fun to continue.

Chalky said, "Everyone round to my place." Nobody needed persuading. We were all in a party mood.

It was past midnight as we got into the car to leave Chalky's house. I knew the police would be out on patrol, so I drove back on the highway, avoiding the coast road. The police seldom set up roadblocks on the highway.

Our car park had one entrance and one exit and a police vehicle blocked the exit. We had not escaped danger. I parked and told her, "Gilly, keep quiet and let me answer all the questions."

The police sergeant left his car and sauntered over to us. I rolled the window down and he held out his hand. "Papers!"

Gilly opened her bag to take out her papers and I stopped her. I told her, "Leave now and go straight up to your apartment, use the stairs and don't look back. Once you get inside, lock the door and don't open it. I will knock twice so you know it is me. If I don't come in ten minutes, go to bed."

The police officer, I assumed, would not talk to a woman in a public place if she was accompanied by a man. He would not call her back. I was lucky, that was exactly what happened. He ignored her as I took out my passport copy and permits. He pointed to the back of the car and said, "Open." I opened the boot. He searched and found nothing illegal. He opened each door and raked the inside. He was searching for alcohol. He left my car and walked towards the apartment block and I followed. When we reached the entrance, he turned to face me and held up his watch so the time showed. He tapped the watch face and repeated, "Madam, madam."

I must have looked mystified because he tapped it again, then put his hands together close to his right ear and said it again. I understood what he meant. Madam should be in bed. I apologised for the error and grovelled once more. "I won't keep her out late again. I promise, sir."

He gave me my papers back, and I headed for the stairs to Gill's apartment. I knocked twice and stayed the night. The police might still have been watching the block for any suspicious activity, such as me leaving one side of the block and going to my apartment via the other lift or steps. It was a lucky escape.

It would be a good story to tell the cast members at the next rehearsal. The show got tremendous reviews and played for a week. Expatriates from all over Kuwait came, and the Americans in the audience appreciated the very professional production.

The excitement of Oklahoma was soon overshadowed by the pressure of work. As the gas plant neared completion, they hired additional engineers to fill the jobs it created. The general manager asked to see Kenny and me again. I did not expect to be sacked, but someone might have complained about two bachelors living in a family block. We entered his office to hear some not very good news. He spoke with a voice of authority. "Sorry, gentlemen, but you have to move out of your apartment." He did not give a reason or give us a chance to ask for one. He said, "Check out the new apartments in Fintas and, if one of them is acceptable, then you can move in." I felt relieved.

The Fintas apartment block was impressive. It was built close to the coast road and was surrounded by more new ones. It was not in a busy commercial area, like the Dabbous block, so it was an ideal location. Police would not pay too much attention to anybody who lived here. We moved in a week later.

Being a family-only block, we were careful, we needed to get accepted by the caretaker and the other residents. No one minded us being there, as we were able to supply alcohol, plus we didn't hog the pool area. I only swam in the luxury pool when accompanied by Gill. After a while, Kenny volunteered us to be dog-minders for residents going on holiday. We panicked when a dog decided it missed its owners, escaped and romped off into the desert to find them. To our relief, it gave up and returned after two days, dusty, hungry, thirsty and wagging its tail, so pleased to see us.

Although some expatriates worked here for twenty years or more, most only stayed a short time. Conditions are harsh and not to everyone's taste. After five years, I quit. The experience I gained would help me get a decent job back home. Mike, our neighbour from the Dabbous apartments, suggested a change of job might be better than trying to settle back into the UK. He arranged an interview as a calibration engineer with an American company. It would be similar work to what I did at Ferranti after I left the RAF. They offered me a job, but I turned it down. The pay and conditions did not tempt me to stay, and I prepared to leave Kuwait.

My lathe operator wanted to retire and when Younis and I discussed what present to give him, I asked, "When you retire, will you return to Pakistan?"

He was quick to answer, "No, I don't want to go back there, it freezes in the winter and I will die from the cold. Kuwait has been my home for more than half of my life. I need to live someplace warm."

The team bought Anwar a silver plate with a picture of the Kuwait Towers engraved on it and a personal message of appreciation.

I also got a present, which I have to this day. Anwar made me a model in brass of an electrical transformer. I felt emotional as Younis presented it.

Complaints were not uncommon, but there was a sense of community spirit in this country and my workplace. It had taken me years to get used to the culture. I discovered that the men I met and worked with were not unlike me. They had their beliefs, their habits, and there was a respected hierarchy. Like me, they would have a good moan now and then. People are so similar all over the world.

As I boarded the flight from Kuwait for the last time, I knew I would miss it and the characters I met. I gave little thought to my future or where I might go from here.

CHAPTER 9

A NEW WASHING MACHINE

Gilly left Kuwait and got a job back in Yorkshire as a supply teacher. In Kuwait, she got paid in sterling and the exchange rate did not affect her salary, so she had saved enough to put down a deposit on a house. We married and moved into our first home together in a small village, only a few miles away from her parents.

I came home after five years with a wealth of experience, but broke and unemployed. After two weeks, I secured a job offer as a maintenance engineer for an oil company based in Nigeria. When I telephoned the recruiter to check on the progress of my visa, I asked him a question that I should have asked earlier. "Why did the person I am replacing leave?" Silence followed. I said, "Are you still there?"

He sounded uneasy. "He had an accident."

"What kind of accident?"

He hesitated. "Bandits killed him."

That ended my interest in working in Nigeria.

A few days later, my passport arrived with a Nigerian visa. I would not be using it. Unemployment was a less dangerous way of life.

I posted my CV out to hundreds of companies. Just like when you wait for a bus, word of two interviews came on the same day. One for an adviser position at a power station in Pakistan, and the other, for an electrical trainer in Sarawak. Both interviews would be in London.

The Pakistan job interview came first. Two recruiters interviewed me, and it went well until one asked my view on preaching Christianity to Muslims. This guy was a bible-pusher and I replied, "Life is valuable to me, and anyone doing that would be stupid." There were no more questions on that subject.

During the Sarawak interview, the interviewer asked about electronic governors. I had no experience with them and told the truth. I did not think he would offer me that job now, but to my surprise, both offers came in the same post. The Pakistan job meant desert conditions with a high salary. Armed escorts would accompany me outside the security compound, and that put me off. The Sarawak job interested me the most. A car came with the job even though there were few decent roads in the tropical rainforest. Gilly would be allowed to come out after I satisfied the probationary period of three months, and then I could be employed there for several years. There was no contest, I chose the Sarawak job. The salary was less, but the prospect of experiencing Malaysian culture and living in a tropical rainforest zone far outweighed any monetary gain in Pakistan.

The island of Borneo is divided between three countries: Indonesia, the Malaysian Federated States of Sabah and Sarawak, and Brunei Darussalam. The inhabitants are ethnic Malays, Chinese, Indian and indigenous tribes. The nation boasts an unparalleled mixture of ethnicity and culture. The Dayak is one of the native groups of Borneo. There are over 200 riverine and hill-dwelling ethnic subgroups in the central and southern interior. Each group has different dialects, customs, laws, territory and culture. My job would be to train Sarawakian workers for Shell Oil Company. I would be based at Lutong, a small village a few miles from the oil town of Miri. I looked forward to the challenge.

That evening, Gilly and I did our homework and decided that I had made the right choice. She finished by saying, "It sounds a fascinating place, but there is one thing I must stipulate if we go to live in Sarawak."

"What's that?"

"You can have a car, but I want a washing machine!"

Gilly had never owned a washing machine, and I knew she wanted one. I put my arms around her and promised. "Darling, you will have the best washing machine in the world." A month later, we kissed goodbye, and I flew to Singapore.

Mike, a tall, well-set man with fair hair, met me at Singapore airport. After sitting in an aeroplane for over 12 hours, I wanted to walk and stretch my legs, then get some sleep, but Mike had other ideas. First, we had forms to process. I had to sign my contract because my salary would start from the day it was signed. Contracts were signed outside the UK and Malaysia because of some legal requirement. I signed it in the hotel lobby, then Mike suggested we go out to eat. I wanted to experience this cosmopolitan city and agreed to meet at 7pm. After a short nap and a refreshing shower, I felt fully awake when we left the hotel.

Singapore is a busy city, with Malay, Chinese, Arab, Indian and English cultures. The buildings were a mix of old and new, with signs of prosperity all around. We went to a hawker market in Chinatown for dinner. Mike explained the many dishes, which included chicken rice, fried kway teow, satay, chilli crab and the healthy yong tau fu dish. I had never heard of these dishes and my brain was suffering from jetlag. A thousand people were talking loudly and that added to my confusion, so I asked Mike to order. I was not disappointed by his choice. The array of dishes was delicious, some sweet, some sour and noodles in a spicy sauce. My taste buds were awakened and sang with appreciation after the bland aeroplane food.

Next, we made our way to Raffles Hotel, renowned for the stance people made there during the Japanese invasion. As the invaders arrived at the hotel, an orchestra played 'The Last Waltz'. Guests were on the floor dancing to it and others sat sipping pink gins in the Long Bar. That is where someone shot and killed the last Singapore tiger. After a beer in these exotic surroundings, Mike said, "Are you tired?"

"No, just got my second wind," My watch was still on British time so, for me, it was mid-afternoon.

He seemed pleased that I was still awake. He cried out, "Super, you can sleep in tomorrow. We're on the late flight, so let's go to Boogie Street."

He didn't look like a man who liked to dance.

The sign read Bugis Street. It was a busy precinct with restaurants, bars and shops. We selected an outside table and ordered a beer from a young woman wearing a colourful pinafore around her waist and a sailor's hat on her head. Within seconds, we were joined by two women with heavy make-up, long, jet-black hair, shapely legs and wearing tight dresses over their slender bodies. The woman placed a drink in front of each of the girls. She then pushed the ashtray to the side and stood a board game on the table.

"Do you want to play Connect 4?" asked the lady who looked like a model.

I speculated that the question related to sex. I'd heard tales about this city, but she meant the board game. I lost the game, in fact, I did not win any games. It occurred to me that the ladies' voices sounded strange. I looked at Mike for guidance.

He quietly explained. "They're not women, they're ladyboys, transvestites. They're paid by the bar owner to play these games. If you look at the bill, it will show two extra drinks."

Leaving them sitting at the table, we found another bar. This time, I ended up losing at noughts and crosses to a ten-year-old boy. My first experience of South East Asia was shocking but nice, and Mike paid the bills. I ended my long day with a good night's sleep, dreaming of home and Boogie Street.

Our onward flight stopped for forty-five minutes at Kuching, the capital of Sarawak. The terminal building didn't have air conditioning and the humid heat made my body sweat. I looked out of the terminal window onto lush green jungle. The insect noise could be heard from where I was standing. When we took off again, I was shivering because of the freezing air in the aircraft. As we disembarked at Miri airport and I stepped out onto the tarmac to walk across to arrivals, sweat poured from my face and body. With these extreme changes in temperature, I must have lost a kilo in weight since I left home. Mike's car was parked at the terminal and he drove us to the Park Hotel, where he made sure I was checked in before he left. I headed upstairs to my room and bed.

A traditional bacon, eggs and beans breakfast helped to clear my hangover. I did not hear Mike arrive because a noisy film called *The Green Beret* was playing on the TV that was fixed on the opposite wall. After he finished his breakfast, he drove me five miles to the Shell offices at Lutong. At the admin office, a business-like lady called Lucy discussed my contract, ending with, "Are you satisfied with your terms?"

"Yes, I am."

"Good, welcome to Shell. Mike, you can take Andrew to his workplace."

Mike introduced me to John, the department head, and then left us. As John read out extracts from my CV, I realised someone had changed it as soon as he said, "I am glad you're an expert on electronic governors." I thought I had swallowed my tongue because no sound came out of my mouth. After a few seconds, he said, "Peter, our training manager is in England on leave so you can't meet him yet. If you follow me, our chief instructor will show you around and introduce you to the rest of the staff."

Another tall, fair-haired man called John welcomed me to the team. Within fifteen minutes, the tour had finished. John knocked and entered the electrical classroom to introduce and leave me with my work partner, Eric. He had an accent I recognised as being from Nottingham. We returned to our office, and he made coffee. I felt relaxed and relieved that I'd chosen this job and not the one in Pakistan.

Trainees came from mixed backgrounds with Malay, Chinese, and tribespeople being dominant. They had to complete eighteen months of artisan training before being assigned to either an onshore or an offshore installation. Lessons were in English and we developed our own training materials. Visits to other installations and offshore platforms were necessary to conduct training and carry out training needs analysis.

This appeared to be an outstanding job, and I had to be clear with Eric about electronic governors. "What is the connection to electronic governors?" I asked.

"We needed someone experienced with electronic control systems, I am experienced on mechanical systems, not electronic."

"I'm not familiar with electronic speed governors but I have experience with electronic systems. If you like, I will prepare the notes and conduct those classes."

He looked relieved. "I'm pleased about that."

Eric went home for lunch, so Bloomers, the instrument instructor, invited me to go with him and a few others to

Lutong market for lunch. We arrived less than ten minutes later. I felt sick when I saw meat being sold that was covered with flies and smelled rotten. Four of us took our seats around a wooden table with an ashtray in the middle. Flies buzzed all around us and I could smell the drains. Within a minute, a round-faced Malaysian woman around thirty years old took our order. Bloomers said, "My usual please, Cherry."

The others ordered fried mee and a drink. I ordered egg and chips and a Pepsi.

Cherry did not write it down and moved off to take further orders. I asked, "How does Cherry remember everyone's order?"

Jeff replied, "Cherry has a photographic memory, she remembers everything she hears." A young man placed a pot of tea, small cups without handles, four small side plates and a fork and spoon wrapped in a tissue on the table. I wanted a drink, but not hot tea. Jeff patted him on the shoulder. "This is Cherry's brother, Sam. He remembers nothing you tell him, unlike his sister." Sam ignored us and moved onto the next customer.

Bloomers filled four cups with tea and the others held their plate and cutlery to one side and poured the tea over them. I said, "Why did you do that?"

"Because kitchens here have no hot water, washing with tea helps to remove the bugs that give you a sore tummy."

"Thanks for the advice." I followed suit.

People at the other tables were also washing their utensils using the tea. I turned to look at the rest of the market and my heart pounded. A rat appeared from a drain hole, but customers ignored it. I have to admit; I enjoyed my egg and chips, and my stomach caused me no problems afterwards. This was the place you were brought to boost your immune system against every bug you could encounter in Sarawak.

In the afternoon, Mike collected me to go to Miri town to apply for my permits. As he approached the outskirts of the town, he pointed to a wooden structure on a hill. "That is the Grand Old Lady, the first oil well drilled in 1910."

A tour of Miri followed and that took barely ten minutes to complete. With a population of 150,000, only one shop sold western food. I saw two banks, a dentist, two medical clinics plus an outdoor market. Most building walls were concrete with red or blue-tiled roofs, and others were wooden with corrugated iron roofs. We stopped at a garage to collect my new white Datsun car. I followed Mike back to the Park Hotel and parked the car there before rejoining him to continue the tour.

He drove to three clubs. The golf club, the boat club, and Gymkhana Club. We stopped for a beer in the boat club then another at the Gymkhana Club. I got automatic membership of the boat club and Gymkhana Club for an annual fee. There was a waiting list to join the golf club. No cash transactions took place at any of the clubs. Members signed a chit for what they purchased and paid the bill monthly. Construction was in progress for a new bar and squash courts at the Gymkhana Club and families were gathered around an international-size swimming pool. They named it the Gymkhana Club because, in the past horses lived there, but they died and were not replaced. I knew Gilly would like it here, this country was so much better than Kuwait. It would suit us perfectly, we would be happy here. At dinner, I chose Chinese dishes from the buffet, watched *The Green Berets*, then headed upstairs for a good night's sleep.

I got to know Miri and its people because I explored everywhere from the airport to the Kuala Baram ferry terminal, a distance of around 20 miles. Just after the airport, the hardtop road finished and a dirt track disappeared into the jungle. There were no roads beyond Kuala Baram where a ferry terminal on the mighty Baram River was located. Ferryboats crossed over to Brunei and smaller boats headed upriver to the longhouses on the river banks. Another road, the Krokop road, followed the river from Lutong to Miri. On the way, it passed through the centre of a Chinese cemetery surrounded by white magnolia trees. At night, I drove quickly through the trees in case there were ghosts.

Sarawak has an average daily temperature of thirty-two degrees centigrade with high humidity and, because it is tropical, it feels warm-to-hot all year round. Despite the heat, high humidity, heavy rain, rats and cockroaches, I still enjoyed being here. In my letters, I wrote the facts down truthfully, the good and the bad things I encountered. Gilly wrote back, *'I don't care about the insects and humidity, I'll get used to them. Just make sure I have a washing machine'*.

Peter, our manager, telephoned and asked me to go to his office. It would be our first meeting. He welcomed me to the team and then informed me my probation period was over. I thanked him. I was so happy and I knew Gilly would be over the moon to hear she would be with me soon. Eric suggested I talk to John as he had just moved into a new villa in Pujut, and there was one more available.

I followed John home, and he introduced me to a Malaysian lady called Chong. Her family owned five villas in a cul-de-sac. She lived in one with her husband, Aho, and their three children. Aho's father occupied the villa next door to hers. An English couple and their two children lived in the corner house, and John, a bachelor Scotsman lived in the one next to it and the vacant one next to John's was for rent. The villas had arches over the patio, making them look Spanish in style. Chong showed me inside and explained she would put in temporary furniture until the new stuff arrived from Singapore. The villa had a sitting room with two steps leading to a dining room with a breakfast bar and kitchen next to it. I was told a washing machine would arrive with the new furniture. Outside, the garden looked a mess, but she read my thoughts. "Not the right month for planting, later I will plant the gardens with trees and bushes."

Gilly flew into Miri Airport two weeks later and four weeks before my probationary period should have ended. I prepared her new villa well. As she entered through the patio doors, her face lit up. "It's terrific," she cried.

"Go to the kitchen. There's a big surprise waiting for you."

"My washing machine," she exclaimed, jumping to the top of the two steps and heading across the dining room to the kitchen. She hooted. "Is this it, a blue bucket and a scrubbing brush and a sign that says, 'Washing Machine'?"

I gave her a big hug. "Your new furniture and washing machine has arrived from Singapore but is still in the port. You'll get it delivered after a week."

She raised her eyebrows. "You rotter, tricking me like that."

I sensed she would enjoy living here.

CHAPTER 10
THE GAME HUNTER

It took Gilly a week to settle in. She found a job teaching at an international school and made friends. She needed her own car so we bought a Nissan Micra. The benefits of having my salary paid to a bank in the UK soon became apparent. With Gilly's teacher salary plus my allowances, it meant my salary reduced the mortgage quickly. We still had enough left over to enjoy the activities we liked and travel to see more of the world. Both of us liked Malaysian food so we did not have to buy expensive western food. Some western items that were scarce, we still bought and when new stocks arrived, the jungle drums sounded and we joined the race to buy HP sauce, biscuits and baked beans. They were necessities.

South-East Asia became a worthwhile existence. We both had good jobs, a villa planted with mango and papaya trees, two cars and heaps of friends. It had its downside, too, packs of wild dogs roamed the streets and they concerned me. If you got bitten by a wild dog or a snake, it could be fatal. Residents walked around and took no notice of the dangers. The government banned cockfighting years earlier, but this cruel sport thrived. Those involved kept their prize birds in cages in the garden or on the patio. You didn't require an alarm clock to wake up.

The good side was when the new bar and squash courts opened at the Gymkhana Club. The squash courts had a gallery that enabled spectators to watch the games and that created interest from Malaysians. A group of us set up a serious squash league with thirty boxes of five players in each. I reached the top league, box one, but was unable to maintain it. The young Malaysians taking up the game learnt quickly. Their enthusiasm and skills were tremendous, and they soon set an elevated standard. Squash turned into an immense aspect of our lives both socially and as a competitive sport. Gilly became a skilful player and gained the status of number two women's player and competed in box three against the men.

One time, after a hard-fought game, some ladies watching it talked to her.

One of them asked her, "Are you from Australia?"

"No, I'm from England."

"Would you teach us to play?"

That became the start of more friendships.

On the eve of Chinese New Year, I remained on the balcony to view a sublime display of fireworks, which were banned in Sarawak. The next day, spent firecrackers littered the roads. There was a strong smell of cordite in the air and it appeared to be foggy, but that was the smoke left over from the displays. Some customs are not dissimilar to those in Scotland. Luck plays a large part in people's customs and lives all over the world. My Chinese friends told me it is unlucky to sweep your house on the first day of the new year in case all the good luck is swept out. I explained to them if they were the first visitors to my home on New Year's Day, my home would have the best of luck for the rest of the year because of their dark hair. Another custom concerned debts. All debts have to be settled before the start of the new year. I visited Chong and her family at the new year and asked, "Where is your dad?"

"He is with his pals playing mah-jong, no doubt to incur new debts."

I smiled as I gave out little red envelopes containing coins to the children. "Thank you, Uncle, for my ang pow," they called out. It is a mark of respect if parents allow their children to call you uncle or aunt.

Recruitment of trainees was not one of my duties. I returned from a class, and Eric had left me a note. Two potential employees would arrive for an interview and we had to conduct them. A few days later, Peter brought over the two candidates, both were in their late teens or early twenties. He introduced them. "This is Daniel and Jacob, I'll leave them with you. Come and see me before they leave."

Both young men wore jeans, T-shirts and safety boots and carried a small holdall. They looked anxious, so Eric invited them to sit while I got them some water. I wanted to chat with them first, aiming to put them at ease with this interview and exam.

My first question was, "Where do you live?"

"In our longhouse," Jacob replied.

"How did you get here?"

"By boat."

"How long did it take you to get here?"

"Two days."

They were able to communicate easily in English. "Who taught you to speak such excellent English?" I asked.

Daniel answered, "The missionaries."

They were shy but understood all the instructions we gave.

Their first test was a multiple-choice question paper that covered general knowledge and arithmetic. It took them until noon to finish and neither of them passed. After lunch, they did practical tests and these were a big improvement. After they finished, I got the brush and swept the floor while Eric gathered up the tools. Daniel interrupted him. "I am sorry, sir, but these tools belong to Jacob and me."

It caught me off-guard when I recognised these good quality tools hadn't come from our tool cupboard. "I'm sorry, where did you get them?"

"The head man in our longhouse gave them to us for our test. He wanted us to have them so we would make our longhouse proud."

Eric and I gawked at each other, everyone in their longhouse must have contributed to buy these quality tools. I said, "We'll be back soon."

After a short discussion, we returned to them to give them their results. They had travelled a long way and the hopes of their tribe was resting on this moment. Eric smiled. "You both passed and we hope to see you again soon to start your course."

A month later, Daniel arrived without Jacob. Daniel chose a career in operations and not electrical. Almost two years later, I met him at the market. As he shook my hand, he placed his other hand over my wrist in a mark of respect. He introduced a young lady with him as his girlfriend. The next time I met him, the same young lady was his wife. Later, on a visit to an offshore platform, he showed me a photograph of his wife and son.

Regardless of whether they live in a longhouse or city, it is in the people's blood to hunt in the jungle and fish in the rivers. It is a characteristic part of a Dayak's life. They go to the interior to hunt for wild boar and fruit bats. The largest bat is the flying fox. These fruit bats can be 16 inches long and weigh around two pounds and have a wingspan over five feet. They have enormous eyes and exceptional vision. In the daytime, they hang from branches by one or more of their feet and wrap their wings around their bodies to shield and keep warm. At night, they become active and search for food. I saw my first flying fox at a dinner party. It was the main dish on the menu and was served with rice and vegetables. It tasted like venison.

Jeffery, who looked like Tarzan, was going to the jungle at the weekend to hunt boar and promised me some of his kill. On Monday I looked for him at work, but he failed to turn up. He appeared on Thursday, with his leg in plaster. I was direct. "What happened to you?"

"I had an accident."

Homemade shotguns used by hunters were ancient, often with only one barrel. Injuries were commonplace. His leg did not look as if a gun caused it. "What happened?"

He related the story. "Darkness fell and this big wild boar appeared."

"What happened?"

"I shot it."

"That's good."

"No, it ran away."

"What did you do then?"

"The trail of blood led to the river and it must have swum to the opposite side."

"You mean it got away?"

"No, I knew it would return home to its territory after it recovered and felt safe.

"Did it return?"

"Rain started, so I made a shelter in a tree to keep dry. I had a good view from the tree and waited in comfort for it to return."

"What happened?" I wanted him to get on with it.

"I fell asleep."

"What then?"

"A noise woke me up, and I pointed my gun to shoot."

"Don't tell me you missed it?"

"The gun fired, and I fell out of the tree."

"Where's the boar now?"

"In the freezer at home."

"What happened to your leg, did you hurt it falling from the tree?"

"On Sunday afternoon, I played football, and someone tackled me and broke it."

Tarzan might have told a 'porky' because he didn't want to admit that he fell from the tree, but he remained my hero because of the delicious boar.

Miri expanded. A Park and Shop supermarket and a pub called The Bounty opened at Piassau Gardens. New places to eat and drink started up in town. Mamma's Grill became our preferred place to eat and served quality meals. The Ranch was a boisterous pub, popular with younger customers because it had live music, and then there was the Barrel for those whose passion was karaoke. Sarawak people love music. Our night's out ended at the disco, and we returned home at sunrise with the sound of the fighting cocks singing in tune. Our social life could be hectic if we chose it to be. Miri was expanding and being brought into the twentieth century.

This job gave us so many opportunities in Sarawak itself and also when we went on leave. Instead of flight tickets straight to Heathrow, I got the cash. We had spent hours planning a different route home to the UK. We flew around the world with stopovers in the Philippines, the Hawaiian islands, Vancouver, London and back to Miri.

As the aircraft circled Honolulu, I was not impressed; there were too many skyscrapers and highways. It was not the place I imagined it, I could see no volcanoes or beaches with crashing waves and people riding surfboards. It looked like any other big city I had been to. Because the Hawaiian islands are part of America, we passed through American immigration and customs checks there. The long flights, plus crossing the Date Line made us tired and irritable. We had landed thirty minutes before the time we had taken off from Manila! We were time travellers as well as globetrotters. A tourist adviser with a nametag that read Susan asked if we needed help. After a brief decision-making conversation with Gilly, I explained to Susan that we wanted to escape Honolulu because it looked like a concrete jungle, and my first impression was not good, therefore I didn't want to stay there.

"Do you have any travel preferences; things you'd like to see?" she asked.

I told her, "I want to see a volcano."

"Me too," Gill said.

Susan smiled. "Leave your luggage with me, go have a coffee and I will arrange a holiday for you."

"Okay, sounds good to me." I was too tired to say anything else. I put my confidence in Susan, only time would tell whether this was misguided and we'd been conned.

Twenty minutes later, after a cup of strong American coffee, we returned. Arrangements had been made because new tags dangled from our luggage. Susan approached us. "You are very special guests and I have arranged a holiday that is usually reserved for Hawaiian residents."

I whispered to Gill, "Where have I heard that before?"

Susan gave details of the package. "Your flight will leave in an hour for the big island of Hawaii. Outside arrivals, you will see a booth that has the name MacDonald on it. They will provide you with a car and information about Hilo and your hotel. After three days, you will return the car and board your flight back to Honolulu. Look for the same MacDonald sign and collect your car and instructions to get to your downtown hotel."

"How much do I owe you?"

Susan gave me the figure, and it startled me so much that I fully woke up. I looked at Gilly and she looked as surprised as me. I expected to pay an outrageous price, but what she quoted was a cheap price, a bargain. I signed the papers, hugged Susan, put my arm around Gill's shoulders and entered the departure lounge.

On our way to the big island, we landed on a smaller island in this Hawaiian group. Disembarking passengers were greeted by young people who placed a garland of flowers around their necks. We were given the same welcome when we reached our destination. As per

Susan's instructions, outside arrivals, we quickly spotted the booth displaying a MacDonald sign. I showed my passport to the operative who handed over a car key for a left-hand drive Toyota, a map and clear instructions. I drove left-hand drive cars in Kuwait so the car didn't bother me. Gilly read out the directions to our hotel in Hilo, a small town with 20,000 inhabitants and no high-rise apartments. A receptionist explained the hotel layout and mealtimes, then a bell boy put the luggage on a trolley and showed us to a spacious room containing a huge double bed. I fell asleep in minutes.

The sun, streaming through a gap in the curtains, woke me. I slid out of bed onto the carpeted floor and opened the curtains. A huge volcano filled the windowpane as if it were a picture on a wall. It was an impressive sight. It didn't look very far away. I expected Gill to wake as soon as the sunlight hit her, so I half-closed the curtains again. She hadn't stirred, still fast asleep, and I had to wake her.

After a breakfast of cornflakes and scrambled eggs, we got into the car with our map, a tourist guide book, a large bottle of water and a bag of mint humbugs. Ten minutes later, we headed along a deserted road to the volcano information centre. After thirty minutes, we stopped at a roadside café to have a drink and look at the view. A middle-aged couple owned the café. We were the only customers, so we chatted and were told that they were Canadian. They had visited this island five years ago and liked it so much that they bought the café. We only had coffee, but the owners enjoyed our tales from the jungle. We drove a little further to the information centre and watched films and attended lectures on Hawaii and its volcanos. Both of us were glad that we met Susan.

Americans are the best in the world for tourism. A lava road led right to the edge of a volcanic crater. The smell of sulphur gas in the air nauseated me and, as I pressed my body against the barrier to see into the crater, my nostrils burned. Rumbles and the acrid sulphur smell that emanated from the crater scared me, but I put on a brave face.

We toured the island in the daytime and at night took in the shows. We got to bed late and relaxed, but I think that was more to do with the Hawaiian cocktails than the shows.

It was so peaceful here I wanted to stay here rather than return to the busy high-rise life in Honolulu. It was not to be. After we landed in Honolulu, we followed the exit signs and found the MacDonald booth. Within minutes, we'd taken ownership of the hire car and were on our way to our downtown hotel. This time, the journey was not to be simple, and we ran into trouble because of busy roads, traffic jams, and a strange one-way system. We could see our hotel and drove past it a few times, but there were always signs informing us we could not turn right. Eventually, I found the road that led to the hotel car park. I slammed my hands on the wheel and cursed to vent my anger about the road system. "That's it! I refuse to drive anywhere in this city. This car is staying put until we leave for the airport."

Gilly remained silent. She knew when to leave me to cool down. Later, over a well-earned alcoholic drink, she told me she agreed with my decision.

As we walked to reception, we passed a giant aquarium built into the wall. The fish were magnificent with so many varieties, there were even two sharks. Fish are supposed to relax you, but this time they did not change my mood.

The receptionist smiled as they always do and welcomed us to Honolulu. I handed her the reservation details form and whispered to Gilly, "Now it is all going to go wrong. We had a bad start with the car and now it will go from bad to worse."

While the receptionist looked at my passport, I thought, *this is it, we don't have a room*. Wrong again, my fears were unfounded. "You are Hawaiian guests; therefore you've been upgraded to a superior suite that has a balcony that overlooks Waikiki Beach."

I felt uneasy and frustrated by this island, I just wanted to stay in the room, but we had to eat. The restaurant we chose was plain but nice and very busy. Steak in Sarawak was not good because it came from a buffalo. Hawaii is part of America, so I figured the steak would be brilliant. The man asked how we wanted it cooked. Gilly ordered a medium, I ordered well done. I never ate meat unless they cooked it to a crisp. Why? On one occasion, I got food poisoning when I'd eaten undercooked meat.

We chatted about our holiday while we waited. I joked, "Where are the coconut trees and beautiful girls in hula skirts?"

Our waiter interrupted and placed the food on the table. It looked good until I cut the steak and blood oozed onto my plate. No way would I eat that. Gilly insisted, "Complain, you asked for it to be well done." It is not in my nature to complain. This always annoyed Gilly and this time, it cast a cloud over the meal. She was annoyed at me. "Don't complain about it to me, tell them." I ate everything on the plate except the steak. I expected the server to ask me why I hadn't touched it, but he didn't. After Gilly finished her meal, he picked up the plates and took my steak away. The bill arrived, and I paid, but just the required amount. He didn't get a tip. I knew that I'd upset Gilly and spoilt the holiday atmosphere. It took a few beers and cocktails before we relaxed and enjoyed ourselves again.

After a breakfast of pancakes lashed with maple syrup, we went by taxi to the tourist area at Pearl Harbour and booked a group tour along with ten people. Female guides dressed in naval uniforms explained the safety procedures and the tour highlights. As we visited the exhibitions, our guide gave detailed information on each exhibit. I felt sad when she described the events that sank the USS Arizona and for the people still entombed in the ship. Overall, I enjoyed the tour but found parts of it distressing. What was amazing was that the biggest percentage of tourists were Japanese.

That night, we dined in the hotel and selected from the buffet. I would not order steak tonight. After dinner, we watched a colourful show featuring Hawaiian dancers, and on the way back to our room, we lingered to admire the fish in the tanks.

On our final day, we went to Waikiki Beach. Mobs of bathers were bathing on the golden sand or relaxing in the water. There were no public conveniences and so I commented, "I want to pee in every ocean of the world before I die. Looks as if that's the only option here." She punched my arm and rebuked me.

I would miss Hawaii, but not Honolulu.

We then flew to Vancouver to visit Elma and Dave. This was my first trip to see my sister and her husband, who emigrated to Canada just after they got married. I liked Vancouver from the moment I landed. Dave drove us around the place and we enjoyed great family times. We travelled by ferry to Victoria, the capital of Vancouver Island. It looked like a city back home. I was amazed to see double-decker buses and red telephone boxes, just like the UK.

I wished I booked more time there. I was pleased to see their success after the hard times in the past following their arrival in Canada. Their two boys were truly Canadian, with no memory of the birth country of their mother and father. Canada would be a place I could live.

On the flight back to London, my tooth hurt. I had crossed the Date Line twice and suffered from jet lag. A baby in the seat in front bawled all the way and two fillings in my teeth dropped out. Now, I just wanted to get home.

I returned to Sarawak and work, while Gilly stayed to enjoy the last weeks of the warm English summer.

CHAPTER 11
CAVES AND COCKROACHES

The lack of decent roads in Sarawak meant you reached most places by boat or a four-wheel-drive vehicle. The Bintulu road turned into a dirt track just past the airport, but it was possible for a car to reach Niah by driving carefully. Gilly and I were determined to visit this historic site. We managed the drive without mishap. Now for some footwork. It took an hour to walk along a boardwalk from the car park to the caves. To explore them properly required a full day and that meant a night's stay at the communal hostel.

We had read up and prepared well for this expedition. Evidence, such as paintings and artefacts, proves people inhabited the caves for over 4000 years. They are well-known to tribe people as a place to collect bat guano to sell as fertiliser and swiftlet nests to supply the Chinese market with bird nest soup. They still practised traditional methods to collect the nests. Somehow, they suspended planks below the cave roof and ascended over a hundred feet up ropes to harvest this produce. The lucrative trade in nests provided a livelihood for many people. As dusk arrived, swarms of swiftlets and bats flew out of the cave to hunt for food in the forest.

It was a long, sticky walk through the jungle, along a rickety plank walk. We had been warned and so chose to wear long-sleeved shirts and full-length trousers to protect our bodies from the myriad of insects. There were poisonous plants and animals all around us. As we entered the cave, we switched on our torches to make it possible to see the height and the bird's nest collecting structures that swung perilously above our heads. The floor teemed with hundreds, probably thousands, of insects. The 'no touching' rule applied to these creatures. They were gruesome but admirable. In this place, there could be the answer to many of the illnesses that circulated in the world. Before our visit ended, we saw someone begin the dangerous climb to the nests.

It had been an exhilarating adventure into the rainforest. Later that night, fishermen came to the hostel to sell fish and vine leaves stuffed with rice that were a tasty addition to our tinned food dinner. There wasn't a plush coffee shop here. Groups of visitors drank coke or beer and exchanged stories on the veranda as they listened to the sounds of the jungle. Fireflies that lit up the darkness were another highlight of my day. The hostel caretaker collected a few in a jar so we could inspect them. We went to our bunks soon after the generator was turned off at 9pm. It was pitch black and silent. The jungle sounds soon filled the silence, making it difficult to sleep. It was spooky. Before we left Niah, we zoomed up the river in a noisy longboat powered by a large speed boat engine, on an awe-inspiring two-hour trip.

Caves much bigger than the ones at Niah were talked about that night. Although these caves existed, expeditions never reached them until the late seventies. They are in Sarawak's Gunung Mulu National Park, in the heart of virgin jungle which made it dangerous and difficult to reach them. Only permit holders were allowed to go there to safeguard this pure jungle from an onslaught of tourists. One lunchtime, I sat with Liang, our safety instructor, and hinted that I wanted to explore them, but knew it wasn't possible without a permit.

"Andrew, if you want to go you must come with me, my village is near to the caves. We'll stay with my family."

"Have you been to Mulu caves?"

"My father took me there to shelter from the rain when we were out hunting with our blowpipes."

This man was a native hunter who spoke Oxford English, which he learned from the missionaries, just like Daniel and Jacob. Unfortunately, the plan never materialised. It would have been an opportunity to visit the village people in the rainforest, to see their lifestyle and have a guide to the caves.

In 1986, almost two years later, I planned my visit to the Mulu caves accompanied by Jim, a colleague and keen photographer. A year earlier, the national park opened to the public and a travel group based in Miri ran the tour for fifteen people. We would depart on an express longboat from Kuala Baram at 6am on Saturday. Our instructions were to pack only a small overnight bag. Food and water would be supplied and there would be a brief stop at Marudi for snacks and soft drinks. Jim carried his camera bag on his shoulder, which the boat driver accepted right away, but he checked my extra holdall. He smiled after I showed him the contents of the bag and explained why I brought it. He stowed it carefully in a waterproof spot.

Everyone arrived on time. Our boat driver and guide helped us to cross over other boats to find a seat on ours and gave everyone a cushion to sit on. We left at the stated time and headed up the mighty Baram towards Marudi. By 10am, I was seated in a Kedai, eating chicken rice accompanied by a mug of tea.

Four hours later, the longboat pulled into a small jetty and we stepped out, glad to stretch our legs and ease the discomfort in our backsides. As Jim and I made our way towards a longhouse a short distance away, we saw several women tossing the rice in large woven trays. Jim prepared his camera to snap the scene, but I interrupted him. "Jim, I think you better ask permission to take photographs, you might offend someone."

"Oh yes, I forgot."

He approached one of the woman. "Is it all right for me to take some photographs?"

"It is, have you come from Miri?

"Yes, we work for Shell at Lutong."

"I am a teacher at a primary school in Miri. It's school holidays, that's why I am back home in my longhouse."

"Small world," I said.

We chatted about the Miri boat race and people we knew, then she gave us a tour of the longhouse before we left to continue our journey.

Two hours later, we left the mighty Baram and joined a smaller tributary. At first, the riverbed was visible through the clear water, but the current became so strong it became murky. Soon we were in rapids and our guide slid over the side of the boat and tried to push against the fast flowing water. No way would he manage it alone, so the other male passengers followed him into the water. A hard fight against the current ensued. Once we reached calmer waters, the boat stopped to allow the men to rest before pushing on. I dozed off for at least an hour and woke up when the boat suddenly jolted.

Our journey was over, the boat pulled into the jetty at the Mulu visitor centre. Everyone was relieved to be away from the sound and smell of the longboat, and to place our feet firmly on solid ground. There were several dormitories and few visitors, so we did not have to share with strangers. We rested while our guides unloaded the boat and cooked chicken for dinner. We were amongst the first westerners to come here as tourists. The excitement associated with this place was exhilarating, we were deep in the interior of a pristine rainforest. When our guide asked if anyone would like to go to karaoke, I thought he was joking. Sarawakian people love music and this modern leisure pursuit was very popular everywhere. I had not expected it to reach the depths of the jungle. We followed dutifully behind him and joined other guests who joined in enthusiastically with the event. With three days to explore the most magnificent cave formations in the world, I looked forward to every minute.

At the time of my visit, little factual information, like guide books, was available. We only had handwritten notes. What I remember is the vastness of the caves.

Our guide accompanied us as we cruised up the Melinau River in a longboat to reach the Cave of the Winds. Our guide flipped a switch and on came the lights. Once inside, I felt a cool breeze as I admired the stalactites, stalagmites and rock corals. Coupled with the limestone figures, it was outstanding. You certainly needed to be fit to reach the caves and to explore them.

After a short hike, we arrived at Clearwater Cave with many tropical plants I didn't recognise around the entrance. A subterranean river ran through the centre and the guide once more threw a switch and the river area lit up. They had installed a few walkways and a bridge for the convenience and safety of visitors. I looked from the bridge into the crystal clear ice-cold water below. I was tempted, but did not dive in for a swim. The river had gouged out the rock to form beautiful, multicoloured curves, which were incredible. The grey pinnacles with jagged edges looked like a rock formation, but were bacteria that had built-up over the years. My guide notes listed the length of the cave system; it was at least 200 kilometres long.

Early next morning, we set off for a two-hour trudge to Deer Cave. It holds the world's largest cave passages and is home to over three million bats and swiftlets. Raised wooden boardwalks were erected for safety.

Walls, more than 100m high in some places, offered a haven to wildlife and protected them from predators. Our guide warned us not to pick up insects or to disturb any wildlife that we came across. We had to think about our safety and preserve the area. The floor represented the biggest pile of 'guano' (bird shit) in the world. Nobody knew what was hidden or alive in or underneath this mountain of excrement. When a twelve-inch centipede scurried across the guano, I froze and let it pass. Inside, there was a strong ammonia smell, but, with our trusty guide, I felt safe and eager to explore and learn the secrets of these wonders of nature.

Almost a kilometre inside, I stopped to study the green oasis of what has been entitled the Garden of Eden. Adam and Eve's unique shower heads spouted columns of water thirty metres to the riverbed below. As I dragged my weary legs out of Deer Cave, I looked into the daylight and saw a silhouette of Abraham Lincoln, which was a natural feature in the limestone. The guide said it was time for a rest and gave out the packed lunches. I appreciated this pause and needed food to re-energise. I sat on a fallen tree to wolf down all but one of the chicken and tomato sandwiches and felt ready for the next stage.

We explored until late afternoon then set off for Lang Cave, with its stalagmites, stalactites and limestone scars. This smaller cave made it easier to see the bats as they roosted on the roof and walls.

Afterwards, we followed our guide to an observation point to wait for the mass exodus of bats at dusk. When they flew out, it reminded me of a typhoon I experienced, as the sky became black with clouds that swirled in the atmosphere. But these were not clouds, they were bats dipping and weaving in search of mosquitoes and other insects. It was here that I ate my saved sandwich. Our epic exploration was at an end and we headed back to enjoy another chicken dinner.

For me, the highlight of our tour was not the caves, but a visit to a small village. We reached it by following our guide along a dense jungle path. A previous exploratory expedition to the park came across a tribe of people living near the caves. With the help of Malaysian government officials, the people were persuaded to come and live in a purpose-built village and join civilization. I was about to meet them.

The village contained a longhouse style hut with outbuildings where natives were weaving cloth garments and making simple souvenirs for us to buy. By this endeavour, the villagers earned cash to buy things that would help them survive in the modern world. One man guarded thirty women and children. Would they be pleased to see us or wish they were back home in the jungle? This was the dilemma that I pondered. Was their life improved and happier since their discovery by modern man, or would their lives have been better if they had been left to follow the lifestyle they had lived for hundreds of years? As we approached, two mangy dogs stirred and growled. Was this an answer to my question coming from the mouths of the dogs?

I visited several kampongs (villages) in the past, and I knew you should always take a gift. I sat at the top of the steps and removed a packet of biscuits from my extra bag that had been stowed in the long boat on our river journey. I took one out and ate it. The children gathered around and accepted the biscuits I offered. I opened the packet up and placed it on a table for the women to help themselves. One woman gave a biscuit to each dog to keep them quiet. I opened another packet, as well as a packet of sweets – liquorice allsorts – my favourites. I studied what the natives made and talked to them, in my own way with hand gestures, facial expressions and the smattering of words I'd learnt in my time in Sarawak. They looked at the photographs I took out of the bag and wanted to see more. Before we left, the man gave me two bracelets made with coloured beads. He would not accept payment, so I gave him the remaining goodies that were left in my bag.

We were about to start our walk back along the jungle path just as two men appeared. They held blowpipes in their hands and one carried a dead monkey across his shoulders. This was a scene from their natural way of life before modern man entered to improve their lives. I had experienced meeting a tribe of people who had only witnessed what we call civilisation two years before. I still doubt whether society's intrusion had improved their tribal jungle culture.

After eating chicken and rice, washed down with a can of beer, Jim suggested we go for a walk along the riverbank. We would decide later about the karaoke. We both felt gloomy, as it was our last night. Wearing shorts, T-shirts and trainers, we started along a path close to the river. Not long after we set off we came across two little girls, youngsters, pulling a boat to the river's edge to take them across the river. I could hear music from a wooden shack on the opposite side. "Is that where you are going? If it is, can we come with you?" I asked in gesture language. One of them pointed to the boat, so we helped pull it in and hitched a lift. They were young, but this was their normal way of life, so I could trust them to get us across.

We reached the other side and tied the boat to a hitch rail, then followed the girls up the bank to the shack. One girl gestured for us to follow them inside and introduced us to their parents who invited us to stay. Men and women dressed in traditional clothes sat at tables or on the two benches set against a wall. A few were eating food, but most were drinking glasses of tuak, the Sarawakian name for rice wine. The strength of this alcoholic beverage ranged from strong to very strong. The mum came over and spoke one word: "Heineken?"

"Yes, please."

She opened the door of an American-style refrigerator. I am sure Jim heard me gasp in surprise and I heard his intake of breath. Inside were cans of Heineken stacked from top to bottom.

For two hours, we listened to a combination of western and Malaysian music, and ate peanuts coated in salt then baked. Celebrations kicked off after a native gave us a glass of tuak and said, "Cheers." To reciprocate this gesture of friendship, I asked the bar lady to give everyone a can of Heineken. Close to midnight, two natives played out a tribal dance. When they finished and the applause died down, I crossed two parangs on the floor and performed a Scottish sword dance. An uproar of appreciation and applause followed. More natives got up to perform and Jim followed up with the Highland fling. I felt favoured to have been invited to dance the night away with natives whose ancestors were headhunters.

Feeling inebriated, I took care of a truly sensible tab, and the dad paddled us back across the river and ensured we could walk to the hostel. We showed up without a moment to spare, the boat was preparing to return us to civilisation.

I was always ready and willing to help people and when a colleague asked me for a favour and take his amah to the Kuala Baram ferry on Sunday because he was going offshore for a work stint, I agreed. I knew his amah, she was the daughter of a longhouse headman and everyone called her Princess.

I jumped out of bed immediately as the alarm rang at 6am, dressed and arrived ten minutes later. Outside the villa stood the eighteen-year-old Princess and a girl dressed in a school uniform who I took to be around twelve years old, waiting on the pavement. I stopped the car and greeted them in Bahasa. "Selamat pagi, Princess, and who is this?"

"Mr Andrew, this is my sister, Christine."

"Hi, Christine, are you going home?"

Princess answered. "No, she goes to school at Marudi. She came to stay with me for the school holidays. School starts tomorrow, so it's time for her to leave."

They looked sad, so I shut up.

Marudi is almost a hundred miles upriver from Miri. It is a busy bazaar town whose traders supply most of Sarawak's northern interior. Different ethnic tribespeople come here to buy and barter for essential supplies like oil for their lamps and casual wear. Some parents send their children to study there.

I bought some soft drinks and crisps to cheer them up. No one spoke until Princess stood up. "It's time to go."

The next ten minutes were the longest ten minutes of my life. My eyes followed these two young people cross over two other boats to reach the Marudi express. I watched as Princess put an envelope in her sister's hand and embraced her. She did not look back as she crossed the other boats to where I waited. I tried to hide my tears as I consoled her. After the boat left, I drove into Miri and treated her to a slap-up breakfast, but I don't think it helped. Miri had happy times, but today was not one of them.

Telephones irritate if you don't wish to wake up to answer them. The darkness made me want to go back to sleep and ignore the noise. I covered my head with a pillow; it didn't stop. No one telephoned me at this time of night unless someone rang my number by mistake, or children playing tricks dialled arbitrary numbers and screamed horrible things into the receiver when you picked it up. I switched the light on; the clock read 1:10am. The noise did not stop. I wanted to smash the phone but picked up the receiver. A female voice sounded distressed.

"Mr Andrew. Help me, please!"

I recognised the voice of another colleague's housemaid.

"What's wrong, Jennifer?"

"Mr Andrew, my head is painful, will you take me to the hospital, Mr Ken is not here."

"Give me a few minutes. I'm on my way, wait for me outside."

It only took a minute to dress, dash downstairs and I reached the house inside five minutes. I helped her into the car, then set off to get the ferry to cross the river to reach the hospital. Her pain must have been severe because she bawled and thumped her head on the dashboard. The time it took to reach the hospital depended on which side of the river the ferry was berthed. I knew it operated twenty-four hours for emergencies. Luckily, it was tied up on our side, so there was no delay.

The bright lights in the hospital made her cry more. I needed to register her and guarantee to pay any bills, then a nurse carried her into the treatment room after she collapsed with the pain.

Our only hospital served around 150,000 patients. My worldwide company medical insurance policy covered me, but few employers insured the amahs who came from the longhouses to seek employment in the oil-rich town. Amah allowance was only paid if you were a senior employee. Some amahs did not live in their employer's home. They came from the villages near the Baram River and did cleaning jobs to earn extra cash.

The receptionist gave me a large mug of sweet tea, then I flipped through the pile of magazines on the table to take my mind off Jennifer's agony. It was 2:20am, and the silence made me uneasy. Over an hour passed before one of the double doors opened and the nurse stepped through and held it open. I jumped up from my chair and crossed the room as Jennifer appeared in the doorway, followed by the doctor. I felt comforted because she smiled.

"Doctor, how is she?"

"She is fine now. Her ear is sore, but I have given her painkillers."

"What caused the pain?"

"I examined her and found a cockroach had crawled deep into her ear. This resulted in the pain and made her unsteady."

"Thank you, I was concerned for her health."

"No need, she is well now, bring her back in a few days and I will check there are no complications."

I shook his hand and thanked him once more. I paid the bill and dropped her back home at 3am. On my lunch break, I called in to check on her progress to find two of her friends were visiting and caring for her. I was relieved that she had company and was recovering from her ordeal.

My life and work in Sarawak was idyllic, I would have stayed for decades, but it was not to be. The worldwide economy was about to crush my Eden. In 1976, a barrel of oil was sold for twelve American dollars. In 1983, oil prices had risen and sold for twenty-nine American dollars a barrel. In 1986, the price tumbled once more to twelve American dollars, caused by overproduction. Cost-saving measures were imposed and, as usual, the first thing to be chopped was training. I lost my job.

I will never forget the night before I left, an ex-trainee gatecrashed the party. With him was an elderly man who walked with the aid of a stick. It was Lim, an ex-star trainee. Someone stopped the music as I welcomed them.

"Lim, I am happy you came to say goodbye."

"Mr Andrew. I am sorry that you must leave us."

"I am sorry too, Lim, but the economic situation is bad. One day I hope I will come back."

"Mr Andrew, I have brought my father to meet my professor, who taught me so much."

I shook hands with Lim's father as a lump formed in my throat.

I flew out of Miri, and the lump was still there. Gilly and I felt as if we were leaving home.

CHAPTER 12
WE DON'T THROW STONES ANYMORE

Job hunting began immediately. I didn't want a long period of unemployment to diminish our bank balance; that would spoil our plans. Only one offer as a trainer landed on the doormat. It was not the best country to go on married status, but the job market was bad and I had to grasp any offer going. I flew to Yanbu in Saudi Arabia to train Saudi nationals.

The company housed me in a furnished bachelor apartment with modern furniture, appliances and TV tuned to only receive Arabic channels. I borrowed censored films from a central library and ate my meals at the company restaurant. I knew several people there who I worked with on previous jobs, one of them, George, played the clarinet in his spare time. He invited me over to his apartment to listen to him play, but when I knocked on his door, he did not answer. As he was expecting me and I could hear clarinet music, I banged harder on the door and entered. You did not need to lock your door in the complex because the crime rate was very low. He was sat at the far end of the room, facing out of the open balcony doors. He was naked as the day he was born. Net curtains blew back and forth in the cool breeze. He heard me enter, lowered the clarinet from his lips and called, "Put the kettle on, bonny lad, make me a tea."

As I put the hot tea on the floor, I saw the scene beneath the overhanging balcony through the rippling drapes. Seated on the grass was a group of grown-ups and kids listening to George and his clarinet. He had lived there a while, so I bet this was a regular occurrence for this family. Good job he didn't decide to play standing up, that would have made front page news in the UK newspapers.

Yanbu village was nicknamed 'Neutron City', because at weekends and holidays scores of individuals vanished to return home to their family or visit Jeddah or Riyadh. Our canteen at work served inexpensive five-star food. Being on my probationary bachelor status, I ate all my meals there. The food was so good that Saudi families came there to eat at weekends.

After being there for only two weeks, the personnel manager summoned me. "When is your family arriving?"

"I have not made plans because I have to complete three months' probation."

He brushed my explanation to one side. "Unnecessary, make your arrangements. Your family is most important."

I was over the moon with this news. I knew Gilly would be happy that we would be together again. I was confident she would deal with the restrictive life that females had to endure.

The number of inhabitants in Yanbu is under 200,000 and life there is more traditional and austere than the bigger urban areas of Jeddah and Riyadh. Islam's two holiest cities, Mecca and Medina, are also close to Yanbu. After six weeks, I travelled to Jeddah to meet Gilly. It took that long because I had to wait for an apartment to become available at Arabian Homes. The homes were in a secure compound between the refinery and Yanbu town. The environment had an ambiance of coolness and calm. Women could wear normal European dress, even shorts, in the freer atmosphere of this living accommodation. Residents shared secluded pool areas with spacious sundecks, where Philippine staff served soft drinks whenever you wanted. Tended gardens with an abundance of tropical flowers and trees made you think you were in paradise. Gilly was happy there. There were plenty of activities to occupy her time and she could pop round to friends' houses for a coffee and a chat. You could almost forget the world outside the compound gates, where rules and codes of behaviour were strict.

The squash courts in Arabian Homes were the chief attraction for Gilly. Outside the compound, she was not permitted to play against a man. Females were not allowed to reveal any part of their body, so outside the compound, she wore a long black abaya. Men still tutted their disapproval because she did not cover her hair. One day, I went to play squash at a venue outside the compound and Gilly came along to spectate. She was not allowed to enter the building even though she was draped in her long black attire. It was illegal for her to watch men playing this sport. She offered to stay in the car while I played the game. No way would I let my wife be ostracised and have to suffer the heat in a parked car, while I enjoyed myself. I apologised to my opponent and took her home. Saudi Arabia is administered under Islamic law, and life there is more conservative than in the west. Westerners find it difficult to work and live there, and a high percentage never complete their contract.

Yanbu town was a conventional fishing town before the oil companies showed up. Now, it is a city of apartment blocks, vehicle parks and bazaars. I never ate there before Gilly arrived because restaurants were for families. Bachelors or married men whose wives were not with them were isolated from any female company. Westerners dined out in town at Ali's. The religious police seldom entered Ali's but precautions were still needed. At prayer time, those with a meal could continue to eat, but those without food needed to wait until prayers finished to order their meal. The menu was very brief and given orally. The three choices were chicken that was cooked either 'not spicy', 'spicy' or 'very spicy'. We ate with our fingers, there were no vegetables or other side dishes. It was chicken and flat bread, freshly cooked in a clay oven. It was extremely delicious.

Every non-Saudi was warned not to go into town on Fridays because after Friday prayers, admirers accumulated at the town square to watch decapitations. If Westerners were in town, the police forced them to observe. It sounds terrible, and it was. A Saudi explained this brutal practice to me.

"If you steal in Saudi Arabia, people say that you will get your hand chopped off. This is not true, a surgeon amputates it and only after the thief has been given many chances to reform."

"What about murderers? Don't you think that chopping someone's head off in public is savage?"

"In Saudi, anyone executed has committed very serious offences against the people or the state and they are sedated before they are executed." This man was experienced and mixed in the company of westerners. He carried on. "We have strict guidelines to follow for administering punishment. However, the way they are applied may not be as humane as you would expect. For instance, the most awful crime is an assault against children. If somebody rapes or kills a child, they may not be sedated or decapitated. We could take them up in a plane and toss them out the door as they pass over the desert below. This is how solid Saudi individuals manage crime against youngsters."

He made me nervous. "I get stressed that, on the off-chance, myself or my wife should make a genuine mistake."

"Andrew, if someone breaks the law in these circumstances we will forgive them."

He may not have wished to answer this question, however I needed to ask it. "Do you still stone women for committing adultery?"

He smiled. "Andrew, don't believe what you read in the newspapers. We don't throw stones at a woman anymore. They are calmed, and a lorry heaped with stones is tipped over her."

I tried not to react to this explanation. Was this considered to be more humane? "Thank you for telling me, it makes me more mindful of your traditions."

"No problem, Andrew, if you need help please ask me."

The group of lads in my class were an elite bunch, I say 'lads', two of them were over forty years old. Hashim, with his jagged face, long facial hair and a passion for eating sunflower seeds, was a mosque leader. We respected each another, and I felt honoured when he requested I supervised some work taking place in the mosque. Once I built up our relationship, I was able to jest with him. I never moaned about the seed shells he littered the workshop floor with. At exam time, I said, "Hashim, I trust you are prepared, if you eat too many seeds, it could slow your brain down."

He smiled through his long facial hair, pointed a finger at the sky. "Don't worry, Mr Andrew, I am ready."

One of the practical tests involved maintenance on a bank of batteries. He kneeled on the floor and peered underneath to detect if there was a leak. No other trainee did that. He came top of the class.

One time, he came to my office; I invited him to sit, but he declined. I stood up. "Hashim, you look sad. What can I do to help?"

"Mr Andrew, my daughter is sick. She has water on her brain so I may have to leave without notice and go home to attend to her."

He stayed behind after class had ended to explain his problem to me. It was unusual for a Saudi to talk of family issues with a westerner and I felt honoured that I had been trusted with this confidence.

My patience was often tested, and I found it difficult to comprehend and acknowledge their habits. I had to be aware all the time that a word out of place or an improper action might upset someone. To cite western norms as an explanation for an action or a wrong word would be unacceptable. To give the class a different way of learning and rest from my voice, I played an educational video for them to watch. A window allowed me to see into the classroom from my office, and it gave me a chance to do some administration work. After ten minutes, it was too quiet and I went to investigate. "Why is the sound turned down?" I inquired.

Hamid replied, "The programme has music so we cannot watch it with the sound on."

Hashim didn't comment.

To differentiate between the Mohammeds in the class, I gave them nicknames they were unaware of. One of them was 'Big Mohammed'. I knew that he also liked music.

Big Mohammed said, "Don't worry, Mr Andrew, we don't need sound."

I asked Hamid, "Do you watch television?"

"Only news and religious programmes."

I had to have the last word. "Okay, but you need to study for the test."

Not long after this, Hamid came to see me. At first, I thought he wanted to complain. He surprised me when he asked for permission to leave because his wife had no baby milk and the baby was crying. I could not understand why she could not get the milk. Then I remembered. This is Saudi Arabia, not the UK. She couldn't get to the shops by herself. She was not allowed to drive and she would never travel alone with a man other than her husband. "We can't let the baby cry. Please go for milk."

I learnt to make allowances for the rules and etiquette of Arab culture.

Our American general manager regularly checked the gate log and came down hard on latecomers. He complained to me about my group's poor timekeeping and threatened to take action if it happened again. My class were good timekeepers, but not on a Wednesday. On this day, they always returned late from lunch break. I accepted it because it was the whole class. I explained my predicament to them. "I am in a difficult situation because you guys get back late."

Big Mohammed replied, "Don't stress, Mr Andrew, you can come with us and see with your own eyes we're not wasting time."

The following Wednesday, Big Mohammed slotted *Sounds of the Eighties* into the tape deck and drove us to his home where nine of us had been invited to lunch. His mum prepared a mountain of delicious food and asked everybody to sit and get started. We showed our appreciation for his mum's first-rate cooking by eating everything. This took quite a long time, so we were late returning to work. This regular lunch occurrence had to be solved diplomatically.

The current situation warranted a telephone call to the general manager to explain our late return. I got through on the first attempt.

"Good afternoon, Andrew, what can I do for you?"

"Ken, you need to extend the lunch break on a Wednesday."

"Why? What's wrong with it as it is?"

"Ken, neither you nor I can resolve the circumstance that results in my learners return late back from lunch on Wednesdays. We will be in conflict with Saudi custom if we force the issue."

I expected he would fire me for my forthright behaviour. There was a long gap while he considered my request. He obviously saw the truth in it.

"All right, Andrew, just don't let them overdo it."

That was one problem solved amicably.

Wives needed written permission from their husband to leave the country on their own. This also applied to Western women. My company always allowed a husband time off to travel to Jeddah to meet his incoming family in case of visa problems. The first time Gilly flew from Yanbu to UK without me, I saw her off at Yanbu Airport. We sat in the family lounge before she left to enter the departure area. During our wait, I never held her hand or put my arm around her and would never have kissed her goodbye, because of a paranoid fear of retribution for my behaviour. However, ladies would breastfeed a kid and no one objected. We parted, and I heard from her later that she had difficulty finding her departure gate at Jeddah. Seeing two westerners, she walked behind them and whispered, so nobody noticed, "Are you on the BA flight to London?"

"Yes, follow us." There had been no eye contact, nobody would have known that a conversation had occurred.

A couple of weeks later, I followed her on a Royal Jordanian Airlines flight. They provided a model in-flight service and flights that showed up on schedule. When the aeroplane landed at Amman airport terminal, I exited via the rear door. A woman ahead of me, dressed in an abaya and niqab, carried a baby plus two bags. Fearful she would trip and hurtle down the stairs, I wanted to support her. I placed a hand on her shoulder, which I ought not to have done and she turned round. As passengers brushed past us, I tried to make her understand I wanted to help and she should give me the bags. I thought she understood, but she pushed the baby into my arms. I put my bag down on the steps to take a proper grip of the infant as she headed down the stairs and got on the bus. A passenger behind me picked up my bag and carried it for me, but passengers stood in my way and the bus drove off without me. I saw the mother and the rest of her family waving from the bus window so I panicked and rushed after it, but too late, the driver did not stop. Anxious about my reception at the other end, I got on the second bus, and the man with my bag stood up for me to let me sit and hold the baby. I relaxed a bit and tickled the baby under her chin so that she laughed. I put my face close to hers so no one would hear me and jokingly whispered, "You are mine now." It made her chuckle again.

Thankfully, it all ended well, her family waited for us in the arrival lounge. As I passed the infant to her mother, her husband spoke in impeccable English, "Thank you for what you have done to help my family."

"No trouble at all, happy to help. You have a beautiful daughter."

He shook my hand, turned and moved off. I sighed with relief, I'd been caught 'holding the baby'.

I learned to expect the unexpected. For instance, a Saudi came into my classroom and plonked himself down at a table. I thought he was waiting until I finished the lesson to tell me what he wanted. I was wrong, he continued to sit there silently until I had to say something. "Good afternoon, how can I help? What's your name?"

He looked at me shyly. "Me electric." Then he continued the rest of his speech in Arabic.

Hashim translated for me. When a sheik, or somebody significant, visited his village, the young man asked for a job and the visitor said, "What job do you want?"

He replied, "Me electric." This visitor must have been important enough to pull strings to influence the oil company to employ him.

"You had better stay then." I knew better than to question the referral system.

It doesn't make any difference why they gave him a job. This was the first day of this young man's development and in two or three years' time, he would communicate in English and do maintenance work on sophisticated plant and equipment. He would be subjected to Western influences and be expected to help bring Saudi Arabia into the twenty-first century. I was hired to help him, and others like him, to accomplish that end.

When it was time for my students to graduate, Hashim, on behalf of the group, invited me to a graduation supper. Westerners seldom get invited to a Saudi home for dinner. As per his instructions, I drove my car to the supermarket car park where he met me. He greeted me with a smile and shook my hand. "Andrew, before we go to the party, I want to take you to my home to meet my daughter, she is much better now."

I felt honoured. "Hashim, I would like to meet her."

His home was a large villa in a zone where only Saudis resided. I removed my shoes and followed him into the hallway, then to a room where various sizes of cushions were placed around the walls.

"Mr Andrew, please sit and I will return in a moment."

He returned a minute later and sank down on a large cushion. As he did so, a watch fell on the floor. I picked it up and saw that it was gold with an inscription engraved on the back. I tried to hand it to him, but he waved my hand away.

"Hashim, this will get damaged."

He retorted, "Andrew, the American bosses should know that a Saudi man cannot wear gold on his skin. If you like, you keep it. I don't want it."

"Thank you, Hashim, but I am sorry. I cannot accept it."

A lady with no face covering and holding a little girl by the hand entered. Hashim stood up, and I did the same.

"Andrew, this is my wife and my little girl."

Mum welcomed me to her house and spoke to the little girl who looked sleepy. I expressed gratitude to her in Arabic and in English. "I am glad to meet you."

The youngster spoke English. "Thank you for coming to visit me."

This was the young lady who had been very ill and caused Hashim to leave my classroom suddenly and frequently. We spoke for a while, then Hashim accompanied them and returned dressed for the graduation supper.

We were last to arrive at the dinner venue. When we got there, it was as if I stepped back in time. Nine men dressed in Saudi evening dress sat around the cushioned reception room, waiting for us to arrive. They stood and came to greet us. I shook everybody's hand as they welcomed us.

I was led into another room, large enough for twenty people. Hamza poured tea into small glasses and passed them round. When I finished, Abdul wanted to know if I liked the tea as it originates from the mountains and is beneficial for health. He offered me more. I thanked him and he brought the teapot over and topped me up.

After tea, I followed them into another furnished, carpeted room where an extra-large wooden tray lay on the floor. Everyone gathered around it and sat down. I was opposite Hashim. A servant placed an orange at the side of each diner and added a spoon next to me. Two servants carried in a whole lamb, which I assumed was spit-roasted. They set it down on the wooden tray, then placed bowls of humus and rice in front of each guest.

Being careful not to offend, I held back, waiting to see what the others did next. Hashim said a prayer before they took meat from the carcass. As I leaned over, someone tossed a piece of meat to me. I looked across the table and Hashim indicated I should eat the meat. Someone else repeated the action. I didn't have to pick meat from the carcass. I think this was because I was the honoured guest. Once the meal finished, the diners ate the orange and washed their fingers in bowls of water, and I copied this social protocol. Contrary to what is said to be a tradition, no one gave me the eye of the sheep and I did not see anyone else eat one. We moved to another room for coffee and dates. I enjoyed the experience. On the way home, I felt light-headed. Was this from the effect of too much caffeine in the coffee and tea?

Less than a month later, we moved from Arabian Homes to Camp Delta. I heard gossip that the owners wanted more rent for our idyllic housing compound, and my organisation refused to pay. From now on, there would be no more squash games for my better half. Her friends would no longer be a stroll away, and her other freedoms would vanish. She would be isolated in the apartment from the time I left for work until my return. She had the choice of going on the ladies shopping bus on Mondays and Wednesdays. Life would be more difficult for both of us and now would be a good time to move on and I handed in my notice. Gilly happily flew home weeks before my departure.

CHAPTER 13
SMELL THE SCENE

On my return, I contacted Arnold who welcomed me home and asked if I would like to go back to my old job in Sarawak. He told me Delton had taken a Malaysian partner and I would work for them. He asked about my availability, and I did not hesitate. "Arnold, I can leave tomorrow!" This was a stroke of good luck, no break in employment.

The entry process to Sarawak was the same. After an overnight stay in Singapore, I checked into the Park Hotel, which had not changed at all. *The Green Berets* film still played on the TV. A driver came and took me to the Shell office to see Lucy who asked me the same question: "Are you satisfied with your terms and conditions?"

"Yes. I am."

"Pleased to see you back, Andrew. You know your way to Wong's office."

After the pleasantries, Wong explained the changes that took place during the oil crises. "Most of the expatriate staff you knew have returned home. We amalgamated technical skills with soft skills, and I was promoted to head both departments. Andrew, have you read your contract?"

"Yes, it's fine, almost identical to my previous one."

"Good, now forget that. I need you to go offshore and to the terminals at Labuan and Bintulu to support and train inexperienced workers. I would also like you to get involved with development courses and you will have two instructors I would like you to mentor."

"Sounds like a real challenge, but I am up for it."

"Andrew, that is why I wanted you back here."

I knocked on my previous office door and Eric called, "Come in." Wong requested he come back from the field job they gave him after the oil price crashed. With no suitable secondary school in Miri, he would leave as soon as one of his children had reached secondary school age. Likewise, Roger, Bloomers and Jeff were called back. Bloomers had not arrived yet. Bunyak and Alfred joined us from a nearby power station, and they were the Malaysian instructors I would mentor.

I walked from the hotel to Delton's partner at Sikom Supplies office. Four administration workers busied themselves at tables covered with files and reports. Two smaller rooms were at the back, one had an open door where a woman sat behind a huge office desk.

I followed an assistant to meet her. "This is Andrew, our new trainer."

The lady behind the desk appeared to be in her thirties, however, I was never any good at guessing female ages, I never got it right. She stood and held out her hand. "Andrew, welcome. Tea or coffee?"

"Coffee, please."

"I am Jacinta, the administration manager, and next door is Philip, our operations director.

She wore smart office-style clothes and had a look that made me apprehensive. I was not used to female workers and she would be my first female boss.

Jacinta enlightened me about Sikom and their role in the joint venture. They employed two other expatriates and Bloomers would join us soon. She handed me a set of car keys. "There is a company car outside for your use." She did not say if anyone else shared it. Before I could thank her, she stood and moved towards the door. "Come, you need to meet Philip."

Philip was shorter than Jacinta and did not have much to say. Perhaps he preferred to stay in the background until there were important decisions to make. With all the arrangements completed, I stayed for a few minutes longer, then shook their hands and made my way down the stairs to check out the car. The biggest wreck I had ever seen was parked on the road outside. Memories of the mistakes I made with the Kuwait job came to mind.

Throughout the two weeks that followed, I called into the office a few times and remained just long enough to collect my mail. As I was about to leave, I heard Jacinta call, "Andrew, do you have a moment?" She spoke first. "How do you find the job and life in Miri?"

"It's good, just like the last time I was here."

"How is the guest house, any problems?"

I moved from the Park Hotel to a guest house, and I was the only one living in the four-bedroomed villa. An amah kept the place clean, and I ate out. "No issues," I replied.

The crucial question was next. "Good, how is your car?"

That disastrous vehicle was the one thing I hated, I feared for my life every time I got into it and I wanted another car.

"It's acceptable."

Jacinta gave a short giggle. "No, it's a disaster."

"It does the job."

"Andrew, you are a gentleman. Your new car arrived at Miri port earlier today."

I laughed. "Is it red?"

"Andrew, it is."

That was the beginning of a phenomenal relationship. Whenever new individuals joined the organisation or there was an event, I was always invited to dinner and the proceedings that followed, and my car was red.

The villa I rented when I was last here was occupied, so I needed to find another. The one I found had a large open plan living area that made it ideal for Gilly. There was space for her to have her friends round to do yoga and aerobics. Her friends were pleased to see Gilly back. The squash league was tougher, because many young, fit Sarawakian people had taken up the sport. We had returned to our paradise after the harsh years in Saudi Arabia. Life was happy and good again.

One of my regular trips was to Labuan Island, just off the coast of Sabah. It is only ninety-five square kilometres, but a car was needed to get around. I flew there with Roger in the company aircraft and he drove a pool car to the terminal. Several ex-trainees greeted me, then introduced me to the site manager. When work ceased for the day, we followed the workers' bus back into Victoria, the capital of Labuan, and checked in to the hotel.

The Labuan Hotel, the only four-star hotel on the island, definitely needed a facelift and Roger agreed. "It needs modernising and yet it's expensive."

I suggested eating out and we agreed to meet downstairs at seven and go to the market to eat.

The walk to the market was fascinating. There were no electric street lights. Oil lamps of different shapes and sizes either free standing or wall-mounted lit up the streets. They can be decorative, but the ones I saw were practical and smelly. Hundreds of them illuminated the shops and stalls. I could not see the stalls clearly because of poor light and fumes. As I walked down the street, I compared it to a movie, but in a movie you cannot smell the scene. Tonight reminded me of an old movie, but I was smelling the scenery. The mixture of kerosene and other oils, coupled with the aroma of spices from the hawker stalls, smelled sweet and smoky. Sometimes it was pleasant, sometimes the opposite.

We dined on freshly caught fish with fried rice, washed down with bottles of Anchor beer to round off a good night. At 10pm, the lanterns were extinguished, and the stalls packed up for the night. As we passed the outdoor cinema, the end credits moved down the screen. Cinemagoers rushed out to catch the last of the food stalls before they closed.

Before we left, Roger gave me a guided tour of Labuan. I didn't realise there was a Commonwealth War Graves Commission graveyard there. It has 3,900 graves and two commemorations. I contemplated what these soldiers, some of them unknown, had suffered and gave their lives for during the Japanese invasion.

I next visited the oil town of Bintulu. It had electric street lights, but very little else to boast about. I booked in to an old wooden inn because I'd heard it was popular and it had entertainment. One night, I remained a while after the show ended. The quiet and darkness made the room feel ghostly. Suddenly, somebody turned the lights on. The blaze of light startled me and I almost leaped out of my skin. Rodents – rats – were scuttling around the floor and I saw more emerging from holes in the walls. They were out foraging, benefitting from the bits of food that clients had dropped on the floor. This mass of squirming bodies disturbed me and I could not sleep. I remained awake, as I was fearful that my room would have a similar invasion if I fell asleep. I was glad to exit the hotel and return to Miri and my rat-free home.

Wong asked if I would take on a project. A government department decided that under the Factories and

Machinery Act of Malaysia, all operators of gas turbines and large diesel engines would be assessed for competency. They had done the first assessments in Bintulu, and none of the operators passed the test. This embarrassed our senior management, and they wanted to discover the reason for their failures. Wong appeared to be concerned. "Andrew, you must find out why they failed and put it right."

I was surprised that he asked me to do this. "Wong, I am electrical, this task needs a mechanic."

"It's your skills as a trainer I need. I am confident you can do this. I will send a mechanical instructor with you to help on the mechanical side."

Ling, my partner, turned out to be a decent guy, and we worked well together. We quickly determined the reason for failure: it was complacency and language difficulties. On the day of the retest, my partner was unable to travel, so I had to go on my own and I was nervous. Two examiners carried out the oral test, while the general superintendent in charge of the testing, and I, observed the candidates. Amongst the six operators were two who spoke very little English, so the examiners asked their questions in Bahasa Malay, their native tongue. Some operators found it difficult to give answers because they did not understand the question. Twice I asked the superintendent if I could assist and he agreed. After the tests finished, he complimented me on my ability to extract information from candidates who spoke little English. When they tested the second group, the superintendent let me work with the examiners and the third time I had shown my competence for the task and I was allowed to conduct the tests by myself. When the results were announced, there was a one hundred per cent pass rate and this result eased the pressure on my boss.

Months later, as the competency project neared completion, I had a disagreement with my partner, not about the job, but an animal. Chinese people believe that if they eat parts of certain animals, they will have good health. As I drove along the dirt track towards the terminal, a monitor lizard crossed the road, and I slowed down to allow it to cross. Ling shrieked, "Kill it! I want it, kill it!"

I pushed down hard on the accelerator and the car shot forward. The tyres screeched and created a dust cloud behind us. An excited Ling jumped up and down in his seat, still shouting kill it. As we approached the lizard, it looked towards us, too late to get out of the way. As I closed in for the kill, in that instant, I realised the stupidity of my actions, so I slammed my foot on the brake. The car turned at an angle, skidded and stopped only feet away from the creature. It remained motionless, silent, and stared at this strange metal animal. It blinked and flicked out its tongue as if to say, *thank you for not killing me*. My passenger was furious. He raged at me, then fell silent. He never spoke to me from that day onwards.

Three years on, I felt I was doing a brilliant job, people respected my work ethic and expertise. Unfortunately, the good times ended when government policies and the economy changed. After a stay of three years, my job ended and the instructors I had been mentoring took over and I left for home.

CHAPTER 14
WONDERS OF THE DESERT

One month later, I boarded a train to London to attend an interview for an instructor's job in Libya. The interview was straight forward. A young Libyan read questions from a sheet of paper he held under the table. A second man wrote my answers on his paper. My answers must have been suitable because the job was mine. To get the job, they had stipulated a degree qualification, and I did not have one. The older man at the interview looked at my City and Guilds Full Technological Certificate and took a copy. He returned and commented, "You don't need a degree if you have this. City and Guilds are the best qualifications."

Ten minutes later, I was in a taxi travelling to the address I had been given to attend my medical. The doctor looked to be as old as the clinic. He stuck his hand between my legs and said, "Cough," then, "Open". I assumed he meant my mouth. An ancient leather couch stood against the rear wall. I worried in case he asked me to lie down, but he didn't. He signed a sheet of paper and handed it to me. My eyes focussed on the important bit: 'Andrew is fit to work in the desert'.

Two weeks later, I flew to Malta, then on to Benghazi.

When the Air Malta flight disembarked at Benghazi airport, I followed the passengers. I saw several big sheds that could have once been aircraft hangers, but nothing else that showed that this was an airport. There were no parked aircraft or buses to ferry passengers. A queue formed outside a small door built into the larger hanger door through which passengers were allowed to enter. I stepped inside and a uniformed man pointed to a book on a table. I entered my name and passport number and signed the book.

Passengers passed through customs, followed by currency control. Several men, who I assumed were workers just like me, were lined up behind wooden tables. As I approached, the customs officer opened the bag of another passenger to look inside. He put his hand into the bag and removed three articles, a *Sun* newspaper, a *Men Only* magazine and another item that looked like a beer kit. Before he could ask what it was, the passenger cupped his hands to the side of his face, closed his eyes and made a snoring sound. The packet was returned to the bag, and he zipped it up. I was not surprised by anything I saw during my travels.

I opened my bag and the officer emptied the contents onto the table. He rummaged through my belongings, picked up a newspaper and placed it on the pile of confiscated newspapers. When he held up my two bags of sweets, I copied the actions of the previous passenger and acted it out. I showed him they were for eating and gestured that he could take one. He placed one into a drawer and helped me repack my bag.

I stayed three nights at the company guest house in Benghazi to get my work and residence permits, and another medical. An administrator filled in the forms and escorted me to the immigration office. After I finished there, the minibus pulled up outside a run-down building with a heavy entrance door. He pulled a knob fixed on a brass nameplate and I heard a bell chime inside. Less than a minute later, a small window in the door opened to check who we were before allowing us to enter.

A woman in a nurse's uniform greeted me. I recognised the accent as being Eastern European. The doctor also spoke with an Eastern European accent. The clinic contained advanced medical equipment even for my eye test. I donated a pint of my precious blood and sat down to a cup of tea and cake. Back at the guesthouse, the administrator gave me forty Libyan dinars that was of no use to me because there was nowhere to spend it.

The oil company employed me directly and this made a big difference to my conditions. They gave me a rotation of twenty-eight days in the field and twenty-eight days off, I must be careful not to break UK tax laws. I was allowed to spend ninety days in a single year in the UK. This meant I needed to spend some of my leaves outside the UK and Gilly would fly out to join me.

As I travelled to the airport in the minibus, I felt despair at my surroundings. Most shops were barred and shuttered. Those that were open appeared to sell only washing powder, cleaning materials, cigarettes, tobacco and Pepsi. I noticed one butcher shop displaying a few pieces of lamb and chicken, then a bread shop with a long queue of people lined up on the street. The cars were old and the traffic lights did not work. Blocks of unfinished apartments filled the horizon. The materials and tools were not available to complete them. This was the era of the world trade embargo against Libya. It certainly had a big effect on business and the general population.

I left the guest house to go to my place of work in the desert, minus my other packet of sweets, which I gave to a staff member for taking care of me. His children would appreciate the sweets more than me. On the way to the airport, we were stopped twice at roadblocks policed by individuals wearing army-style uniforms or jeans and T-shirts. They bore arms and held them in positions that looked like they were ready to use them. The airport looked like any other small airport except for the many men toting guns. Once inside, I relaxed a little but stayed close to the departure gate, ready to make a quick move if it was necessary. A small café sold soft drinks and snacks, but I had a small bottle of water with me and made do with that.

Leaving Benghazi was easy. I showed my passport and work permit and left through a different shed to the one where I arrived. A twin-jet aircraft with Libyan markings took me to the oil terminal at Sarir. As we flew across the desert at a height of around 30,000 feet, I peered out of the window at the desert below and saw giant trucks with large, wide wheelbases and huge tyres suited to desert conditions travelling in a convoy. A group of Bedouins with their camel train crossed the dunes not far away from them. As we flew further on I spotted a structure that looked like a sewage works. I was puzzled at this. Why was there a sewage plant way out here? Just before we landed, we flew over a desert compound that appeared to be a military installation. As the aircraft circled the runway, a high barbed wire fence that surrounded the site where I would live and work came into view.

A fair-haired man wearing a white short-sleeved shirt and casual trousers greeted me when I left the aircraft. He introduced himself as Arthur and welcomed me to Sarir and took me to the site manager's office. The site manager was a very tall and lean fifty-year-old man. After welcoming me, he called the safety officer to complete my site induction, a process that lasted less than three minutes. The most important thing the safety guy told me was that I must remember not to get into the shower, then turn the tap on because the water tanks were on the roof and exposed to direct sunlight. I could end up with third-degree burns because the water would be boiling.

The site buildings were constructed from concrete and creosoted wood, similar to the ones I lived in at RAF St Athan. I had to bed-hop until they allocated me a permanent hut after two years. Arthur introduced me to the key people as we toured the site. A Pakistani doctor staffed the medical centre, and he was sitting cross-legged on a table in his baggy pants and white shirt. The room contained two hospital beds. Any equipment to deal with an explosion, fire or any other emergency was missing or had never been there.

The final stop was the training centre. The equipment available for me to utilise looked familiar. Its appearance and dustiness showed that very little of it would be in working order. The total number of students was sixty.

They were separated into groups by their discipline and the level of study covered. I would have twelve students. Because of the rotation of workers in the field. I would have ten students in one class and two in another and be required to stand in for other instructors when necessary.

My first day in the field passed smoothly. By 5pm, I had showered and changed for dinner. Arthur banged on my door for me to accompany him. We called at another hut where a dozen people were gathered, all of them held a homemade beer in their hand. The man who had been ahead of me at Benghazi airport customs handed me a glass of beer and said, "Welcome to paradise!" This pre-dinner ritual was much appreciated. I drank two glasses of beer before thanking my host and making my way to the dining room with several others.

The oil workers were multinational, but all the cooks were Turkish. Food was nutritious and plentiful, and this disparity of resources made me think of the poor people queuing for basic food in Benghazi. During the meal, I said, "What's the purpose of the sewage works that I observed from the air?"

Arthur answered, "That's not a sewage works! Those are the sprayers for irrigating the desert. They grow fruit and vegetables there. That's where your melon was grown."

This astounded me. "Where do they get water?"

"It is pumped from vast underground lakes."

"That's amazing."

Lewis continued, "The Great Man-Made River project is Gaddafi's dream. He wants to provide fresh water for all Libyans and to turn the desert green, making Libya self-sufficient in food production."

This sounded like a beneficial project. "Gosh, I'd like to see that when it's finished."

"If it ever gets finished. The sanctions make it impossible for Gaddafi to finish it. Also, politics come into it. The Egyptian government believes it will drain the River Nile."

After dinner, I accompanied Arthur to a different hut and chatted to people, again with a beer in my hand. They called this gathering, and the one before dinner, 'Fives and Sevens'.

To become a member of the club, I would need to prepare my first brew on my next rotation. I managed this, and that is how my social life in the desert continued.

After a course of study with trainers like myself, the students took City and Guilds examinations in their respective disciplines. Despite the lack of equipment and training aids, the centre examination success was remarkable, with a success rate of over sixty per cent.

My first month passed quickly, as did my twenty-eight days at home. Because of sanctions, Libyan Arab Airlines and Air Malta were the only airlines flying to Benghazi. It often meant a one-night stopover in Malta because onward flights were full.

Several expatriates had worked here for a long time, some as long as twenty years. Despite Libya's problems, most expatriates liked it. Since birth, my group had only experienced life after Colonel Gaddafi took over. Young people either loved him or hated him, but most loved him. I was very interested in Libyan people's opinion of other countries and cultures of the world and their views about their own country.

As I got to know my students better, and vice versa, they trusted me and described their lives and living conditions in Libya. I listened and never made a political comment. An expatriate should never get involved with local politics. It was a dangerous thing to do, as you never knew who was listening and who would pass your opinions on to others. Their biggest fear was being drafted into the army. During the war with Chad, captured Libyan soldiers were mutilated and dumped back across the border.

One lad from my group of two informed me he would not come to the field on his next rotation. I joked, "Have they conscripted you into the army?"

"No, Mr Andrew, I am going to Austria."

"For a course or a holiday?"

"Neither, my mother is ill. She needs treatment so the government will pay for us to go there."

I gave my best wishes to him and his mother, but I wondered how the government could pay for medical treatment for one person, but not for training and equipment that would benefit the wider population and the prosperity of the country. Was my student connected to or a relative of somebody in the Libyan hierarchy?

Three months later, I was teaching the subject of electrical fuses and their characteristics. I got as far as fuses with time delays. These fuses are called 'slow blow' fuses, their purpose is to allow a surge in electricity for a short time before the fuse blows.

Mohammed, back from his Austrian trip, jokingly summed up his short stay in Europe. "Mr Andrew, short time in Austria, very expensive!"

I heard about Nafoora from people who I met at Sarir. An opportunity arose to take a trip to this base deep in the Saharan desert, and I volunteered to go. You would have expected me to have learned from my time in the RAF never to volunteer, but I was always eager to experience new situations, so I volunteered. At 7am the next day, I shook hands with Mehedi, my driver, and gave him two packs of Marlboro cigarettes, following Arthur's advice. This present would ensure that he would drive safely.

Mehedi, a wrinkle-faced old Bedouin, looked like he should have retired years ago. I checked that the Land Rover was in good working condition and had everything essential for a desert journey. The tread on the extra-wide tyres was in sound condition as were the two spare wheels. A twenty-five litre plastic water container and a jerrycan of petrol were lashed down in the back and two smaller metal water bottles and two packed lunches were on the front seat. A toolkit and a foot pump in the rear, plus two thick woollen blankets completed my checklist. Then I remembered an important item. "Where's the radio?"

Mehedi looked puzzled. "We go now?"

I assumed the transport department would never allow a vehicle to travel without a serviceable radio. Trusting my life to Mehedi, I put my overnight bag in the back, smiled and called, "Let's go, partner."

He drove at a steady pace and, for the first two hours, stuck to the track that ran alongside the pipeline. The estimated journey ranged from 200 to 400 hundred miles and five to ten hours. Time and distance was not important in the bleak landscape of the desert. We travelled for three hours with the pipeline visible on my right side. As I put the canteen to my mouth to take a swig of water, I felt the Land Rover veer to the left then straighten up again. The track disappeared as we shot off at right angles to the pipeline. I called out, "Everything OK?"

Mehedi lit a Marlboro. "Good," he called back.

There were dunes close by and I was bothered about getting stuck, but the desert we were driving across felt solid beneath the Land Rover wheels. Suddenly, reflections from the desert floor blinded me and there was a loud crinkling sound, like broken glass, as the wheels crossed the start of this shiny area. This sound was a signal for Mehedi to drive in a loop to avoid the obstacle, whatever it was. He stopped the vehicle and pointed to the vast sparkling expanse. I stepped out to examine this spectacle. It was a field of crystallised glass. Thousands of pieces of clear glass crystals littered the desert. Some looked like coloured pebbles from a beach, but most of all they reminded me of kryptonite from a Superman film. All I needed was a pair of tights, a cape, and a big 'S' blazoned on my chest. Was the outside world aware of this natural phenomenon? It could be ranked as one wonder of our world, a natural spectacle created by the heat of the sun. I turned to Mehedi and smiled. He raised his thumb in agreement with a look of pride on his face. This was a man who had shown me how proud he was of his country.

An hour later, I saw something in the distance. As we got closer, a tent containing metal stands that held barrels of fuel and lubricants appeared. It was nowhere near as exciting as the last stop. A Bedouin was waiting for us to pull up. Mehedi greeted him. "Salaam alaikum."

"Alaikum salaam." And, as was their custom, they kissed both cheeks. The Bedouin turned to me. "Salaam alaikum."

"Alaikum salaam."

He pointed to his chest. "Me, Saleh."

I placed my hand on my chest. "Me, Andrew." I held out my hand, and he shook it, but, we did not kiss.

First, Saleh offered water and then tea, offering water was the golden rule when you encounter travellers in the desert. He must have fired up the kerosene stove when he spotted us in the distance. While standing and sipping tea, I smelt the aroma of spices and meat being cooked. I guessed it was camel or goat.

Whatever it was, it proved to be delicious. He served it in a metal bowl and later held out fruit and dates to round off the meal. I didn't speak, but my two Bedouin companions had plenty to talk about.

Once Saleh had filled the tank with fuel, we were ready to leave. I took out two packs of Marlboro from my bag and gave them to Saleh, who appreciated my gift. Perhaps he would kiss my cheeks if we ever met again!

We arrived at Nafoora mid-afternoon. The site manager escorted me to meet the maintenance supervisor, who thanked me for delivering the test equipment. I spent the next hour chatting to the supervisor and telling him about the crystallised desert we crossed. The electrician came in and reported that the test equipment I brought showed where the fault was and the turbine was now back online. They housed me in the guest hut and invited me to Fives and Sevens. It was good to quench my parched throat with a cool beer and pass the time with a different bunch of men. Everyone was interested when I told them about my detour and the crystals.

After an early breakfast and a few goodbyes, I waited for Mehedi to arrive at 7am. I checked the Land Rover and this time I saw the radio tucked out of sight underneath the glove compartment. I handed over my bribe of two packs of Marlboro and we set off.

We stopped briefly at the refuelling station and bypassed the field of glass. I knew Mehedi had taken a detour to show me this wonder of the desert. After two hours, the temperature rocketed. It felt hotter than the day before.

As I dozed in the heat, a loud bang jolted me awake. A blowout made the vehicle lurch. I helped Mehedi retrieve the spare wheel from inside and placed it beside the damaged one. I wanted to help change it, but Mehedi brushed me away, he would not hear of it. We were out in the open at a temperature that must have been close to forty-five degrees. As I waited, huge red ants crawled out of the desert and onto my legs. They must have smelt food – me – and they bit me and it hurt. I brushed my legs hard with my hands to get them off. I could not see a reason why ants lived in the middle of nowhere and why they came after me and not Mehdi.

An hour later, I heard another bang, and, once more, the vehicle lurched. Another tyre had blown out. Panic – mine alone – set in. Mehdi merely shrugged his shoulders. "No problem."

He removed the wheel, and I grabbed it and immediately let go; the hot wheel burned my hands. I wrapped rags around it before attempting to move it and put it into the back of the Land Rover. There were no ants, but I picked up a few pieces of what looked like bits of coal, another desert wonder. They were pieces of petrified trees, millions of years old, dating back to a time when the Sahara was a lush green forest.

With no further breakdowns, we reached Sarir three hours later. I enjoyed my astonishing experience in the Sahara Desert.

Another event terrified me. Because of a lack of office space, we were permitted to do administration work in our room if we didn't have a class. I informed Arthur I would work in my room for a few hours the following morning. I saw him at breakfast and reminded him, then returned to my room to begin my paperwork. After an hour, I felt dizzy and nauseous, so entered the bathroom to wash my face. It was then I passed out, cracking my head on the basin as I collapsed to the floor. How long I remained unconscious and how I got outside, I do not know. Some workers spotted me wandering close to the security fence, bleeding and confused. They took me to the clinic, and the doctor, after diagnosing my ailment, put me on a drip for two days. I made a full recovery and returned to work after he gave me a clean bill of health. He guessed my illness was caused by a dangerous virus and it could have been the end of me. I was ready for my leave after this.

I never knew the real reason the airline never confirmed my onward flights from Malta to London. I assumed it was because of political reasons, or unreliable flights. I hated the mad rush to get to the transit desk when the flight landed at Luqa. Luckily, I always got a seat, I had learnt the technique of pushing. One time, I got chatting with some of the airline staff and bought them a drink. I asked them if they needed anything from the UK. Twice, to the delight of the check-in girls, I obliged. From that point onwards, no matter where I was in the queue, I always got a seat.

On one occasion, my company informed me the Malta flight was not available and I would fly Libyan Arab Airlines from Tripoli to London. This meant an overnight stay at the guest house in Benghazi before flying the next day to Tripoli. I would have preferred to fly with Air Malta because I was not confident flying on a Libyan Arab Airlines flight. Their safety record was questionable.

The first flight out was a seventeen-seater aircraft, which arrived the day before and parked at the Sarir airfield overnight. At 6am, passengers waited, but no aircrew appeared. A passenger left the waiting room to find the pilot and co-pilot. He had to drag them out of bed. They arrived bleary-eyed, dressed in jeans, T-shirt and sandals. Despite their appearance, no one cared, we just wanted to get home. We were airborne less than fifteen minutes later.

The flight to Benghazi was uneventful, except for the thick fog of cigarette smoke in the cabin, the dirty toilet and the lack of tea or coffee. We landed sideways at Benghazi, and the pilot blamed the wind, but as an experienced former RAF electrical mechanic, I knew better. In this profession, you get used to these things, but it doesn't make it any easier. I made it to the guest house in time for breakfast.

Someone I recognised, but could not for the life of me remember his name, came into the restaurant carrying a holdall. He looked pleased with himself. He opened the bag and took out a beautiful, cuddly teddy bear. He spoke in an excited voice. "If anyone wants some cuddly toys to take home, the big supermarket just down the road have hundreds of them and they're very cheap."

I grabbed my holdall from my room and went to the supermarket, grasping the forty Libyan dinars the company gave me. The supermarket was a shed with almost empty shelves. The shelves with items displayed held bread, milk, rice, cleaning products, and cigarettes. In one of the far corners, I spotted the cuddly toys. There must have been at least a thousand of them piled onto sheets spread out on the floor. I caught a shop assistant by the arm and showed him my empty bag and told him to fill it.

I spotted a Hippopotamus with a label on it with the name 'Pot Belly'. Its eye was damaged, and I felt sorry for it, so I placed it in the bag. The assistant didn't want me to have it, but I insisted. I returned to the guest house with a full holdall and two extra bags the supermarket assistant gave me. I had spent some of my worthless currency, only fifteen dinars remained.

The guest house steward gave me an old suitcase that someone had left, and I packed the toys into it. There were teddy bears, monkeys and Pot Belly. All were top quality, 'Made in Korea' toys.

Passengers passed through customs and currency control on the way in and on the way out at Tripoli. My happy mood changed when a rather large and round-faced customs official said, "Open!"

My hands shook as I tried to open the suitcase. I'm sure he suspected I was smuggling contraband. His face turned red when he saw the cuddly toys, but I reacted in time before he blew up. I put on a big smile and crossed my arms like I was holding a baby. "I have many babies. Do you have babies?"

The guy looked about 60. I think he was overcome with surprise as I removed one of the soft Monkeys from the case and offered it to him. "For your baby." I knew the art of persuasion. I am an expert in diverting awkward situations.

He placed the toy under the table and helped me close the suitcase.

Gilly could not believe her eyes when she saw what was in the suitcase. She loved Pot Belly the most.

Having spent five years in Kuwait, I was well acquainted with the dangers of living and working in the desert. Two of the most dangerous times are a sudden sandstorm or flash flooding. Sandstorm conditions are also ideal conditions to bring on rainstorms and flash flooding becomes a threat. Desert sand does not soak up water quickly, so, without warning, heavy rains can produce flooding. Dry channels, ditches and wadis fill quickly and the resulting deluge can be strong and violent. More people drown in the desert than die of thirst.

I enjoyed the beauty and fear that the desert can bring if things go wrong. Whenever I ventured into the desert, I always carried out a checklist – thoroughness prevents accidents. I never considered I was in any kind of danger in our camp, other than getting stung by a scorpion or picking up a virus. However, I discovered how wrong I was to be so confident. As I made my way back to my hut after dinner, a distance of around 200 metres, a strong breeze picked up, and sand blew into my face and body.

Birds flew past me, searching for shelter, as the sky turned black. From my experience with storms at sea, I knew that once birds seek shelter, the storm is about to hit. Dressed in trousers, a T-shirt and sandals, I ran. Dressed as I was, my body was not protected against what hit me. Sand pelted my body, and the pain became unbearable, and my vision was blurred. My situation would become dire quickly and if I did not make it back to my hut, death would be the outcome. It was impossible to reach my hut. Somehow, I got to the nearest hut and banged my fists on the door, but no reply. My attempt to break it down failed, and my only alternative was to get underneath the hut. Wooden posts two feet high supported the huts. I squeezed my body underneath, but only a few feet because of the cross-beams. I shared the space with sheltering birds.

The sandstorm reached a peak, a full-blown assault that threatened destruction. The pain I was feeling alarmed me as the sand now reached below the hut and threatened to rip the skin from my body. If I did not get my face covered quickly, it would blast off my skin, blind me and I could drown in the sand as the granules entered my lungs. I crouched with my back to the onslaught, but it didn't help. With difficulty, I removed my T-shirt and wrapped it around my head. Blood ran down my face as I tried to cover it. The crossbeam would protect my exposed torso if I could get beyond it. I scraped away the sand with my hands enough to allow myself to succeed. My idea worked; once I was behind the beam, my breathing improved. The birds followed me deeper inside.

Almost an hour passed, and I thought I would die from thirst or pain unless I got medical help. Another hour passed, and some birds left the safety of the hut. Their departure was a signal to me that danger was passing, the worst of the sandstorm was over. As I edged myself to the outside, one bird fluttered against my body, as eager as I was to escape this enforced imprisonment, it was shaking and too scared to fly so I placed it safe. I could just see outside the hut where the sun shone through the hazy sky. I crawled back to check on the bird. It appeared to be still alive, but too afraid to leave. I moved my hand to get a hold of it, to let it out and set it free. Trying not to hurt the bird, I lowered my hand and its claws circled my finger and it held on tightly. I whispered to the little desert lark, but it would not fly off straight away. Perhaps it needed to get its bearings to find out which way to fly to join the flock or maybe it was just exhausted. I released it from my finger and placed it safely out of sight, to let it recover in its own time.

The siren sounded the all-clear and that meant I must report to my muster point. The roll call proved that there were no fatal casualties, but several people, myself included, had to report to the clinic for our wounds to be cleaned.

The site manager gave instructions for key personnel to return to their workplace and the uninjured were to take part in 'Operation Clean-up'. The injured should make their way to the clinic. I helped with the cleaning of the clinic until it was my turn for treatment.

Two rotations later, my old boss in Sarawak Shell called me. I waited patiently until the introductory chit-chat ended. My prayer was answered when he said, "I need you to come back to Sarawak."

I breathed a sigh of contentment and happiness. My escape from the desert had arrived. I was to go from one extreme to another, the aridity of the desert to the lush greenness of a tropical rainforest.

CHAPTER 15

MODERN-DAY PIRATES

My happiness and joy bubbled over as I stepped off the aircraft at Miri. I was back for the third time. Lucy was pleased to see me back. Wong had briefed me on my work requirements during our previous telephone conversation. My role was to ensure the smooth handover of the Samarang offshore platform from Shell to Petronas Carigali. Here, 120 technicians and operators would learn theory and go offshore for on-the-job experience. After training, they would go to the platform and replace Shell's employees. 'Political dynamite' was Wong's description. It would involve three expatriate workers. Jeff, who I knew well, was the coordinator. Steve, who would be my back-to-back on twenty-eight days on and twenty-eight days off rotation, I had not met before. Our job would be to assist and support Shell staff to carry out the practical on-the-job training phase.

He was very clear. "Andrew, this is a very important project for both companies. The date for handover is 31/03/1995 and we must meet it."

"Wong, I won't let you down."

"I know that, Andrew. That's why I wanted you for this job."

The Samarang field is in Sabah waters, forty-five miles northwest of Labuan. Because of the lack of beds on the Samarang platform, the on-the-job training would be carried out at Erb West, Samarang's sister platform. My employment would last three years.

I arrived on Erb West to a tumultuous reception from my ex-trainees, who were now long-term employees. Their enthusiasm was emphatic. "Don't worry, Andrew. You taught us well so we will help your new trainees." This was an enormous relief to me, Jeff and Wong, as it was vital that I got cooperation from the employees.

My job was interesting, I worked with almost everyone on the platform and I felt part of both the Shell and Petronas organisations. Nobody treated me as just another contractor.

Every report I made was scrutinised by the Petronas managing director. I found this out when the supervisor called me to the control room. "Andrew, tomorrow you are on the chopper to Labuan and then on a flight to Kota Kinabalu, the MD wants to meet you."

The next day, when I was sitting in the MD's office, he said, "Andrew, I asked you here because I wanted to meet you. I've read all of your reports. You are very honest with your reporting and have been a big help to me and my team."

"Thank you."

"In last month's report, you lowered one of the trainee's safety mark from five down to four, and you wrote you did it because of horseplay. Do you want me to punish him?"

What he said surprised me, because I did not think someone as high as this would read my reports. "No, that's unnecessary, it was an isolated case and I can assure you it won't happen again."

"All right, Andrew. I will call him in and give him a verbal warning when he comes in from his shift."

We chatted for a few minutes before he thanked me for coming and I left feeling appreciated. It is good to be seen by the boss and to be praised for hard work.

My trainees accepted discipline. I was tough on them because their lives depended on the success of their training. They were going to take over a platform where they would work in an environment fraught with danger. It was not only the technical stuff I dealt with; I dealt with their personal problems. One lad received a telephone call from his pregnant wife telling him she had visited someone whose son was suffering from measles and she worried about their unborn child. I sat with him for two days until the scheduled helicopter arrived to fly him back to his loved ones. It was expensive to fly in a helicopter just for him, and the supervisor would not justify this as an emergency. Other times, I cheered up those who missed their girlfriend or children, or who didn't enjoy being away during a festival or other occasion. Life was tough, but it was also rewarding.

Presentations were a training activity I introduced. Small groups presented a system or platform operation they would work on. They had to do the presentations in front of their peers and if they were not up to standard, it would delay their move. On one occasion, a group presentation was about to take place and a major shutdown happened. There was no rest for anyone.

It took two days to fix the problem, and once the platform was up and running, the supervisor told everyone to take turns and get some sleep. My trainees thought I was joking when I insisted they still had to complete their presentation two days later. The following day, the Samarang supervisor called me, wanting to know why my trainees were requesting information on the platform so soon after a shutdown. I explained that this was an opportunity for them to learn what it was like to work under extreme pressure just to meet deadlines and he agreed with me. The presentation was perfect, and they transferred to their designated positions with no further delay. Shutdowns were not the only problems or dangers they would encounter in their working lives. These young men had to be ready for anything.

My favourite movies were *Treasure Island* and *Pirates of the Caribbean*. I loved the characters and the costumes. The skull and crossbones filled me with dread. Movies are fantasy so any fear ends when the movie ends, but that is not real life. The Sabah oil and gas platforms were close to the Southern Philippine islands, known to be a hiding place for modern-day pirates. There were procedures to follow should they attack a platform or terminal.

I knew what had happened at Lahad Datu, a township on the remote east coast of Sabah, rarely visited unless you are a deep-sea diver. One evening, in September 1985, a group of armed men clad in jungle green uniforms invaded the town. Mercilessly, they opened fire on the residents as they raided the bank and airline office.

The attack was soon over, but police blocked the road back to the boats preventing a quick getaway. They wounded two of the raiders, but most of the gang escaped with over 200,000 ringgit (£50000 sterling) of loot. They left behind a trail of blood and twenty-one dead bodies, including a pregnant woman.

Weeks later, after this horrendous loss of life, I landed at Labuan Island and saw jet fighters fully equipped with missiles. As I left the twin otter, I commented to another passenger, "They look like they mean business. Somebody is in trouble."

"It's revenge for the slaughter in Lahad Datu."

We heard nothing for some time, but gradually information filtered through. The smoke that we had seen in the distance rising from one island resulted from a carefully planned rocket strike. Many died, the numbers were unknown. This revenge attack was only briefly reported in local newspapers and wasn't reported in international newspapers.

Working for four weeks offshore was not perfect, often I felt downhearted and homesick, but there were also times of utter pleasure and amazement at the beauty that surrounded my artificial island. Each morning, as the sun came up, I exercised, walking from my living accommodation to the wellhead and back. I paused on my way to gaze down to the sea to view the many species of fish swimming below. If I gazed towards Sabah, Mount Kinabalu, with its peak at over 13,000 feet, was visible through the white clouds. Once, I was peering down into the blue depths, when into view came two giant stingrays swimming side by side. It was one of the most beautiful sights I ever saw.

After this amazing, calming episode, I looked forward to a perfect day. Today was not normal, because we received a visit from some army officers. It appeared to be just routine, and our supervisor confirmed it at the daily meeting. A few days later, he informed me several more people, and myself, were returning onshore and the helicopter would arrive in thirty minutes. "Sorry, Andrew, VIP visitors are arriving today and we need accommodation because they are staying overnight." Who could they be? I was curious to find out, but the supervisor would not give me any information. All he would say was, "Your guess is as good as mine."

"Thanks, I will get my bag and go to the helideck."

Although training new people to work on platforms is essential, it takes second place to production and VIP visits. If a bed was needed, I got a welcome break from the isolation of the platform and a trip back to Miri.

I spotted my manager getting off the chopper. It was impossible to speak to him, but his body language meant, "Why the hell are you leaving?"

On the helideck, with rotors running, there was no way I was going back.

When I arrived back onshore, I let Jeff know our training manager was on the platform, and it surprised him. Everything became clearer when the report came through. "Last evening, pirates attacked Erb West, taking a Filipino worker hostage."

Two days later, I flew back and the supervisor briefed me about the event. It turned out not to be a real attack, but an exercise. Everything was kept secret, not even the supervisor was let into it. Apparently, I was to be the hostage, and the supervisor had scuppered the plan. The whole exercise was to test the emergency services and included international help from services in Kuala Lumpur and London. I discovered who the replacement hostage was; it was a Pilipino worker. When I talked to him, he reported that the attack by the army pirates was very realistic and terrifying. Everybody was imprisoned or tied up. He was threatened and manhandled after it all kicked off. In retrospect, I am pleased the supervisor sent me to Miri. I often think about how I would have reacted to being taken hostage.

Once a month, the emergency shutdown (ESD) was tested. Everyone on board had a role to play. The most common exercises were a man overboard, a fire, a helicopter crash on the helideck or a severe injury. Exercises involving piracy had never happened before.

Approaching the halfway mark to the deadline, Shell sent their trainees to the platform. Experienced personnel would train as multi-discipline technicians. The motto was 'jack of all trades, master of one.' Permanent staff would now be outnumbered by trainees. Using the experienced permanent technicians to help the inexperienced, I promoted the motto and with everyone's cooperation, safety was never compromised.

A lesson I learned was never to judge people by how they behave. The trainee whose safety marks I docked for misbehaving was a splendid example. It was coming near to the time he was to transfer. I was going through some salient procedural points with him and he burst into tears. I was taken aback. Here was someone with their entire future in front of them, crying.

I decided not to call the platform supervisor, but to just sit it out to see if he recovered. Eventually, he calmed down. He was insistent. "I don't want to move to Samarang."

"Why not? You are doing well here and can do the same there!"

"I can't go there."

"You don't need to go. No one will force you. What is making you upset? Tell me the reason and I will help."

He was silent for a minute, then blurted it out. "I am afraid of the noise."

I sat there stunned for a minute, then suggested I discuss his case with the platform supervisor. I hoped he would answer yes because this would need reporting.

"I don't want anyone else to find out."

After further discussion, I found out he enjoyed working offshore, but when he entered a noisy area, such as the turbine house, he was afraid.

I reported the problem to the supervisor, and the lad moved to Samarang with only a few people aware of his problem. Later I met him at the handover dinner and he thanked me for helping him.

In life, people believe in the supernatural, things that cannot be explained. I have experienced this myself. When I fell ill one time, I was visited by dark angels who never spoke to me, I was not afraid as I felt they were there to make me get better.

Belief in superstitions is as old as humans. The old, the young, the educated and the uneducated believe in superstitions. Human nature is the same everywhere, despite scientific progress and increase in education, some people are still superstitious. Some of us believe there is only one god, but others believe there are many gods and spirits that affect our everyday lives. Such beliefs or knowledge are rooted in human nature.

Many have allowed their beliefs to change as new theories and ideas on the concepts of life have emerged, but deep-rooted superstitions and the supernatural is still with us. For Dayak people in Borneo, the sense of the supernatural is always there, and its influence encompasses every action of their daily life. The spirit world surrounds them on every side; voices speak to them and tell them where to build a house, warn hunters of danger and tell them where to plant paddy. As a child of nature, they believe in nature worship. The Dayak hears what he believes to be the voices of nature and obeys. Before the missionaries came, they had no sense of sin and the voices of nature guided them. Petara is the name of their deity and denotes endless spirits. Each person and animal has their own petara or guardian in the unseen world.

Evil spirits roam the jungle in various forms and keep the people in a state of terror. Every illness is blamed on evil spirits who will devour their human prey unless a sacrifice of food is made to appease their anger. Sacrifices of rice, eggs, plantains, bananas, fruit and fowl are put on a brass salver. If they are out hunting, they construct a sacrificial altar made of sticks fastened with rattan and a roof of nipa leaves. If the food remains untouched, they say that only the husk is there and the invisible essence has been consumed by the invisible spirit.

Sacrifices are made to secure successful farming; a blood offering is the essential element to achieve the desired result. A fowl or a pig is killed, and the blood sprinkled over the ground, or a newly sacrificed bird is waved in the air over the paddy field. If it is an illness, the sacrifice is offered by the medicine men, who are called priests. Occasionally, the chief of the tribe, or some old man, is chosen to perform the rite. The superstition of omens is one that keeps them in fear. Animals, birds or insects may bring him the warning he dreads, but birds give the most important omens, and they have become an object of worship. Would I ever experience one of the Dayaks' sacrificial rites?

As we were approaching the end of the project, I needed to spend more time onshore staying at one of the new hotels in Miri. On Friday afternoon, the telephone rang. It was George, the new owner of the Bounty pub who wanted to check if I would be in the pub later. He said it was his birthday and I must go to join in the celebrations. I told him I would be there.

The evening passed with fun, entertainment and lots to drink. A successful birthday party. I fell into a deep sleep after this session. Loud banging on my door interrupted my dreams, and I woke with a pounding hangover. When I opened the door, George stood outside, grinning. Why was he so chirpy when I felt so dreadful?

"Come, Andrew, get dressed, we are going for roti canai."

I often joined friends for an Indian breakfast, but never on a weekend. Why come today? I invited him in and made him coffee while I showered and dressed. I hoped I would feel better after dousing my head in the water.

He drove us to our favourite Indian restaurant on the waterfront and I felt better after my breakfast. It was true; a full stomach can improve or cure a hangover. As usual, the restaurant was busy, and I knew several of the diners from my visits offshore. I was surprised to see so many of them together as they would usually spend every moment of their precious leave time with their family. With good food and relaxing chat, no one was in a hurry to leave. Then Samuel looked at his watch and called out, "Andrew, George, time to go."

"Where to?"

"To the kampong."

I knew not to ask why, I was invited and I didn't want to appear rude questioning the reason.

At the village kampong, a surprising sight met my eyes: over one hundred people were sitting around on chairs in front of a raised circular open stage covered with thatch. An event was going to happen here. This was the reason for my visit. We stepped up onto the stage and sat down, as did a dozen others who had been dining in the same restaurant. What was going to happen here? We appeared to be the centre of attention. I sat down with a good view of the people below me. I recognised many of them, but why were we all gathered here? I knew it wasn't a public holiday, so not that.

I did not have long to wait to find out. A man, who I recognised as being a manager in the company I worked for, came on to the stage. He wore a traditional costume: a woven skirt, loose-fitting black trousers and a shirt with gold and red trim, a silver belt, and, on his head, a woven hat decorated with feathers. The reason I was invited was about to begin, but why was I not in the audience watching?

There was music but no chanting, nor did I see anyone conducting themselves in any way that could be described as traditional dancing. The man placed a mask on his head and spoke at length to us. I did not understand the words, however, my neighbours nodded in agreement and uttered responses to his words and gestures. He removed a chicken from a cage and gripped it in his hands, lifting it high above him. He moved around, waving it in the air. I was part of a ceremony that I guessed was to do with offshore workers. Later explanations of the event proved I was correct. He slit the throat of the chicken, then moved close enough for the chicken blood to spray on each worker. I knew then that this was a spiritual ceremony to protect us from harm.

The ceremony finished with young people performing traditional dances and a lot of tuak, strong rice wine, and food. My hangover had disappeared, but I was about to get another one. People congratulated me, and my friends thanked me for joining them and receiving the blessing. I was now protected from evil spirits that could hurt me offshore.

It was a big honour to be part of this ceremony. It showed that I was accepted as a friend and part of their culture. I thanked my friends for this invitation and they replied, "You are welcome, Andrew."

I knew in my heart that I was part of a serious ceremony that I should not question or discuss. The people who witnessed and the people who took part in the ceremony were Christian, yet they believed in what took place. I learned an important lesson that day. Life is not just about my beliefs, it is about what others believe and how I, and the rest of the world should accept and respect each other's beliefs and traditions.

With only a few days to run before the handover dinner and my return home, I received a telephone call from Arnold. "Andrew, I have some good news for you. Can you fly to Hong Kong to get a visa and then take the ferry to China? You will like this job."

The graduation ceremony was a lavish affair held at the Tanjung Aru Beach Resort. Ex-trainees who were off shift were there, dressed smartly in Malaysian formal dress. As they helped themselves at the buffet, they were only going to the table once. Puddings, cakes, salad, vegetables and meat were stacked high on one plate.

During the speeches, several individuals were thanked for a job well done, but not Jeff or me. I felt disappointed. Jeff and I were outside having a smoke when Wong approached and asked us to go with him.

We entered a side room where the VIP party had gathered. The principal guest, a government minister, gestured that we should join the group.

As we approached him, he congratulated and thanked us. "Jeff, Andrew, thank you for helping to make this project a success." All the other personnel began clapping and agreeing with the minister's words. Our hard work had been appreciated. He had wanted to thank us directly and personally, not in a crowded assembly hall. I felt so proud and elated.

It was tough saying goodbye to my friends, but I was a contractor and they moved on. I boarded a Malaysia Airlines flight bound for Hong Kong. In my offshore bag were my formal batik shirt, trousers and shoes that I bought for the presentation reception, my toiletries, spare underwear and the gift set I had been awarded. I was wearing jeans, a T-shirt and trainers. I never needed a jumper or jacket in Sarawak.

CHAPTER 16
IT'S 5 O'CLOCK SOMEWHERE

The flight time from Kota Kinabalu to Hong Kong was three hours and during that time I had a few beers and a tasty inflight meal. I felt relaxed until the 'no smoking' and 'fasten your seat belt' sign came on. This was a notoriously dangerous runway to land on. I had a window seat and a good view of the terrain and could see Kai Tak Airport below as the aircraft circled and the pilot announced for the crew to take their seats. The runway jutted into the sea and we would approach it directly over the city. Fear gripped me as the aircraft buffeted and flew between blocks of apartments. I felt as if I could wave to people in their kitchens, we were that close to them. This airport was famous for its closeness to habitation and many passengers closed their eyes as the plane came in to land. It unnerved me but it was a fascinating experience. Thankfully, this was a problem-free, safe landing.

The only way British and American visitors could enter China was to get a visa in their country of origin or purchase one in Hong Kong and this would take up to four days. British and American visitors did not need a visa to enter Hong Kong. I arrived on Friday and that meant it would be Tuesday before I could leave for the mainland. No way was that acceptable, as hotels were expensive and I would not get paid until I arrived at work. As soon as I cleared immigration and customs, I telephoned our company agent and he was waiting for me at the hotel. I handed over two photographs and my passport. At 6pm, he returned with the visa I needed to proceed to the port of Shekou in mainland China. I could not have got a visa in such a short time without the help of the agent – a Mr Fix-it!

Life in Hong Kong moved at a faster pace than in Sarawak. People rushed along streets like ants in search of their next meal. Jeff warned me about the cost of living and to be careful where I bought my everyday necessities. Food cost little, but beer could be five times the price than back home. This proved to be untrue. I found a place that served food and because it was 'happy hour' beer was at a discounted price and reasonable. The other customers were relaxed and did not appear bothered about the prices. My first visit to the island passed quickly, and I had a good night's sleep.

Daily temperatures in Sarawak ranged between twenty-nine and thirty-three degrees centigrade. This morning, the temperature in Hong Kong had only reached eighteen degrees and, being jacketless, I felt cold in my jeans and T-shirt so I hurried to the taxi rank to keep warm. It dropped me at Sim Sha Tsui ferry terminal, where hundreds of people dashed around buying tickets and making their way to the various departure points. The tannoy gave instructions in Chinese, but the signs in English helped to make it easier for me to buy my ticket and find my departure point. I sailed on the mid-morning ferry for Shekou and it took an hour to get there.

The ferry was almost full of people going to China on business or to work. I had no problems when I reached immigration and no one stopped me at customs. I followed Arnold's instructions and changed some American dollars to Chinese yuan then, took a taxi to Chiwan Training Centre, a fifteen-minute drive from the ferry terminal. We drove through an industrial area and the port before climbing a steep hill that led to my destination. Inside, two young ladies introduced themselves as Cycy and Helen. They both spoke impeccable English. Cycy escorted me to another office where I met Jim, the senior instructor. He invited me to join the weekly meeting about to start. Nine other staff members were there and after the introductions, I sat for the next hour, cold and bored. After the meeting, I expected Jim to give me my induction into the company. Instead, he asked me to wait in the secretary's office.

Both girls were busy, but Cycy saw I was shivering. "You look cold, Andrew, do you have a jumper?"

"No, I didn't need jumpers in Sarawak and I haven't had time to buy one here."

"Never mind, let me get you a nice cup of coffee; that will keep you warm."

Work finished at 1pm and I followed the others as they piled into a minibus. I assumed that this was how I would get back and forth to work. We dropped off Helen, Cycy, Craig, and Alex, then Jim called out, "Andrew, we are going to the beach bar. I guess you are ready for a drink."

"Yes, I could do with a pint." It would also be a time for me to throw out questions to learn a little about the job, the area, shopping and everything I would need for my life in China – like some warm jumpers!

The driver stopped as close to the place as he could get. There were a dozen outside tables near what looked like an old shack. It was not the warmth of an inside bar I had envisaged. So far, my knowledge of Shekou had been given by Helen, who told me that four million people lived in the Special Economic Zone. My opinion, so far, was that this was a town with a population of several thousand, not millions. I heard Jim say, "You guys get started. I will take Andrew to the Nanhai and get him checked in."

The Nanhai Hotel was close to the ferry terminal. We entered through a back door that led to check-in. A receptionist, wearing a dark blue uniform, checked me in and told me my company would pay the bill. She added the restaurant served a buffet lunch and I could sign and put my room number on the bill. The buffet looked popular, judging by the numbers eating there. I dumped my offshore bag in my room and returned downstairs to where Jim was waiting. There was a cold breeze as we walked back to join the others. I sat down just as a young woman delivered four large bottles of Tsingtao and David poured me a glass of beer. Another woman in her forties brought dishes of food that looked similar to the dishes I had eaten during my time in Malaysia.

My new colleagues were forthcoming with information about Shenzhen and my workplace. Shenzhen was a tiny fishing village until it became a Special Economic

Zone (SEZ) in 1980. The population grew from 3000 to four million in ten years. State officials, entrepreneurs, technicians and skilled workers came here to make a new life for themselves and their families and they made up thirty per cent of the residents. The other seventy per cent were temporary migrant workers from rural areas who came here to escape from poverty and the old communist ways. Most of these workers were women working in the many factories built to improve China's economy. Shekou, where I was based, was part of the Economic Zone and remained unaffected by the growth until now. This was about to change because the government had plans to develop it for tourism.

Cycy joined us, carrying a paper shopping bag in her hand. She offered it to me. "Here you are, Andrew, this should keep you warm." She had remembered my plight and bought me a present. This was the beginning of the kindness I experienced from her and others in China.

I opened the bag and pulled out a jumper, not my favourite style or colour, but who cared. It looked warm and cosy. I put it on and thanked her. Now I could stay longer to get information on what there was to do here.

Someone mentioned the city of Guangzhou and Jim said, "Andrew, you'll have to wait a bit to go there. You need to get your permanent residency identification." Every country has red tape so, once you had the essential paperwork and stamps, life could progress smoothly.

Alan said, "There is a fence that prevents unauthorised people from entering or leaving the zone. You need your passport, and not just a copy, if you leave."

"That seems harsh."

"Yes, it does, but if there wasn't a fence then millions would come to the area to seek work and the place would be overrun with unemployed people."

"Andrew, if you wish to go to Guangzhou, I want to be your guide."

"Thank you, Cycy, I'll remember that."

Jim was full of praise. "Andrew, don't worry, you're in expert hands. The two girls will keep you right on everything to do with your job and China. They are the best."

The social gathering broke up and an early night was going to be next, but Wayne and David had other ideas. They were taking me out tonight.

After my social induction to Shekou, I telephoned home and spoke to Gilly. She said, "Are you okay? Your voice sounds strange."

"Must be jet lag."

"There's no time difference between Malaysia and China, have you been drinking?"

"No, it's cold here and I'm shivering."

It was nice to hear her voice, but I could tell she didn't believe a word I was saying. She recognised the voice of an inebriated Drew. I think Gilly was unhappy with me because I had only been in China for a few hours and I sounded as if I was drunk. I didn't tell her I was going out again in a few hours' time.

I woke up with a bit of a hangover, showered and made my way to the dining area and ate from the buffet. I spotted my new colleagues when they arrived at reception and went to greet them. Wayne came from Australia and was not wearing shoes and never did. I considered that to be bizarre and dangerous and that he must be crazy, or had he lived in the outback so this was normal for him?

We proceeded past the security barrier and within two minutes, stopped for our first beer at a bar called the Red Rooster. It was owned by an expatriate and his Chinese partner. We decided not to have a second beer and left. As we turned a corner on the main road, we passed the Anchor bar and Casablanca restaurant and both were full of customers. After a minute Wayne said, "Cross the road, we are at the bus stop!"

I could not see a bus stop. I hoped I didn't have to get on a bus if Wayne or David couldn't speak Chinese.

We crossed over and entered a shack. This was the Bus Stop. It was a bar, and we remained there a while.

It was approaching 10pm when we passed the Casablanca for a second time, and now it was almost empty. We filed through the door of Joe Bananas, a nightclub with live music. It was packed with partygoers and the music was deafening. I can't remember leaving.

On Sunday morning, I woke up with a hangover, but still wanted to explore Shekou. After a shower and dressing, I exited the hotel through the rear door. I passed the places I visited the night before and a few minutes further on, I stopped at the Park and Shop supermarket and saw it had a good stock of western food. Five minutes later, I reached a square surrounded by shops, apartment blocks and offices. On the corner was a McDonald's, something I never expected to see in China. I had missed breakfast, so I ordered a spicy chicken burger, which tasted as good as the ones at home. It was an area with decent shops, including, a photography, a souvenir and a bread shop, and a grocery store. Across the square, I could see the beach and a cargo ship that was landlocked.

Strolling back along a block-paved footpath on the seafront, I stopped for a coffee at the Seagull restaurant where several families were picnicking between the trees. As I passed the beach bar, the woman who served us the day before waved. I returned to my temporary home in the Nanhai and spent the next hour eating and recovering from the night before. Once I felt better, I decided to investigate what lay beyond McDonald's. It was chilly, but my new jumper kept me warm. After a quarter of a mile, the traffic stopped as more than a hundred young girls dressed in identical working uniforms and riding bicycles exited the gates of the Sanyo factory. I assumed this must be the end of the early shift. Soon after that, I came to the main police station and a covered market. A little further on were streets with more shops and restaurants. I zigzagged between the shops in these streets, which sold industrial goods, clothes or electronics. Apartments for single people and families were close by and beyond that, the principal part of the town had several supermarkets and large stores. This was where over a million residents lived and it was buzzing with activity. Shekou was not the one-horse town of my earlier impression. This was good news; Gilly would have plenty to do when she visited during the school holidays. She was teaching full-time in Yorkshire and needed relaxation and interesting new experiences to recover from the rigorous changes occurring in education. A new national curriculum was currently being introduced to schools in the UK.

The training centre was owned by the Chinese National Offshore Oil Company (CNOOC). Four oil companies, Chevron, Texaco, Mobil, and AGIP had formed a consortium and hired the centre to train their future offshore workers there. The trainees made my job easy because only one of them was not a university graduate and they were all keen to learn. One had been a doctor and gave it up when the opportunity came for him to work for an oil company. They were the cream of the Chinese education system. All of them held good jobs before coming to Shekou in search of a better standard of living. They received intense English training from Alex and Craig before starting their trade training. It was early days, but I was already glad I accepted the job.

English was widely spoken in the oil sector, but I needed to learn Mandarin to visit outside the wire. My tutor, Mr Wu, a 72-year-old ex-Chinese Navy man, made me work hard. After six months of learning, I understood the intricacies of pronunciation and vocabulary. I appreciated my success with the language and could ask and answer basic questions and ask for directions and help. The first test of my ability came when I was walking into town. I passed a hawker selling exquisite Chinese clay teapots. I greeted him by saying nǐhǎo, which meant 'hello'.

He said nǐhǎo in reply.

"Duōshǎo qián yi?" How much for one?

I guessed his reply was the price.

"Tài guì le." Too expensive. "Nǐ shuō wǒ néng dǎ zhé kòu ma?" Will you give me a discount?

He unwrapped two more and placed them on the pavement. I assumed, 'yes, if you buy three'.

I sat down on the pavement, facing him and examined the three teapots. They were flawless and beautifully shaped.

I told him I was a teacher and he was keen to do business, so we started bartering. An hour passed before we completed negotiations. I paid, and the hawker then wrapped twelve exquisite teapots in old newspaper and placed them into plastic bags. When I stood up, I noticed a dozen people had gathered to watch the negotiations. I smiled at the group and prepared to leave, when of the bystanders came forward. "Excuse me, how long have you lived in China?"

"A year."

"I'm Chinese and I couldn't have bought those teapots at a better price. You are good at bartering."

"Xiè xie, thank you." I shook hands with him and waved to everyone before I headed back to an executive apartment, which I now shared with Alex and his Malaysian wife, Lisa. Her cooking skills outclassed mine, and she encouraged me to speak Chinese so I didn't mind her living in the apartment.

To learn a language, practice it and become proficient, Chinese learners of English asked me to explain the meaning of words, so I used the same method and asked them to check my pronunciation. Most of the time, they wanted to find out about Britain and I had to steer the conversation back to China. To do that, I asked questions like, "Who is the most famous poet in China?"

Many people didn't know the answer, but I had researched it and found out that one of the famous poets from China was Li Bai. I asked them how he died. I knew he had a love for alcohol and after a drinking session, he fell overboard from a boat and drowned. People were keen to tell me more. I learned fast because I did not get disillusioned if I got something wrong.

The people I became acquainted with openly expressed their views and knowledge about their country. They spoke respectfully when referring to their government and political system. Western reports I read covering the one-child policy were damning, but people here agreed with their government that population growth had to slow down. They openly told me about the policy that was instigated by Deng Xiaoping in 1979. People referred to him as 'The Father of Shenzhen'.

They clarified that the one-child policy applied to Han Chinese living in rural areas. It did not apply to ethnic minorities. Over ninety-one per cent of the population is Han and over fifty per cent of those live in rural areas. Furthermore, families could have a second child if the first one was a girl. Families observing the rule were rewarded with higher wages, better schooling, and government help. For those who violated the policy, there were fines, wage cuts and employment termination. Families approved to have a second child had to wait for three to four years after the birth of the first child before conceiving a second one. This was harsh, but my friends did not complain. I wanted to know more and my friends wanted to tell me. One of them told me that China would never invade another country to gain territory. Likewise, they would never give up territory they considered to belong to them. I said, "What about Taiwan?"

"Andrew, your civilization in the west has only been here for 2000 years. We have been here for 4000 years, time for us is not important. China will take back Taiwan. First, they will try peaceful means, but they will take it back when the government chooses to do so."

China may be the oldest civilisation in the world and time may not have been important in the past, but now it does not appear that way. Today it is like a movie on fast-forward, high-rise blocks of apartments and industrial units are being built at breakneck speed with the population of Shenzhen rising by a million every two years.

I saw the development plans for the economic zone. Over the next few years, the Chinese government would spend billions of dollars on its development. They would join Hong Kong to the mainland by a bridge, and SEZ districts would have a metro system. After completion, the new airport would have a ferry directly to Shekou. The ship called *Minghua*, would be marooned in reclaimed land and would become a centre of entertainment and a mini-golf course would adjoin it. Shekou Bay would be reclaimed from the sea and hotels, shopping and business centres built on the land. I thought it was a fantasy, but I was proved wrong. All these things happened.

To reward my hard-working group, I splashed out and treated them to a day out. We drove towards the nuclear power plant and onwards to a small beach resort where we spent the day swimming and playing volleyball.

We all enjoyed the day and on the return journey, we stopped at a restaurant of my choice. I could tell from their actions and remarks that they approved. I let Yang order the food, and I added six large bottles of beer. His food choice was amazing, there were plenty of appetising dishes and after six more beers, there were a few trainees with red faces. Most Chinese people turn red in the face after drinking alcohol.

After we finished the meal, I spoke to the person sitting opposite me. "Yang, mai dan." This meant 'bill'.

Yang asked for the bill and a fāpiào – a receipt.

I said, "Yang, no fāpiào, I am paying."

He looked upset. "No, Mr Andrew, you cannot pay. The company will pay."

Before I could protest, Yang took a collection from the others then paid for the meal and got a receipt. Everyone thanked me for a splendid dinner.

Concerned that the group would not allow me to pay, I talked to Tony Xiang who had joined us from the China National Offshore Oil Corporation (CNOOC) a month earlier to oversee the business side of the training centre. He said, "Yang came to me with his receipt and told me of your generous gesture. In China, it is the custom for company managers to treat workers. It helps to compensate for low wages and makes for good relations."

"I did not realise that."

"Andrew, your group speaks good things about you and they appreciate what you do for them so don't worry. I have paid Yang.

Before Tony could say more, I apologised, "Sorry, Tony, I will ask your permission future."

"Thanks, Andrew."

I had learned a lesson.

Part of my trainees' development was to go to another company to see and learn from their operation. I knew that the nuclear power plant visit would be an impossibility, so I asked Cycy to telephone the manager of a neighbouring power station to arrange a visit. An hour later, Cycy knocked and entered my classroom and waited until I looked towards her.

"Andrew, I told the manager that one of our British instructors wants to visit his power station with some trainees."

"What did he say?"

"Look someplace else, you can't come here."

Perhaps he was wary of my intentions and suspected I was a western spy. I wanted to arrange a visit. Each day on my way to work, I passed a very large electrical substation that looked suitable for a development visit. I asked for a volunteer to go to the Chiwan electricity department office to ask the manager if we could come and look at the electrical equipment inside.

Yang put up his hand. "I will go, can Liu Ji Long come with me?"

"Why? Do you need someone to hold your hand?" I knew he would not be offended and would take the remark as a joke.

"No, not that, the manager may come from a different district to us and pretend he does not speak Mandarin and will speak to us in his dialect if he wants to get rid of us. We will have an advantage of Mandarin plus another two dialects."

"Yes, but everyone in China speaks Chinese don't they?"

"Yes, we do, but we speak different dialects. It became compulsory for schools to teach Mandarin only a few years ago."

Liu Ji interrupted. "My friend married a girl from another district, and for two years they needed an interpreter because they couldn't understand each other."

"Who speaks the best Mandarin?"

"Guo Qing, he studied at Beijing University."

"I think you better take him with you as well."

Three of them set out on a mission.

Two days later, a polite manager, who spoke good English, greeted me to show us around his substation. The visit ended with tea, soft drinks and sandwiches. I had learnt another aspect of negotiation, and my understanding of Chinese business and politics was improving.

I have discovered so much about the life and culture of this vast country. Those who have moved from villages and towns have left their families behind. Some have been exploited, but the majority are treated well by their employers and the government. There is little crime in these zones because wages and living conditions are better than elsewhere. To celebrate Chinese New Year, a high percentage go home to visit their parents. Hundreds of buses depart for the journey home. Journey times of twenty-four hours are common. A friend described to me what it was like. Many buses have no toilet facilities and the time between stops can be hours. Passengers depend on the driver stopping when he needs the toilet. People take containers to urinate in and women wear cotton pads in case they can't hold it in.

One of my trainees asked to get away early, so I asked for a reason. Management did not allow employees to leave early to travel home. This was a logical, serious student who I knew would never try to trick the system to get away early. His reason seemed genuine. "If I arrive in my hometown late at night, I will be robbed.

At Chinese New Year, robbers know people returning home from the Shenzhen area are rich and they lie in wait in the darkness around the bus station area, ready to grab a victim and rob them." I let him leave early to catch a bus that got him home in daylight.

Cycy informed me that there would not be the usual team meeting on Saturday and asked if I would like to accompany her to Guangzhou. This was my opportunity to go outside the wire into what my friends termed 'the real China'. I jumped at this chance and immediately agreed.

The distance from Shekou to Guangzhou is just over seventy-five miles and the coach left at 6:30am. At the zone end checkpoint, we left the bus to have our passports checked and then boarded the bus again on the other side, just like airport security. On the onward journey, few words passed between us as I took in the scenery. It was unspectacular unless you liked very high voltage electricity pylons, cement and brickworks or duck farms. I could see far into the distance and could not tell if this haziness was because it was a misty day or smoke from industrial works. Was this the pollution that the western world constantly rants about? Considering the dense traffic, our coach arrived on schedule at the White Swan Hotel on the historic European-style Shamian Island, along the Pearl River, which was the centre of Guangzhou's historic area. The hotel looked just as luxurious as the private hire bus we travelled on. We did not resist the temptation to go inside and have a look. Inside the foyer, jade ornaments of animals, people and ships built to scale held my attention. The artistic flair of these ornaments astounded me. I was hoping to see more culture and beauty as I sank into a comfy seat to relax and drink coffee on the terrace overlooking the Pearl River.

As we headed across the busy roads, Cycy took my arm to make sure I would not get run over crossing the road. She knew how to dodge and weave between the noisy, impatient drivers who constantly beeped their horns. We safely bypassed the buses, lorries, cars and mopeds of all ages and states of repair. It took me many weeks before I gained this road-crossing skill. She knew where we were going and it was not long before we reached one of the main markets.

As we entered one of the massive sheds, it sounded like a wide awake lion roaring as vendors dealt with thousands of eager customers. The sheds were crammed full of stalls and this left only narrow walkways forcing people to follow a one-way system like soldiers on parade. The deafening chaos made my ears ache and my eardrums throbbed and rang. It felt as if I was standing under a giant speaker at a music event.

Herds of people clambered on top of each other, yelling wildly like vultures as they fought their way through the hordes of flies to get the best bits of meat. Food hygiene was non-existent. Meat lay in the open with no segregation of the type of animal, except wild animals were in different stalls to domestic ones. The stalls that sold animal parts believed to be high in medicinal value attracted the most customers. Some specialised in specific animals, like bear parts. Rows of severed paws, sorted by size, were stacked in crates on the floor. I felt sick when I saw one customer negotiating the price for a bear's head. As we moved along, I was overcome by the stench and noise of the market and wanted to exit the shed. I could see no escape route, not a sign of an exit door, so I held onto Cycy's arm and continued to surge along with the crowd, there was no other option. I passed stalls selling all breeds of dogs, foxes, rabbits, porcupines and animals I did not recognise. Westerners think that eating these things is abhorrent. This eating habit is all about belief. Chinese people believe they can eat any animal that walks with its back to the sun.

As we passed through the different sheds, it became easier to proceed. I was careful not to bump into someone, stare or make loud comments in case someone heard and took offence. Cycy guided me between the gaps of sweaty people, who wore tight trousers hoping to prevent the pickpockets from stealing wallets and purses from their pockets. She asked me, "Andrew, are you sure you're all right?"

Two sheds held my interest, the bird shed, and the reptile shed. I had never seen so many birds of different colours and shapes. They sold most of these creatures for pets, but many would end up in the cooking pot. I could not decide if the peacocks were for eating or for in the garden. Considering most Chinese live in an apartment, I guessed they were for eating. The noise of the birds chirping and squawking added to the volume of sound from the market-goers and vendors calling out their wares and prices. I would never believe it could get noisier, but it did. One vendor sold fruit bats. I had eaten them in Sarawak and when the vendor offered me some, I was tempted as it is tasty meat, but I declined. The lack of cleanliness and hygiene put me off.

The air was clammy, and it was as if all the sounds in the world had come together for a reunion. As we moved to the end of one shed, I saw people sitting between stalls smoking what looked to be opium pipes. A tiny woman sat next to one pipe smoker. She fumbled through scores of bags, ticking items off a list to make sure she got everything she needed.

Compared to this, the snake market in Shekou is tiny. Thousands of live snakes lay quietly in glass boxes and vendors attracted customers by offering cooked samples. I had tasted python, and it tasted just like chicken, so I went to try a piece of a large eel-like snake but Cycy pulled my hand away and called out, "Don't be silly, Andrew." I did not buy a snake or a bottle of snake's blood, I came to look and experience, not purchase. Nor was I tempted to sample the alcohol from the demijohns containing dead snakes.

I felt hot, sweaty and nauseated by the odours of animals and people. Cycy said, "Have you had enough, do you want to leave?" The look of relief on my face and a nod was my reply. We searched and quickly spotted the nearest exit and burst out into the bright sunshine and relatively less odorous air. After all that walking, we deserved a rest so we sat down at a food stall and I asked Cycy what she wanted.

"Ice cream, please."

"Good, I will have the same."

Fully refreshed, we headed to the heart of the city. Cars, buses, trucks, horse-drawn carts and people moved in every direction with no notion of danger. The rule of the road was similar to my experience in Jakarta. At a roundabout, whoever got their nose in front claimed the right of way and drivers used the horn to signal each other and prevent crashes. Afraid for my life, I took precautions, but the locals did not. Worn out motorcycles carrying three or four people, including children, showed no fear as they weaved their way amongst the busy traffic.

China is a large country, but space in the city was in short supply. To overcome the problem, unlike Beijing, where the roads are wide with many traffic lanes, Guangzhou's answer was to build upwards. They built roads on top of roads with huge concrete pillars to support the structures.

Cycy held her hand up to stop me. "Andrew, this is the most famous restaurant in Guangzhou. We can eat here."

I looked at the sign written in Chinese and felt confident about her choice. "Let's go."

The hustle and bustle of the markets and walking for miles made me feel hungry. Huge stone dragons protected the restaurant, but they looked friendly, unlike many of the dragons that guard the entrance to ancient monuments. The doors were tall and shaped like arches and decorated with large knobs and medieval locks. The background paint was yellowed, with narrow red contour lines painted to follow the shape of the arch. Inside, I felt as if I had entered the great hall of a medieval castle where kings and knights gathered to feast themselves on wild boar and deer. The only difference was that red tablecloths covered the solid oak tables, and the room was full of ordinary people enjoying a Saturday afternoon out. The sound of their voices was like hundreds of clucking hens as they conversed and ate their food.

Guangzhou is the birthplace of Cantonese cuisine. A historical Chinese buffet banquet of around 200 dishes was our choice. I followed Cycy to a table set for four. As we waited for the traditional pot of Chinese tea to arrive, a suckling pig arrived at the neighbouring table. You had to pay extra for that. The method of roasting a suckling pig in Guangzhou goes back over a thousand years. The roasting transforms the meat to a golden shade and the meat inside the crust is tender. Cycy told me they had ordered it to celebrate the birth of a son. I wished I was proficient enough in Chinese to ask for myself. We took our time over a scrumptious meal before making our way back to the coach. Ten minutes after we set off, I fell asleep and had to be shaken awake at the checkpoint to re-enter the economic zone.

Changes were taking place all the time during my residence in this part of the world. The planned modernisation of this area was underway and some of my favourite haunts would disappear. The Bus Stop bar was demolished and the rugby pitch was dug up as part of the new development plan. They were replaced by a beautiful park. The reclamation of Shekou Bay and Sea World would be next. It would be at least four years before the construction of hotels and offices near the port would start, but the Chinese people who would be ousted from their current properties under this planning did not object. They saw it as an opportunity to do business. Landlords could rent out ground floors as bars and restrict the bar trade to one area. This would assist the police because they could control any trouble in the bars.

New bars opened, frequented by tourists and expatriates, who renamed the street 'Bar Street'. A renowned club called the Snake Pit had been opened there several years earlier. You could recognise it from its sign outside which was an illustration of a snake wearing a cap and a slogan that read 'It's 5 o'clock Somewhere'. I had never been to this bar, but now I wanted to visit it because I'd heard intriguing tales about how it was run. To be approved as a member there was an initiation ceremony. Without pausing, you had to drink a large glass of liquor poured from a bottle containing a lurid looking liquid and a snake. Everybody present watched as the new devotee was initiated, clapping and shouting their encouragement. Cheers followed and the successful candidate was asked to stand. This was to discover what effect this intoxicating mixture would have on the person. People moved out of the way as the new devotee wobbled and staggered around the room or fell off their bar stool and were assisted back onto their seat while being patted on their back.

Gilly underwent this process on one of her visits during the long summer holidays from teaching. She completed it admirably and remembers nothing else after the event. I told her what happened the next day – that she went dancing round the room, kissing everyone. Some of my stories were true!

Under the rules of the membership, it was necessary to buy tickets to pay for your drink. The membership rules were not long and serious but were strictly kept. If your mobile phone rang inside the bar you bought everyone in the bar a drink and if you stepped through the door wearing your work necktie, a member took a pair of scissors and snipped it in half. One wall in the bar was decorated with neckties of various colours and patterns to remind the members of their misdemeanours. You must agree to the rules before being allowed membership.

Outside were two wooden benches where I sat to relax and people-watch. On occasions, I bought a soft drink and chatted in Chinese to practise my recently learnt vocabulary with the young girl who visited the bars selling flowers. The Snake Pit customers looked out for her and made sure she was OK because she was only fifteen years old.

More bars on the main street opened. Eventually, over fifty bars opened. The best and most memorable times in Bar Street was during bad weather when a typhoon struck. Offshore workers were evacuated from their platforms and as soon as they reached shore, they headed towards Bar Street. Once inside, the doors closed until the 'all clear' sounded. Somehow, they then headed back to work. Typhoons were a welcome break from the hard slog on the rigs.

Many changes were happening, new people arrived and others left, but a hardcore few remained. Two who stayed were Russell and Frank. Russell was the only Brit in a team of five who installed and commissioned the equipment for a new glassmaking plant near Shenzhen. They were all keen dart players, and we met to play in the sports bar.

They invited me to the plant to see the first production of glass. It was a worthwhile experience and was amusing and memorable when Frank's safety boots caught fire because of the heat. After a successful day, we headed back to Shekou in the work's minibus. Ten minutes into the journey, Jeff called out, "Stop the bus, I need cigarettes."

We chatted for a few minutes until he returned, carrying a case of cool Heineken beer and handed the cans to his appreciative colleagues. That day, I learned how glass was produced and it was very enjoyable.

A few months later, Delton lost the training contract and a Norwegian company took over. When I told Gilly, I explained I wanted to remain here for a short time to see what would develop. Actually, I wanted to return to the UK to work, but I was fifty-six years old and with high unemployment back home, I would find it impossible to get another job. It made sense to stay and see what materialised. If this job became permanent, Gilly could join me if she wanted to give up her job at home. There would be plenty of opportunities for her to get a job here. We had to decide and we decided I should stay and she would come out whenever she could.

CHAPTER 17

HE MIGHT HAVE BEEN SHOT

Professional business and government officials frequented a club called the English Corner to improve their conversational skills. I received invitations to go there to help, but I refused to go. It meant I would miss going to the beach bar. I relented one time because they were persistent. They told me that all I had to do was to join a small group around a table and make conversation. I decided I could visit and, the following week, give an excuse and get out of it.

When I arrived at the community centre, a committee member introduced me to a few other expatriate visitors. People sat around low-level tables. One group squeezed along the bench seat to make room for me. The introductions were friendly and polite, but I could not remember a single name even though some had given a European name rather than their Chinese birth name. Then an uncomfortable silence reigned as we sat waiting for someone to make a move. I needed to start the ball rolling and begin a conversation, so I asked them where in China they were from and about the work they did. There were two teachers, a lawyer and a policewoman who worked at the port. The rest were office workers or business people. The city names confused me, but one of them drew the map of China and wrote the names in English. This was a bonus for me, I quickly learned to identify the regions of China and the best places to visit.

A woman picked up a microphone and introduced herself as Wendy. She spoke English and invited one or two people up to say a few words about themselves. When she finished, I continued my discussions with the group. Wendy then requested I should move to another table, and I was happy to do that. This was turning out to be an interesting afternoon, one where I would achieve my aim of learning and understanding other cultures in our world. Each table chose its topic to discuss, and our subject topic was decided quickly by Hui-yang. "Andrew, do you like the Queen of England?"

Few people ever mentioned Britain, they usually talk about England. They did not know the geography of the UK. Unsure why she would ask about the royal family, I said, "She does a good job when she visits other countries. Her visits help Britain and the countries she visits."

That started it, our queen was the topic for discussion. Questions came fast – had I met her, did I like Princess Diana, Prince Charles, and even the queen's dogs were mentioned. The royal family was a favourite topic for discussion.

Another lady called Fran picked up the microphone and announced the rest of the programme in Chinese, then repeated it in English. She gave the name of the restaurant where they would eat. She reminded everyone to follow the English Corner custom – to go 'Dutch'. This meant you paid for yourself when the bill was tallied and split equally at the end. If men wanted to drink beer, they paid extra.

I accompanied two men there and joined fifty others at a long table with a red tablecloth. No one spoke English and when the food arrived, the noise level did not drop. Two glasses of beer later, a heated discussion started amongst the people sitting around me. Fran leaned across the table and called out, "Andrew, ignore them, they are discussing politics."

"That is okay, I am used to it, but I don't discuss politics as a guest in your country," I said it loud enough for the others to hear. The views of others interested me, but I wanted to avoid involving myself in sensitive issues. Full up after the gorgeous food and beer, I wished I had agreed to the earlier invitations.

The following week, I had to miss the meeting, as I needed to go to Hong Kong to renew my visa. Brits and Americans were compelled to leave China every three months because of visa restrictions. I attended the week after, joining Wendy and Fran at the front of the assembled crowd. Wendy started off the proceedings, then handed me the microphone. "Andrew, you try. I don't think they are responding to me."

I, too, found it was difficult to get anyone to come up and speak. I had a flash of inspiration. "Can anybody here sing?" Several hands went up.

"Okay, this is the rule. You can choose any song, but you must sing in English."

The hour passed with several people getting up to sing English songs.

Wendy complimented me. "Andrew, well done, they like your style."

During the weeks that followed, she supported me in getting people up to talk on a range of subjects. Attendance each week steadily increased to 200.

One time, I chose the subject. I couldn't think of new ideas for conversation so during the week I wracked my brains to come up with something unusual. "The topic today is our planet. I want volunteers to come up and explain why our planet is round and not square."

Volunteers gave scientific theories, but the best explanation came from a fifteen-year-old schoolgirl. When she spoke, the room fell silent.

"This is why the world is not square." She paused. "People eat too much junk food and get round and fat." Another pause. "When people feed the planet with pollution, it becomes fat and round, not square. That is what I think."

It was an interesting theory, totally unscientific, but it showed that this young person was concerned about pollution in the world. She made everyone present think. She sat down to applause that lasted longer than any other speaker.

There was no shortage of volunteers. Wendy and I encouraged everyone to speak in English, even if they made mistakes.

One afternoon, I joined a group of young students and discovered their English was of a high standard. Billy told me that learning English in school was not compulsory, but most students studied it. Fran came and sat beside us and introduced each student by their English names and parent's professions. The parents all held prominent positions in the government or the business sector. Billy Tang's father was the Shekou chief of police and gave his support to English Corner when required. They were polite and keen to converse, so I gave them my business card and told them to call me if any of them wanted to chat.

Saturday afternoon at English Corner meant missing my drink and conversation at the beach bar. I did not mind because later I met up with David and Wayne and went to the Hammer Bar, moving on to finish the evening in Joe Bananas. It was always a long session and I got to my bed very late. Because of this, I considered Sunday mornings a time for sleeping and when the telephone rang, I cursed. Who would want to ring me at 9am on Sunday? It was Billy Tang. I did not think any of yesterday's students would call me, or at least not so quickly.

"Mr Andrew, will you come to McDonald's and talk with my friends?"

I wanted to throw the phone at him, but I had encouraged them to call me anytime. However, I did not mean on a Sunday, I would make this clear to him today.

"Give me ten minutes and I will be there."

After a quick shower, a mug of strong coffee and a Panadol sandwich, I entered the restaurant. Five young people around fourteen years old greeted me. Billy wanted to treat me to breakfast, but I turned the offer down. I did not want my friends to find out a student bought my breakfast. For two hours, I conversed with these well-mannered young people.

When we left, Billy spotted someone he knew. "Mr Andrew, please wait a moment."

He sprinted to the other side of the square and pointed me out to a slender woman who looked to be about thirty. Billy introduced the woman who was one of his teachers. The politeness of this group of young people impressed me. The teacher invited me to visit their school.

Several weeks later, I received another telephone call from Billy. "Mr Andrew, please come to dinner tonight at my house to meet my father and mother." I never expected this, but before I could answer, Billy continued, "My father's aide will call you later to make the arrangements."

"Okay, I look forward to it."

Ten minutes after returning from work, the telephone rang. It was Mr Tang's aide. An hour later, I was showered and dressed with just enough time to run down to a flower shop and pick up a bouquet of mixed carnations. When the aide saw the flowers he smiled. "Hen hǎo, Andrew. Mrs Tang will love those."

We drove to an estate in Shekou that I did not recognise. When we entered through an archway into the car park, I saw a dozen three-story high blocks of apartments. Several official cars were parked in the courtyard. These were the homes of the important officials from the Shekou area. I could not see any security, but I am sure it was present.

Billy opened the door and ushered me into a well-furnished open-plan living room and kitchen containing a dining table that could seat eight people. Billy's father stood up and switched off the TV, then came to greet me. His mother joined her husband, and we all shook hands. She smiled and thanked me for the flowers.

I expected his father to be an overweight, balding official, wearing the usual clothing that denoted his status – trousers, white shirt and necktie. I had gained this perception of officialdom from seeing parliamentary broadcasts on TV. I was so wrong. He was wearing jeans and a casual polo shirt, and was not overweight. He was tall, lean and fit. His hair swept back into the style that looked like a duck's tail. This was the duck's arse fashion from the UK in the 1950s. The sides of his hair almost met at the back. He would have been the envy of any teenager in the fifties. Billy's mum was equally casual and modern in the red flowery dress covering her neat figure. She was friendly and had an air of confidence about her. The apartment was of moderate size, clean and well-furnished. I sat on the couch with Billy as his father took a pile of CDs from a shelf unit and handed them to me before plonking himself into the armchair.

My next preconception about him came when I selected the music. All the CDs were pirate copies! I never would expect to see this in a senior police officer's home. I could tell by Mum's movements she was pleased with my choice, the CD, *NOW 35*.

I had no problem communicating with Billy's mum and dad, they could understand a little English and Billy kept us right if there was any confusion. His dad and I shared two bottles of beer while Billy and his mum drank what looked like cola. I enjoyed this home-cooked meal and after returning to relax on the couch, the conversation continued to flow and I discussed my family and hometown. At 10pm, the aide knocked on the door and I thanked my hosts. I was chauffeured home, after an evening that gave me an insight into the life of a more privileged Chinese family.

Once the aide's car was out of sight, I headed for Bar Street and Alice's Bar. Alice, the bar's proprietor, originally worked as a floor manager at the Nanhai hotel but, like many young entrepreneurs, had left her secure employment to make her fortune in the bar trade. As I entered, she removed a can of Heineken from the refrigerator. My favourite bars, where I was a regular customer, kept cans just for me as bottled beer gave me a headache.

"Good evening, Andrew, you're late tonight, have you been out for dinner?"

"Yes, I had dinner at Mr Tang's house."

As she poured the can into the glass, froth overflowed onto the bar top, instead of wiping it, she stared at me in amazement with her interesting eyes. Everyone who owned a bar knew that name. After a long pause, she uttered, "Andrew, you are honoured to be invited to the police chief's home. Usually, officials invite guests to a restaurant. I've never heard of any European who's been to their private family home."

Because of my association with English Corner, my knowledge of China business, and how it functioned, improved. Business people brought me documents and letters written in English for me to interpret or rewrite. I worked hard, and people appreciated my efforts. I received many dinner invitations to restaurants or their homes.

Several times, Mr Tang's aide telephoned to invite me out or go to dinner at his house. One time, we went tenpin bowling, and I tried my best to win. I never succeeded because he had been coached by someone in the national team, one perk of his job. One evening, I was playing darts with my American friends when Mr Tang entered the bar with his aide and four other men. He ignored me as they passed to go to a quiet room. I knew it would not be wise to assume our acquaintance and friendship in public.

A month later, they came again. The owner greeted them and led them to the same room. Shortly after, she came over and in a quiet voice said, "Mr Tang invites you to join him and his friends."

His friends stood up to shake my hand, and the aide introduced them. They were the health minister, the minister for education and the head of security. I found it easy to relax in the company of this group of top officials. I could not think of a reason they would ask me to join them. Was it merely because of my acquaintance with Mr Tang or did they have another motive? When they left, I thanked them in Mandarin for inviting me to join them.

Weeks passed before their next visit and again I was invited to join them. This time, the interpreter was a small, neat woman dressed in a smart pair of tight jeans and a fashionable loose top. She was called Mia. Everyone was relaxed and cheerful except Mr Tang. He did not speak. It would be wrong of me to ask what made him so quiet tonight, so I didn't ask. Mia interpreted quickly and competently so I understood the conversation. When she mentioned aeroplanes and pilots, I said, "In the UK, we have female pilots that fly jumbo jets."

Mr Chun leaned over. "Female pilots here fly fighter jets." I laughed inwardly at his one-upmanship. The rest nodded and then chuckled. This was a minister joking with me.

Mr Tang leaned forward and quietly spoke to Mia who turned to me. She said, "Mr Tang wants your advice." I was about to learn the reason for his silence. He must have been pondering his problem and had finally decided on a course of action.

"I will help if I can."

"This morning, there was an incident at the port involving an American riding a motorcycle."

Only a few expatriates in Shekou owned motorcycles. Most of them owned Harley Davidsons, and they drank in the Snake Pit, so I probably knew the culprit.

"What happened?"

"He didn't stop for the security police. He approached the barrier too fast, weaved around the barrier and entered the port area."

"Did the police catch him?" I had to think quickly and carefully about my reply, because this could escalate.

"No, they let him go and reported it."

"They should have arrested him. Anyone as reckless as that could kill someone or cause a serious accident. Expatriates should not behave in this way."

Mr Tang sat in silence before speaking to Mia. "Andrew, Mr Tang wants you to know that security has certain procedures they follow when anyone enters a secure area illegally. If the police had shot the American, it would have caused an international confrontation."

"He should still be punished; his motorcycle should be confiscated until he learns to follow the rules."

Mr Tang silently considered my suggestion, obviously aware that the incident was a political time bomb. If he should make a wrong decision, it might not only affect the American, but it could also affect his position and his family. "Andrew, if the American apologises for his actions, Mr Tang will forgive him and he can keep his motorcycle."

I felt relief. "I will find out who the culprit is and get him to apologise."

The other officials supported his decision, and the security chief smiled. I felt like a peacekeeper at the United Nations assembly.

I wanted to lighten up the mood after this critical conversation. "We should stop smoking, it's not good for our health." A discussion about the evils of smoking began.

Mr Chun said, "Good idea, if any of us smoke during the next month, they will be fined one hundred yuan." (Equivalent to ten pounds.)

Everyone except Mr Yao agreed. He shook his head and banged his hand down on the table, almost spilling the drink. "If anyone smokes, I will chop off one of their fingers." He looked around at his colleagues, smiled and burst out laughing.

Mr Tang had not laughed since he came in, but did so now. His problem was now in my hands and I had to continue my role of peacemaker diplomatically.

I called in at the Snake Pit and spoke to a committee member about the episode with the motorbike. He would know who it was because he was in the bar every day and would have heard any biker talking, maybe bragging about what had happened. I added, "He probably thinks he got away with it, but this order comes from the police chief himself. If he does not apologise, he will be in deep shit and get deported."

Three days later, the wrongdoer apologised and a warning, telling members to behave in public, was displayed prominently on the Snake Pit notice board.

After four weeks, it appeared the no-smoking pact had been taken seriously. Everyone tried not to smoke, the signs were clear. Mr Tang's nails looked bitten and one or two of the others were fidgeting nervously with keys or their fingers, and the ashtray was empty! Mr Yao said, "Those who smoked will now lose a finger, who smoked?"

"Not me!" We all promised him.

He questioned us, disbelieving that no one in the group lit up a cigarette.

I said to Mia, "Tell Mr Yao I watched his office with a pair of binoculars and saw him smoking."

Everyone laughed at the idea of me watching the head of security with binoculars.

He turned to Mia. "Tell Andrew, one hundred people were watching him and he smoked, so now I will cut off his finger." The laughter continued but much louder.

With that, he picked up his drink, said cheers, and glasses clinked. A minute later, he put two packets of cigarettes on the table and we helped ourselves and smoked. I liked the company but took care when I spoke. One time, I asked the owner if I could pay the bill as I felt bad about drinking for free in their company. She refused, saying, "Don't worry, Andrew. They are government officials; the bill always gets paid. If you pay, it will offend them."

The next time we met, they were all quiet, and I asked Mia, "Why is everyone sad tonight?"

"They are upset because your country once more is critical of China and our human rights policy."

How was I going to deal with this political issue?

"What did they report?"

"That our police smashed down doors and arrested innocent people."

"I am sorry to hear that."

The room was quiet for a minute. Then Mr Tang spoke to Mia and a series of questions, and my replies, took place.

"Andrew, Mr Tang wants to know the population of your city."

"Around 200,000."

"How many live in Manchester?"

"Around a million."

"How many in London?"

"Around two million."

"What is the biggest crime in those cities?"

"Drugs."

"Do you know the population of Shenzhen?"

"Over four million and growing."

"Does Shenzhen have a drug problem?"

"No. Shenzhen has one of the lowest drug-related crimes in the world."

They smiled.

"Andrew, are you aware of what the law is here before two people of different sex can live together in the same room?"

I knew this. "It is against the law unless they are married."

Mr Tang muttered to Mia who interpreted it as, "We do not knock down doors if people are in love and move in together. Our actions are different when police suspect drugs or criminal activity is involved. The west needs to understand that China is not wrong in what they do."

"I am sorry for the way our media reported this."

Mr Su spoke. "Andrew, Mr Tang has told us you are a good man and train people to work on China's offshore oil rigs. You help people at English Corner. Everyone respects you and we thank you."

I said, "I just want to help." By this, I implied that, in the future, I would help in the UK whenever there was a detrimental news report about China. I would tell people what Mr Tang had explained to me.

A week later, Billy telephoned. He sounded excited. "Mr Andrew, you must come to my house tonight,"

I told him, "Calm down, what is so important that you want me to come tonight?"

"I want you to meet my brother!"

"Billy, you don't have a brother."

"Yes, I do."

"Okay, Billy. If your father agrees, I will come."

An hour later, Mr Tang's aide telephoned and came to collect me.

When Billy opened the door, he grabbed my arm and dragged me into the sitting room. I got a big surprise. A baby around one year old was jumping up and down on the sofa. Letting go of the sofa, he clapped his hands and fell onto the floor. I picked him up to console him and wipe his tears.

Billy shouted out, "I told you, Andrew, this is my baby brother and I love him, so does my mother and father. We are happy."

The aide called from the door. "Andrew, I will explain later."

I congratulated the family, but did not ask questions.

On the way back in the car, the aide explained about this new addition to the Tang family. Someone left the baby on the step outside the police station with a note asking for someone to care for the baby as the mother was not married and wanted the child adopted. Mr Tang took the boy home for the night as he was concerned about his well-being. Mrs Tang decided to adopt him.

"What will happen to the mother?"

"Andrew, we could never trace her. In the past year, over a million people came here to work in the factories. It will be impossible to trace her if she does not want to be found. This baby is lucky."

I shook his hand and headed for Bar Street, only this time, I did not say I had just visited Mr Tang's house and never mentioned the baby. I was happy for the family and Billy's new brother. One abandoned baby was to have a very good upbringing and lifestyle. I guessed that the one-child policy would not apply in this case.

I did not visit Shenzhen often, but when I went there, I enjoyed it. The centre was built in the early eighties and was modern, but it maintained some of its former character. In 1979, Shenzhen was a small town with 30,000 inhabitants and served as a customs post into mainland China from Hong Kong. That year, it was declared a Special Economic Zone. Cash poured in from the government and foreign investment and people from all over China moved there. New roads, offices, housing, schools, hospitals, water, power, communications facilities and factories were constructed to cater for a population growing at over a million a year. I loved the shopping centres, markets and food stalls. You could buy everything from pirate software and copy watches to the most luxurious authentic goods in the world.

Shenzhen city itself is devoid of culture, but outside the centre, it has the most breathtaking theme parks. You can spend days in these places and experience worldwide grand tourist attractions and ethnic culture from all over China.

My favourite was Window of the World, a theme park in the western part of the city. It has 130 reproductions of the most famous tourist attractions in the world squeezed into forty-eight hectares. The 108 metres tall Eiffel Tower dominates the skyline. You do not need to travel the world, everything is here: The pyramids, the Leaning Tower of Pisa, Sydney Opera House, Niagara Falls, Buckingham Palace, the volcano Vesuvius, and more, can be seen in proximity to each other.

I visited there in summer, which, on reflection, was a mistake. It was far too hot. The Window of the Word had a monorail to take visitors around the whole site, but I didn't take it, another mistake. The exhibits are built to scale and are extraordinary. The best exhibits were Buckingham Palace and Ayers Rock as they looked so real.

By mid-afternoon I needed food and rest and headed for the Folk Culture Village, another 'must see' attraction and within walking distance from Window of the World. The ethnic minorities in China are the non-Han Chinese. The Chinese government recognises over 50 minority ethnic groups. The exhibits were beautifully designed. One of them was a replica of Mosuo village in Yunan province. The speciality of this region is the exquisite wood houses, delicious food, and beautiful girls. There is a custom with this minority group that will sound bizarre to the Western world. If a young man wants sex, he can knock on a woman's door, and if she is willing, he can enter her room. He may stay overnight but will return to his own mother's home in the morning. Children born from such relationships live with their mothers and there is no stigma attached to the mother or child. This is a normal in their culture.

In another village, the ladies allow their hair to grow so long they can tie it above their head in huge beehive styles. I never knocked on a door where a beautiful lady lived! But I saw classy hairstyles and colourful, symbolic costumes. The highlight for me was the food, the acrobats, and a pretend battle with horses, loud bangs and fireworks. My understanding of Chinese culture improved because of the experience.

CHAPTER 18

CRUISING DOWN THE RIVER LI

I promised Gilly a holiday of a lifetime the next time she came to see me. After an enjoyable taxi ride on a beautiful day, we arrived at Shenzhen Boan Airport and boarded a China Southern Airlines flight to Guilin. The flight took just over an hour and the attendants distributed the in-flight food – a prepacked box containing a packet of dry biscuits and fruit. The hostesses, dressed in smart chequered blouses and tight blue skirts, were efficient, but they spoke too fast for me to understand the safety brief. On arrival at Guilin, the cabin crew bowed to the passengers, and the passengers clapped their hands in response.

We ate dinner at the Li River hotel and took in a magnificent cultural show. We were the only Europeans present, and the staff singled us out. We were invited onto the stage, I declined but Gilly enjoyed getting up and taking part in the dancing activities. We retired early and enjoyed a hearty breakfast before setting off for a long day of cruising.

I don't know how many steam paddle boats were needed to take the several hundred passengers who crowded the wharf on the river cruise, I counted twenty but there may have been more. As usual, the tickets were categorised into different groups, ones for Chinese, and ours, for foreign tourists. The cost included a free drink and lunch.

There was a carnival atmosphere as our four-star cruiser with an upper deck and a viewing deck set off from Zhejiang Wharf to start the journey down the River Li. We sat on the lower deck at one of the eight-seater tables, along with some Taiwanese tourists. They were in a boisterous mood and we joined in because most of them spoke broken English and with my Mandarin, we could communicate. Soon after the boat sailed, a crew member placed four large bottles of beer, two bottles of water, and a pile of plastic cups on the table. The men and Gilly enjoyed the beer while the other ladies drank the water.

We were lucky because our boat headed the flotilla as it made its way downriver. We could see the crew preparing lunch and people making their way up to the viewing deck. The man opposite said, "No need to go up yet, it is hot outside and you get a splendid view from the window here." I followed his advice and sat down again.

We had an English version of the tourist brochure describing the area through which the steamboats wheels paddled. The topography along the river was described as 'karst', which meant a landscape that was characterised by many caves, sinkholes, fissures, and underground streams. It forms in regions of plentiful rainfall where bedrock comprising carbonate-rich rock, such as limestone, gypsum, or dolomite dissolves, forming peaks of great natural beauty.

The English dictionary describes Shangri-La as an imaginary faraway place where everything is pleasant and you can get everything you want. Here, we were in the most beautiful place I have ever seen. Shaped limestone peaks reached high into the sky and stretched far into the distance. Buffalos grazed on lush green grass and bamboo shoots and a bamboo raft floated by with a fisherman and several large cormorants on it. The bird's wings were open to keep cool in the warm sun. Gilly nudged me and when I turned to her, she looked radiant. "What do you think of Shangri-La?" She did not speak but held up her thumb and then squeezed my arm as she pointed to the river's edge. A fisherman looked to be asleep on a ledge in the cliff face. The man opposite called for more beer.

Gilly and I excused ourselves and set off to go up to the top deck and as we arrived, a crew member held out a tray with drinks for us to sample. I got a scare and almost dropped my glass when a figure appeared at the handrail. A man had scaled the hull to sell souvenirs. Of course, I bargained vigorously and successfully purchasing a carving of a water buffalo. A beautiful bargain!

Our destination was Yangshuo, a bustling tourist town with lots of souvenir shops and food stalls. Once we got to the pier, Gilly spotted a man with two cormorants perched on a pole. This was the perfect photographic opportunity for Gilly. She wanted a photo taken with her holding the pole with two large cormorants sitting on each end – like a rose between two thorns! They flapped their wings and stuck their long necks in the air in a magic display. It was a perfect memory of our trip to Shangri-La. By the time the rest of the boats arrived, we had left the pier and wandered around the stalls and bought more gifts.

Our visit was over far too quickly; we were rounded up for the return journey by coach. The boats had to sail back without passengers because of the fast-flowing river currents. The journey was long and tiring and I struggled to keep awake. There was too much excitement on board the coach and so much to see as we made our way through the scenic hills back to Guilin.

Gilly's visits to China were what I looked forward to. She joined me during every school holiday that was over a week long. She told me that when she returned to teaching it was a weird experience because of the effects of jetlag. She felt as if she was looking down on herself as she taught the lessons. On one visit, I invited her to English Corner. My acquaintances had begged me to bring her to be a guest speaker. She was shocked when I handed her the microphone. I knew she would have been nervous and would have had a sleepless night if I told her in advance that she was going to be the guest speaker. "There you are, they will love you, get them talking."

She leaned forward, kissed me on the cheek, and whispered in my ear, "I will get you for this!" She took the microphone and smiled at the audience. "I'm so pleased that you invited me to speak today. I will always remember meeting so many lovely people."

Her words flowed, she proved to be a popular host. When she finished her solo performance, she moved around the room, joining each table for a short chat to discuss every topic, from yoga to what made the world go round. She joined us at the restaurant meal that followed this meeting and thoroughly enjoyed the noise, food and company of the people. It was a taste of real Chinese life and culture for her. More experiences were to follow this one.

Billy telephoned. His father wanted to meet Gilly. During the weeks that followed, we dined several times with Mr Tang and she got on well with Billy, his mother and his new brother. The night before her departure, the aide telephoned me. "I will come at 10am to take you and Gilly to the ferry terminal." What was going on here? Gilly was having an official escort to the ferry terminal.

We were ready when the car pulled up and Mr Tang got out to greet us. He looked very relaxed as he handed Gilly a farewell gift and wished her a safe journey. He ordered the apartment block security guard to load her luggage and held the door open for us to get into the back seat. People were staring in disbelief at two gweilos (Europeans) being picked up in an official car and getting VIP treatment. Smoothly and swiftly, the car zoomed along the road, an official bonnet flag blowing in the wind.

When we arrived at the ferry terminal, Mr Tang escorted us up the stairs to departures. Curious eyes followed our procession towards immigration, probably puzzling who the important guest could be who was bypassing the security system with such ease. The aide asked Gilly for her passport, then escorted her to one of the immigration desks and within a minute, it was returned and handed back. They were no long, tedious queues and scrutiny for my wife.

I am sure she felt important having a police escort to the ferry terminal, but her eyes told me she would have preferred to stay longer with me.

Once again, I was alone and a public holiday was looming. I needed to keep busy. I could not fly home for just five days, so I did some searching and decided to fly to Xian and see the Terracotta Warriors and climb one of China's most sacred mountains. I felt confident that I could speak Mandarin well enough to do this on my own.

The flight time from Shenzhen to Xian took almost three hours, and an early morning flight meant I arrived at my hotel, the Sheraton, located just outside the city walls, in time for lunch.

The tour office billboards advertised several expensive tours, so I ignored them. I knew the main reason for my visit but there would not be enough time to take in the Terracotta Warriors today. The wall of the old city was visible, so I headed towards it to get some exercise and pass the time. I loved wandering around and discovering things for myself.

Before I left the Sheraton, I chatted to the concierge to familiarise myself with the area. For eating, he suggested a visit to the Muslim Quarter and when I was ready, I took a taxi for the journey which took only five minutes. The area was so different from the area where my luxury hotel was situated. There were no proper roads, only dirt tracks with many souvenir shops and food stalls running down the sides. The aromatic smell of fresh lamb hung over red hot barbecues made me hungrier, but the heat stifled me. Hand carts and oil lamps reminded me of Labuan Island. The atmosphere glowed with light and activity. After a scrumptious dinner, I walked back, following the city wall to the hotel for a beer and to listen to music before going to bed.

At 9am sharp, I left the hotel to find a taxi. I never took a cab just outside a hotel because they were the expensive ones. Not too far away, I found a taxi rank. I chose a driver whose cab looked the newest and in good repair. I tested out his knowledge of English to satisfy myself that I would get to where I wanted to go. It had a meter to show the price. I greeted the driver in Mandarin so he would realise that I was no mug and he could not run me all over town to increase the fare. As we drove to the Terracotta Warrior site, we grinned and chuckled at two men having a heated argument in the middle of the road. It looked like there was going to be a punch-up, but as we approached, they stopped and started laughing to hide their embarrassment.

The driver dropped me close to the food stalls, not very far from the entrance to the primary site. Because he had been fair to me and had been a sensible driver, I gave him a good tip. Food stalls were near to the entrance. Barbecued pork fat crackled and dripped on the hot coals, it was very tempting. I succumbed to temptation, and it was worth it. The crispy fat crunched and juices dripped down my chin. It was the best pork roll I ever tasted.

The immensity of the site staggered me. It would take me more than a day to get around the various open-air sheds that protected the excavations, plus all the displays.

In March 1974, some farmers from the Xiyang village were digging a well when they found some unique red soil about six feet down. Further digging led to the excavation of a life-sized Terracotta Warrior, who villagers believed to be the pottery god. They continued digging and excavated more artefacts, bronze arrows, crossbows and broken warrior statues.

News of the find was reported to the Department of Cultural Relics, who sent a team to investigate further. Since then, the Terracotta Army has become famous around the world. It is the buried army of Qin Shihuang, an ancient Chinese emperor. The sculptures were hidden, buried for over two thousand years. A thousand warriors and horses have now been exposed, and the number keeps rising. At least 6000 remain beneath the surface.

I admired the excavation work and the figures themselves. Visitors around me were as enthusiastic as myself and helped me to understand the history. They were proud of their treasure. Yang Zhifa, who dug out the head of the first terracotta warrior, was hailed as the discoverer. Today he was there signing guide books for visitors. On the way out, one visitor came up to me. "Mr Yang Zhifa will sign your book. He is sitting at the table over there."

I looked over and saw a group of people waiting to get their souvenir book signed. Not only did I see the

Terracotta Army, my guidebook was also signed by the man who discovered them.

Sacred mountains in China are associated with Taoism and Buddhism. The ones associated with Taoism are called the 'Five Great Mountains'. The others are referred to as the 'Four Sacred Mountains of Buddhism'. Mountains of both groups are important pilgrimage places.

Huashan Sacred Mountain, often called Yellow Mountain, is an area of outstanding natural beauty. The guidebook claims that once you climb the 7000-foot high granite peak and look down, you would think you were floating on top of the clouds. This was the mountain I wanted to climb.

I agreed on a reasonable price for a day's hire with Lim, my driver from the day before. I found him easy to communicate with and friendly, so easy to get along with. It took two hours to drive to Mt. Huashan near Huayin city and about 120 kilometres from Xian. Because of the public holiday, it was very busy and tour buses were parked along a tree-lined avenue. Lim accompanied me to the base of the mountain. When I looked up at the terrain, I gasped and stopped and Lim stopped too. "It looks a dangerous climb, Lim, maybe I should pay you now."

He grinned. "Andrew, no need to pay me now. No need to climb, you can take the cable car, very safe."

"Thanks, Lim. I like your confidence."

The cable car looked ancient, as if a long ago emperor had ordered its construction. Other tourists were getting on so I risked it. Once the car moved off, I felt giddy and never looked down. When I got out, there was still some climbing to do, but the worst of it was over. Steps were cut into the face of the mountain to make it easier for tourists to climb the rest of the way.

I ascended the north peak, better known as 'Cloud Terrace Peak' and reached a height of about 5000 feet and that was high enough for me. I would never be a mountaineer and hesitantly followed the fifty people ahead of me. We passed a sheer cliff and a long narrow ridge called 'Black Dragons Ridge'. Most people decided that was far enough. They had reached the limit of their energy and courage. I felt going higher was too risky, so I retreated with them back to the cable car and to the safety below. I may not have a head for heights to be a mountaineer, but I succeeded in my goal to climb the most sacred mountain in China, with a bit of cheating.

Lim looked pleased to see me.

I liked Lim. He took care of me and made sure I enjoyed my visit to Xian. We drove to the Grand Xiyue Temple and ate lunch in the garden. There were few visitors around and the temple was magnificent. Lim wanted me to dress up in an emperor's costume so he could take my photo. I declined because I did not bring a camera with me.

Back at the hotel, I moved to get my wallet out to pay him, but he waved it away. "After tomorrow, you pay. I will come and collect you from your hotel. Where do you want to go?"

"I want to see the Yellow River, but I just want to see the river. No need to see tourists." He understood me perfectly. I did not want to go to the main tourist site.

"No tourists, only fish."

"Nine o'clock, then."

We shook hands before I left to go to the shop inside the hotel. I bought sweets and biscuits before taking a taxi to the Muslim Quarter for dinner. I walked back to the hotel the long way, around the walled part of the city to wear off the excesses of a large, tasty meal. I always ordered far too much and consequently ate too much.

I ate a decent hotel breakfast and met Lim at the agreed time. When we got into the taxi, I gave a bag of biscuits and sweets to Lim. "This is for your family."

We headed out on the AH34 highway, a good road. Once we reached the countryside, there were trucks and hand carts but few cars. We passed fields and fields of corn where people dressed in baggy trousers, loose-fitting smocks, sandals and conical shaped rice hats toiled in the open air. Further on, a maintenance crew wearing high-visibility coveralls, jackets and safety boots were digging a cable trench. They must have been hot with all that gear on.

Lim left the highway, drove down a dirt track and stopped at a hamlet, and I transferred some goodies into another bag for the children. However, as we approached the hamlet, all I could see were two mangy dogs. Rabies is rife in China, and dogs don't welcome strangers. Lim spoke to them and they settled just as a door opened and a woman in her later years stepped out. She was dressed similar to the labourers in the fields, except she was not wearing a hat. Lim chatted to her and pointed to me. She came over and held my hand to stroke it, as if I was the first Westerner she had met.

There were five other small houses and several outbuildings, one I assumed to be the toilet. The buildings were built with a mixture of breeze blocks, bricks and mortar and had corrugated tin roofs. Fifty yards away, four pigs and some piglets foraged in the ground. Three elderly women all dressed the same came out and stared curiously at the white stranger.

"This woman invites you into her home, to drink tea."

I felt humble. "Thank you, Lim, I would like that."

I ducked down to get through the door. Once inside, I saw an earthen floor and four elderly men sat around a handmade wooden table playing mah-jong. They looked in surprise to see me, puzzled that someone from the other side of the world was here visiting them. They stood up to greet me. They were wearing heavy trousers caked with dry mud and collarless shirts, just like my grandfather wore in the forties. Their faces looked like they had suffered from years of toiling in the scorching sun.

Lim joined in the game of mah-jong and translated for me. They were delighted with the visit from a Westerner. I handed the woman a bag containing sweets and biscuits, which she happily accepted. I asked Lim if it would be appropriate to give them some money, and he whispered in a soft tone, "No, sir, you will insult them.

When we leave, I will give one man a cash gift, that will be okay."

"Thanks, Lim."

As we drove past more fieldworkers, I reflected about when I was thirteen, and I was taken out of school to work in the fields picking potatoes and to bring in the harvest. Back then, we used digger machines to lift the potatoes out of the ground, but here they were dug out by hand. This lack of progress and modernisation in the countryside was in direct contrast to the modern technological city life.

Sometime later, I saw what I wanted to see, the Yellow River. Lim drove around a bend and there it was. I tried hard to hide my disappointment as we followed the wide river for several miles. It was a dirty reddish-brown, not the crystal clear, yellow colour I had expected.

Fishnets hung on trestles to dry with a few rowing boats tied at the river's edge as we pulled into a small village. There were no children at the previous hamlet, but here I saw several engrossed in a game that looked like hopscotch.

When I left the car to get a closer look, people came to examine the white stranger with a long nose – me. Lim talked to the group for a few minutes then said, "Mr Andrew, are you hungry?"

"Starving," I told him.

"Good, these people will cook fish from the river. It will be the best fish you will ever taste," Lim bragged.

The group applauded when I played hopscotch with the children while we waited for the meal to cook. When it arrived, men, women and children joined us. A woman poured tea from an old kettle and no one washed their utensils with it, like at restaurants in Malaysia and Shekou. There was fish soup, rice, vegetables and steamed fish. It tasted delicious.

When the time came to leave, I told Lim to pay and I would settle with him later.

This was the real China. The poverty was heartbreaking, but I was glad to have seen the countryside inhabitants. Life was so different here compared to the Scottish country life of my youth. I worked hard from a very young age, but not as hard as life was here. The cost of my visit? Lim paid one hundred Chinese yuan (ten pounds) to the first hamlet and 250 Chinese yuan (twenty-five pounds) for the meal. The total bill for the three days came to 1500 yuan (£150). I gave Lim 2000 yuan and the next day he dropped me at the airport for free.

CHAPTER 19

KEEPING WARM IN TIANANMEN SQUARE

I booked China Airlines to return home for Christmas. This meant I had to have an overnight stay in Beijing. When I left Shenzhen airport, I wore a pullover underneath my lightweight winter jacket. I never wore a hat, gloves, or scarf. When I got off the flight and passed through the terminal to take a taxi to my hotel, I felt chilly, but not cold. I knew that my body would protect me for a short time, if I experienced a sudden major drop in temperature. When I flew from Kuwait to Scotland, for the first few days, I never felt cold.

I dumped my bag and rushed out to experience the city. Fixed on a metal structure above a shop, a clock with a temperature indicator read 5:15pm and one degree centigrade. I shopped for my final Christmas gifts and returned to my hotel, showered and readied myself to go out and eat. The guy on the concierge desk advised on where to go and wrote it on a bit of paper to give to the taxi driver. After a few minutes into my taxi ride, I asked the driver, "Is that Tiananmen Square?"

He said, "Yes, but it is closed, you cannot go there."

After fifteen minutes, he dropped me at Sanlitun Street which is where the bars were. I noticed people wore thick, warm clothing, including heavy footwear, gloves, hats and scarves. It did not worry me because I still felt warm and there was a lively atmosphere in the bars and restaurants. I ate dinner in a nice, warm restaurant which had a bar and music. I stayed for almost three hours.

On the way back, I asked the driver if we could stop at Tiananmen Square. Once more I was told it was closed, but that did not deter me. I asked him to stop and when he did, I paid and got out. The misty air felt icy cold. I looked at the clock outside the entrance and it was 10:15pm and the thermometer was minus seven degrees. My body's protection system gave up, and the cold hit me. I breathed heavily and stuck my hands into the pockets of my jacket to protect them against frostbite. Not to be put off, I approached the square. A security guard saw me approach, and he moved towards me. He wore a thick military overcoat, a hat trimmed with fur and in his thick, woollen-gloved hands he held a rifle. His thick clothing restricted his movement, so I considered ducking under the barrier, but thought twice about it. I could create an international incident – the headline could have been, 'Shots fired at British tourist'. I could see a hut with more guards in it and could just feel the warmth flowing from inside. Instead of asking him if I could have a quick look at the square, in my best Mandarin, I asked if I could warm my body at the heater inside the hut.

No doubt he felt sorry for this stupid tourist who dared to be out on a night like this dressed for summer. He let me duck under the barrier and on my walk to the hut, where I could warm my chilled limbs, I saw right into the square. There were no lights so I couldn't see much, but I achieved my target by devious means. After chatting as best as I could with the sentry, I hurried back to my hotel for a hot shower. I sang in the shower, *"I have seen the square called Tiananmen. I tricked a guard to let me pass, but alas, there was nothing there. The best bit of the night, a hut with a brazier, inviting and warm."*

The next time I visited Beijing, Gilly came too. It was at the end of September, not in freezing winter. I booked one of the best hotels in Beijing, overlooking the main street. When we left to go out, we were not allowed to use the front exit. It was closed because the pavements and roads and even the walls of the hotel were being cleaned and prepared for the National Day Parade that is shown on TV around the world. Everything had to be perfect to present the best picture of China. Like every other guest, we exited by the rear door. This turned out well for us because behind the hotel were several small streets with shopping and restaurants. In one restaurant, the range of animals available for eating amused us. We tried the giant frog's legs, accompanied by noodles in a spicy sauce and they were tasty.

On this visit to Tiananmen Square, we had no problem gaining access. We entered the square with hundreds of Chinese and foreign tourists who came to see the military power of China. It was a hot, humid day and a mist of polluting exhaust fumes covered the area until the sun burnt it away. Uniformed and plain-clothed police patrolled the area. They could ask you for your identification and the purpose of your visit, luckily we were not stopped after the initial body and bag search on entry. They had not got my photo on file from my winter visit!

The many attractions in the square took all day to enjoy. The crowds were friendly and proud of their country. They wanted to talk about the history of their capital, the square and, of course, practise their English. One little girl asked, in perfect English, if she and her parents could take a photograph of us together; that made me feel good. I asked a security guard to take the photograph, and he smilingly assisted us. The tourist attractions, the buildings themselves, were beautifully constructed and very historical, but the museums lacked exhibits to admire, as many artefacts had been destroyed during the Cultural Revolution. We viewed, the 'Gate of Heavenly Peace', where we could look down at the crowds that thronged the square. It reminded Gilly of the time she visited Buckingham Palace when she looked down from the balcony where the queen watches aeroplanes fly past on ceremonial occasions and newlywed royals wave to the crowds and kiss on the balcony. We felt like important visiting delegates as we gazed at the panorama of the square. It was there that we bought our Deng Xiaoping watches, which commemorated the formal passing of responsibility for the territory of Hong Kong from the United Kingdom to the People's Republic of China at midnight on July 1st 1997.

We ate a hotel breakfast and left by the back door to find and negotiate a taxi fare for the day. Both of us wanted to see the Great Wall of China. The driver took us to a section of the wall fifty miles from our hotel where there were few tourists. We wanted to escape the crowds at the main viewing site. It was a steep and winding climb up from the carpark where we were accosted by a souvenir seller and bought a guidebook from him. Once on the wall, we walked to the first historical tower. Magnificent unrestricted views stretched for many miles in both directions. I understand you can see the Great Wall from outer space, so I looked up and waved at the astronauts orbiting the earth in their space station.

At our section of the wall, there were no tourist shops or food stalls, but building was progressing at this site. I made do with a comfort stop within four breeze block, roofless, walls, where the word 'toilet' had been painted in English and Chinese. When I entered, there was no water tap, only a line of buckets filled with excrement with the most enormous flies I have ever seen buzzing around. That pee was the quickest one I ever did, and my recommendation to Gilly was, "Cross your legs and hold on until you reach civilisation." We did not stop the driver from racing to the nearest place where we could get a drink and visit civilised toilet facilities. Nearly thirty years on, I am sure the location we visited now has four-star facilities.

For her next visit, I did my homework to find another interesting place to take Gilly. Chinese people like to gamble, they believe in lucky colours and numbers. I don't gamble, but I do like excitement. An opportunity arose, so I booked a top hotel in Macao to give Gilly a surprise weekend away. I decided that this would be a first-class weekend, and that included the ferry. First class on the ferry held no sumptuous charm and perks, it merely meant we would get a free drink and be first to disembark, but it was worth it as we would miss being pushed and hassled by our fellow passengers.

From the pier, it was a short walk into Macao and the Venetian Macao Resort Hotel, the principal hotel for gambling. The area around the hotel buzzed with people, but it took only a few minutes to check in. We followed the bellboy as he carried our hand luggage to the lift. When he opened the door, I followed Gill into our suite. Sheer luxury greeted us. The room smelled fresh, and the massive size of this luxury apartment made me think it was a palace. The bellboy rushed to pull open the patterned curtains, and the light streamed into the room. He tested the huge TV before showing us the kitchen with its high-quality appliances, not that we would need a kitchen. Everything we could want was there: a king-size bed, another TV and more wardrobe and drawer space than we could use. The bathroom was spacious, with double washbasins and a bath big enough for two, which was tried and tested to authenticate my claim. Plenty of fluffy luxury towels, bathrobes and a basket of artisan toiletries completed the splendour of our penthouse suite. I wanted to get the percolator going so I could sit down with a strong coffee and throw my shoes off. No chance of that, we were only here for two nights and there was too much to explore.

Macau was an overseas Portuguese territory preparing to become a special administrative zone, similar to Shenzhen. With a blend of oriental and western influences similar to Hong Kong, the city had an air of romance and nostalgia. Its reputation dates from the 1920s and 1930s, as a place of smuggling, gambling, prostitution, and crime controlled by Chinese triads (crime syndicates). The gambling houses are well known across Asia.

My first visit to a casino opened my eyes. The bright lights lit up the surroundings and revealed girls in skimpy costumes carrying trays of drinks. I had watched movies where gamblers wore evening suits and smoked cigarettes or huge cigars and displayed nerves of steel as they studied the cards in their hand. This scene did not remind me of a movie; casually-dressed punters moved around the blackjack tables, roulette wheels and gaming machines. Possibly a thousand people fed slot machines with coins and seldom did I see anyone win. I was disappointed, it was all too much for me, seeing this mindless squandering of money. The smoke-filled room, packed with flashing and buzzing electronic noises was depressing. I was not tempted to join them. After our two complimentary drinks, I told Gilly I didn't like it. She agreed with me, so we left. I left with a full wallet and the knowledge that I had won. Well, we got free drinks.

We viewed a few of the tourist sites and wandered the streets until evening. We decided on a Portuguese restaurant. It was the one where diners were queuing up to get a seat. We were not disappointed with our choice. We climbed up three floors to reach our table, spying on the diners and their dishes of food as we mounted the stairs, becoming more and more ravenous as we smelt the food. Our visit to Macao was memorable because I was able to spoil Gilly with our luxurious suite and the enticing food.

I wish she could have been there to experience my next Chinese treat, but, alas, she had to return for work. The

Chinese government supports sport and wants to be world champions in every field. This included motor racing. Simone and Jinton, good friends of mine and members of the organising team for the first event to be held in China at the purpose-built racetrack at Zhuhai, invited me to join them at the meeting.

Simone picked me up at the ferry terminal and took me to his parent's house. I knew nothing about his parents and was apprehensive as we pulled up in front of a large terraced house in what looked to be an affluent area. It was separated from the road by a wall with a gate that opened into a neat garden where several fruit trees were growing. I followed Simone through a heavy oak door and along a passage to a living room with a high ceiling that made the room look bigger than it was. Military photographs and memorabilia associated with a woman filled the room. I guessed his mother was once a high-ranking officer in the army. His father never joined us, so I assumed he had either passed away or was working. Simone never mentioned him, so I did not ask questions. Jinton had already left for the racetrack.

His mother was now in her late sixties but still agile. I wished I spoke better Chinese, because I would have loved to have a long chat with her and talk about her career. For a military person, and a former or possibly present important Chinese official, she was relaxed. It pleased me when she asked Simone to show me her military room. I was unable to read the documents next to the medals and took them to be letters of commendation for her service to the PRC. Her uniforms hung in display cabinets and a wall cabinet held a pistol in a leather holster. "Simone, your mum must have been and must still be an important person. I find this room fascinating. It looks like her career was long and distinguished."

"Yes, she was an important person in China's Cultural Revolution and was close to Chairman Mao."

"I think your mother is an interesting woman."

Another display case caught my eye. "Andrew, do you find this interesting?"

"Yes, what is it?"

"It's a fossilised Dinosaur egg. It was a present to my mother from the people of Mongolia. It is at least 150 million years old."

After I thanked Simone's mum for welcoming me to her home, we set off for the racetrack. When we got there, we found Jinton within a few minutes of our arrival. I could see why she had asked for two passport-size photographs as she hung an identification card around my neck. They would be busy until lunchtime and I would be free to wander.

Wander I did. The colour of the cars, the drivers' outfits, the dresses worn by the pretty girls and photographers taking pictures and filming the drivers, captivated me. Marshals guided the public and just before the race started, I took my reserved set in the stand to watch. This was the final race of the 1999 FIA GT Championship and the last one of the twentieth century. The season began on 11 April 1999 and ended 26 November 1999 after ten races in Europe, the United

States, and this one in China. The race featured grand touring cars and awarded a driver and his team the championship. The atmosphere was electrifying as the cars moved into position. When the chequered flag came down, the cars sprang into life as they set off in unison, weaving from side to side to get to the front. Engines roared on full throttle and the air filled with tyre smoke and the smell of burning rubber.

Within minutes, the crowd went quiet. The race was 105 laps of the track and would take around three hours to complete, so I made my way to meet Jinton for lunch. "Are you hungry?" she asked,

"Ravenous."

"Good, you will enjoy this restaurant."

Not only was it a classy restaurant with tasty food, but there was also entertainment. A fashion show took place as we ate. Gorgeous, tall ladies paraded along the catwalk dressed in dreamy outfits. I could afford none of these very expensive designer clothes but Gilly would have loved seeing them. She might have fallen in love with one of the outfits and wanted to buy it, so it was a good job she was not here. Jinton must have been enjoying the show and wanted to see more. She told me to relax and enjoy my lunch. I wanted to take my time; I enjoyed her company, and my eyes were fixed on the fashion show.

The race had an hour to run after my return to the stand. My instructions were to stay put after the race and Jinton would come for me. I was in a prime position as the excitement increased. Porsche, Lamborghini and

Chrysler Viper cars roared around the tight corners and hairpin bends, burning rubber. They flew around the four and a half kilometre track in a minute and a half.

The Chrysler Viper Team Oreca with Olivier Beretta and Karl Wendlinger in their 10L V10 Chrysler Viper GTS-R won the race. What an amazing end to the day. I was very fortunate to have such good friends.

I dropped Jinton home in time to catch the last ferry back to Shekou. I was convinced my bedroom smelled of burning rubber and gasoline. I should have showered to rid myself of the smell impregnated in my clothes and skin, but I got into bed and fell asleep in minutes.

CHAPTER 20

KEEP YOUR CAMERA HANDY

I enjoyed working for Delton in China and after they lost the contract to a Norwegian company, I wanted to quit and go home to be with Gilly. I also wanted to stay because I loved living and working here.

Once the student numbers fell, the stakeholders were eager to make savings, and I was the first to face redundancy. When I received the bad news, my emotion was one of relief – working in China for over three years was difficult. I'd suffered a triple heart bypass and the long separation from Gilly was taking its toll.

On the same day that I received the redundancy news, Cycy informed me that Alf, the Norwegian oil company operations manager, wanted to see me in his office. When I entered, he smiled and greeted me with, "Good afternoon, Andrew, I trust you are well."

"I am well but I am sorry to tell you I will leave China in two weeks. There's no more work for me here."

"Good. I'm pleased to hear that. I have a job for you."

"What's the job?"

"I want you to go out to our new FPSO for a month."

"I would love to, but my preparations are made to go home."

"I know about the difficulties in the training centre. Tell me, have you thought about going into business for yourself?"

"Yes, I have."

"I think you should consider it as an option. We need people like you to continue sharing your expertise. I can help you get started. You will need to register a company, then I can give you work for at least a month. There are opportunities in China, and someone with your skills could do well."

Deep down, I wanted to stay in China and I had always wanted to have a stab at starting a company of my own. This was my golden opportunity, a chance to fulfil a long-held dream. "I'm prepared to start my company and I would like to take the job on the FPSO."

He wrote the figures on a whiteboard as he questioned me about my salary, accommodation allowance, airfares, etc. He wrote his figures at the side of my figures. The total was tempting as it came to double the amount I currently earned. That night, Gilly and I had a long discussion, itemising the pros and cons of my future situation. She was excited at the opportunity I had been offered. She could see that my prospects were good. We decided I should accept the offer. In a very busy three weeks, I set up my company and received my first contract. I renewed the lease on my apartment and did a sea survival course.

The FPSO was sheer luxury compared to the conditions on a platform. I did additional English training and compiled additional notes for the Chinese operators and technicians. I enjoyed it and saw for myself the operation and became an important member of the crew for the next five weeks.

When I returned onshore, I received grim news. The price of a barrel of oil had dropped dramatically, Alf had returned to Norway and his replacement refused to renew my contract. This was a harsh blow to my emerging company. I was now a sole trader with no business or job.

After the initial blow, my confidence suffered a wobble, but my optimism returned as I was determined not to let this setback crush my dreams. All I needed was to get appointments with the right managers and persuade them to give me work. Two weeks passed and my efforts had been futile. I needed advice from managers and people experienced in the business.

Short technical and safety training courses were what I wanted, but most of the enquiries I received were about documentation and technical English.

Tony informed me the consortium would soon give up hiring the training centre and would only send people there if the course suited their needs. The China Offshore Oil Company, who owned the centre, would hand over the running to a private company. If I could get Arnold and Jacinta interested then I should prosper. I told them I had set up a company and wanted to represent them in China. I passed on the information Tony gave me, hoping that they would be interested.

Jacinta arrived in Shekou first, accompanied by a team from one of the largest drilling companies in the world. I knew one of the team members very well, as we worked together in Sarawak. I made the arrangements and went with them to discuss the possibility of a partnership in the training centre. They were ready to invest a million dollars in training, but what they specifically wanted were drilling contracts. Tony could not guarantee this would transpire after their investment in training, so they pulled out. From this negotiation process, I got an insight into how ruthless doing business can be. So far I had acted as a go-between with large companies, but my efforts had produced nil profit.

I was confident that my arrangement with Delton Training Services would pay off. Two weeks later, Arnold and his team arrived to present their case to Tony and other managers. I had made all the arrangements and accompanied Arnold, assisted by Simon and Jane. She had been DTS office representative before they lost the previous contract. This was Arnold's chance to take it back.

After the presentation, Tony invited us to another meeting at the China National Offshore Oil Company's offices to meet one of their most senior managers. When we arrived, I recognised three people who attended the earlier presentation and while we waited to go into the meeting room, they served us coffee and chatted. A man came over. "If you will follow me, please. I will show you the seating arrangements."

Once inside the meeting room, he instructed us where to sit. Finally, a man in his late fifties or early sixties entered and sat in the seat reserved for him. Tony introduced our team, giving a brief description of our positions and responsibilities. He praised Delton for the quality of training we did in the past. The rest of the meeting was taken up mostly by small talk. It is customary with Chinese companies that they get to know and trust you before they sign a business deal. I believe Tony had convinced his senior manager to give the business to Arnold because he was trusted and this was only small talk to complete his decision. Arnold had lost the previous contract because of decisions made by the consortium and not the owner.

We left the meeting not knowing what to expect. As Jane drove towards the Nanhai hotel to drop Arnold and Simon off, her mobile rang. A few seconds later, she cried out, "Delton has the contract."

It disappointed me when Arnold appointed one of his managers to front the operation. I quickly got over any disappointment because I would have been an employee again and what I wanted was to run my company.

Jane gave me expert advice when I asked her, "How do I do business in China?"

"Andrew, you need to understand Chinese culture and business methods. To be successful, people must trust you."

"I think people trust me,"

"Yes, they do. Now you must be patient. Chinese people are very patient and want to know you before they will do business with you. Arnold got the contract because of Delton's record and because Tony, who is a party member, trusts you."

"Thank you for the advice."

It was at this point that it occurred to me I would have been more successful if I had a Chinese partner. I was wrong to think I could do it on my own.

My involvement and my contacts within English Corner could introduce me to several people who could help. One of them introduced me to Wang Yi, the training manager at the Daya Bay Nuclear Power Plant and he invited me to visit the plant. That was a big surprise for me. I had no success in the past organising a visit for my students to such important and secure places.

To create a good impression, I hired a limousine for the day. It took us an hour and a half to get there. Outside the plant, I showed my invitation to the security guard and Wang came to greet me five minutes later.

"Good morning, Andrew. Welcome to Daya Bay. I trust you enjoyed the journey here?"

"Morning, Wang, yes, I did. I am looking forward to my visit."

"Where is your camera?"

I was not sure if he was joking.

He led me into the visitors' centre, which displayed posters and information about the power station. He was keen to tell me about the plant. "Daya Bay is the first ever large commercial nuclear power plant in mainland China. Eighty per cent of the power generated is transmitted to Hong Kong."

It surprised me that China would supply so much electricity to Hong Kong.

"The French National Company, Framatome, designed and built the reactors with Chinese participation. It is French people that train the employees and this is where you can be of help. Our workers don't have as good a standard of English as we would like. Your experience in the oil sector would be a significant help to us. We would like you to work alongside the French trainers. Let me show you our training control room and it will give you a better idea of how we train our operators."

Inside was a replica of the actual control room for the nuclear plant.

Wang could see the surprised look on my face. "Andrew, this control room has to be an exact duplicate of what is in the plant. Those being trained can follow what is happening in the primary control room, but they cannot make any adjustments. They can only follow what adjustments the operations people are making."

"This is amazing."

"Yes, it is, and it helps people to learn. We are very proud of our facilities here."

After meeting some trainees and trainers, I could see why I could be useful to the operation. The trainers from the plant were highly skilled but had difficulty passing on their expertise because the trainees were familiar with English, but not French.

At lunch, he introduced me to several engineers and managers, and the meal was full of friendly chatter. None of them asked if I had a camera so I was now sure he had been joking. After lunch, Wang escorted me back to my limousine and shook my hand. "Andrew, I will be in touch soon."

I felt elated and hopeful as I sat in the rear seat of the limousine; I had paid extra to impress.

A month passed, I heard nothing from Wang, but my patience was to be rewarded. The important telephone call finally came. "Andrew, can you come to Shenzhen with me on Wednesday to meet a very important man?"

"Yes, I am free."

"Good, I will meet you outside McDonald's at 9am. I am sorry, but you will need to make your own way back from Shenzhen as I must go someplace else."

"No problem, Wang. I want to go to Electronics City, so it is a convenient arrangement for me."

He arrived in a company car with a driver to head to the hotel, so I sat in the back seat. I experienced state-owned hotels in Shekou; they are inconspicuous, clean and less expensive than the foreign chain hotels. When Wang checked at reception, they had been expecting us. The manager escorted us to a penthouse suite and invited me to sit.

A woman, who I took to be of managerial status, escorted an older gentleman dressed in casual clothes usually worn for relaxation and not for a meeting. Wang stood up, and I followed his lead.

"Andrew, this is Mr Liu. He is retired now but was the general manager when they built the plant."

I shook his outstretched hand. "I am honoured to meet you."

A young female came in carrying a tray with tea and snacks, then left along with the hotel manager. The conversation with Mr Liu never got around to work, or what services I could offer. It centred on family and the countries I visited.

I knew the introduction was over when Wang said, "Mr Liu is tired and should take a rest now." I was to be left in limbo for quite a while, not knowing if my meeting was a success or a failure.

The wheels of progress turn slowly in China. It would be some time before (or if) I would hear anything back.

With the world economy in such a terrible shape, few companies wanted my services. At Christmas, when Gilly came out to visit, she could tell little progress had been made since her last stay. I tried to reassure her that things would get better because the world economy was improving. After a long discussion, we agreed for me to give it more time.

I visited the British, American and Australian consulates in Guangzhou to see if they could put me in contact with the right people. My first opportunity presented itself when someone at the American consulate got me an introduction to a food company in

Guangzhou. My efforts paid off, and they awarded me two safety training courses, but they wanted me to deliver them. This was not the way I wanted to progress. I wanted to scout for work and place others in charge of delivering the courses. However, I took the work, hoping it would open up new possibilities. It didn't, so I moved on in my search.

At a trade fair, I met people from the Baotou Chamber of Commerce. They wanted me to go to Baotou and offered to help me open an office there. I said, "It's a long way from here, I will think about it."

Baotou is the capital city of Inner Mongolia. I ate in several Mongolian restaurants and had met people from there but I knew little about the area. I had to find out more and I had a cunning plan in mind. In the SEZ of Shenzhen, there were many people from Inner Mongolia who had left to better their life. At English Corner, I singled out a group that had two people in it who I knew were from Baotou. I sat with them and requested that I decide the topic. They readily agreed and I put my plan into action. "Today you can tell me about your hometown and give me reasons why I should visit it."

That got their attention.

"Chen, where are you from?

"Baotou, Andrew."

"Anyone else from the same region?"

Ping raised her hand. "I am from there."

"Okay, Ping, you start, tell us about Baotou."

"My family live there."

"Is it a big city or a small town?"

"It is a huge city." The others nodded in agreement.

"Are there nice things to see and do there?

"No, there is nothing like we have in Shenzhen."

"Is the weather better there than here?"

"No, No. In the winter it is freezing and in the summer it is hot and dry, I don't like it."

"What about you, Chen? What do you like about Baotou?"

"Only my family. There's nothing much to see or do that would interest you, except, perhaps, when the Mongolian horse people come. They put on shows and there are some parks, but nothing else."

"What about work, is it easy to get a job there?"

"Yes, it is easy because there are big industries like coal and steel. Mining is the principal part of the economy."

"What about close by, what is there to see?

"Only the grasslands and somewhere there is a big temple, but few people live there."

Ping said, "There is a big lake, but no one goes there because it is very dangerous for your health."

"Why is that?"

"Because that is where they dump industrial waste."

"So would you recommend for me to live there?"

"No, Andrew, please do not live there."

Chen continued, "Andrew, when it snows there, the snowflakes are not white, they are black. You should stay away from Baotou."

"Thank you, Chen. Thank you, Ping."

This was not an encouraging prospect. I made my mind up, and I decided not to go to Baotou.

When I was working at the training centre, Tony asked me to do him a favour and rewrite some tender documents for a company. Because of this, I became friendly with the owner and several of his staff. Xiao Hong, one of the service engineers, asked me if I would give some English lessons to his friend, June. I agreed, and it paid off. June taught at a private English school and arranged for me to have the use of a classroom whenever I had a need.

Xiao contacted me again because Mr Zhang, the company owner, wanted to see me. I had visited the office before and it was easy to get to, so I had no problem being punctual for the meeting.

"Hello, Andrew, it has been a long time since you came to visit."

"I have been very busy, Mr Zhang, but I am glad that I am here now."

"Andrew, I am told you have set up your own company and you're doing well. I need your help and if we can agree on a price today for your services, you can have the business. Have you got time to rewrite a tender for me?"

"Mr Zhang, for you, I will always make time."

Previous to setting up his service company, Mr Zhang worked as an offshore installation manager and therefore understood the oil business. I worked day and night to meet the two-week deadline for his bid to be submitted. A month later, he was awarded the contract, and I became Mr Zhang's favourite person. Within six months, with my help, he was awarded more business and because of this, I made a regular income. This method of earning was not in my business plan. I wanted this type of work, but I wanted others to do it.

For my next task, he wanted me to accompany him to a pre-tender meeting. I prepared the documentation, and he was awarded the job. Mr Zhang invited me to a 'steamboat' meal at a highly rated restaurant and during the meal, he asked me to join his company as a director.

This was an unexpected turn of events.

"What will it involve?"

"You will oversee all our documentation in English, train our people when required, attend tender meetings and promote my company."

"What about dealing with the Chinese managers? I am not so good at that."

"Andrew, you deal with the Americans. I will deal with the Chinese."

The package was good, but I needed time to consider.

Gilly would arrive in just over a week, and I knew she wanted to discuss my future in China. This would be my sixth year here and I struggled when setting up my company and I knew I needed a powerful partner. Was this an opportunity for me? I needed more time. "Mr Zhang, I will give you my decision in one week."

This was an acceptable strategy. He would not be in a hurry for my decision. For days I had little sleep, I could see a future for myself in China, but because of my age, it was a difficult decision to make. I knew it would be another five to ten years before I would see any real benefit. I needed to consult with Gilly and perhaps take advice from Jane.

Jane liked Gilly and invited us to dinner. She showed us relics from her past and what happened during her childhood. Her family had been very rich as they owned vineyards. She enjoyed a privileged upbringing in a secure, palatial home for many years until her parents lost everything during the Cultural Revolution between 1966 and 1976. Her family found it hard to adjust to their new status, future expectations and the change in their lifestyle. It was a sad story.

I told her about the offer. "What do you think, Jane?"

She looked at me sympathetically. "Andrew, you are too nice to be a business owner." In this simple reply, she was telling me I had not got the attitude that was essential to succeed in China. I was shocked by her bluntness but she was right, I always considered others before myself.

I looked across the dining table at Gilly. I had seen the truth in Jane's words and said, "Gilly, looks like it's time for me to come home. I need to reconsider my future in China and the UK. Maybe it's time to retire." After reviewing the financial gains so far and my efforts to make my company prosper, I hung up my travelling boots. I fulfilled my commitments and gave my notice in to quit my apartment. Mr Zhang understood and I left China six weeks later. It was a sad parting as this was a country and people that I loved. I wish I had been here earlier in my working life when I was a bigger risk-taker.

CHAPTER 21

FISH CAN FLY

Despair came over me. How would a sixty-year-old man, who had hardly ever worked in the UK, get a job? I accepted I would find it difficult, but how difficult would it be? I didn't want to think about it. When I worked on the oil rigs, on my twenty-eight days off, I attended college and got myself a Higher National Certificate in Multi-Discipline Engineering. I was depending on this qualification to open a few doors. I could become a teacher, so I contacted Leeds University to see what I needed to do to achieve this.

They wanted me to teach a class to establish my ability. Eight people, all over thirty, were in the class. I guessed they were teachers. I chose the 'the resistor colour code' as my subject. This was a good choice because it is easy to involve students in a hands-on activity.

The participants were responsive and after my test lesson, Angela, the lady who was interviewing me, said, "Andrew, you don't need to do a teacher training course. You could teach our teachers how to teach." I was flattered by her words and kindness, but nobody would employ me if I could not produce the important proof of competence, a teaching certificate.

"Thank you very much, but I cannot get a college job if I am not qualified. I need to get a certificate that proves my ability to teach. What do you recommend I should do?"

"With your experience, I advise you to do the City and Guilds Teachers Training Certificate and an assessor award. These are the minimum qualifications you need to get accepted for work, and you will not be required to attend full time."

I thanked Angela for her advice. Now I had a plan of action and I did not delay acting. The following day I signed up for these courses at a local college.

I was prepared for this new challenge, but my first day at college did not impress me. The staff were very apologetic about their oversight when they explained that the start date was changed. Nobody had informed me and I was fed up and annoyed. Thirty potential teachers turned up the following day. Most of them were grumbling because, like me, they had not received the updated information and turned up the day before. They were all mature students, just like me. It made no difference that they were all younger than me, I just wanted the qualification. Several worked at the college and the others came from government or training providers. As the weeks passed, I recognised why Angela made her comment about my ability to teach teachers to teach. My lecturers came to class unprepared and with poor quality support materials. This was not my way of teaching. I felt like taking over and showing the lecturer the proper method. This was the way the rest of the course continued. I bit my tongue and calmed myself. I would put up with the poor teaching and resources because I needed the teaching certificate.

The assessor classes had twelve participants in the class. The lecturer arrived prepared and on time. I was encouraged by this start. When he found out I was unemployed he arranged for me to conduct practical lessons in the college workshops. I had to do this because not having a job would have meant that I could not complete the practical aspects of the course. After a few classes, I was offered a supply teacher job working through an agency and I would get paid. I completed both parts of the teacher training and the assessor and verifier training courses in a year.

The people I met at the college were nice, but I felt management accepted minimum standards. Their attitude was 'as long as we are not getting sanctioned, then it is okay'. I was not happy with this attitude, as only the best was good enough for me. I knew I could not follow their example and work at that standard. I would have to take my newly gained qualifications elsewhere.

Monetary gain did not drag me back into the world of the expatriate, our further education system was being destroyed by a lack of investment and by those providing the education. I always gave my best and my students knew this. I was a popular lecturer, but working at the college was not giving me job satisfaction, so when Arnold telephoned and asked about my situation, I was glad to leave. He had offered me a new situation that was more to my liking.

I flew to Abu Dhabi and joined a team of assessors and verifiers on an island in the Arabia Gulf.

The island is just under two square miles in size, and around a thousand workers lived there. Accommodation and food was four-star and when I finished for the day. I could go out for a walk or just relax in my room to watch television and videos. The accommodation, food and work rotation suited me and I never got bored.

Rules were simple: No workwear or shorts in the dining room, all transport must give way to wildlife and it was forbidden to feed the birds. Once a month, all non-essential workers picked up and bagged the plastic waste and rubbish washed up on our beaches and this was transported to Abu Dhabi for disposal. Our company was eco-friendly, and it did everything they could to keep the environment natural and safe. I kept to the eco rules, but could not resist feeding the birds, they were one of my interests and they were part of my relaxation after work. Wherever I had worked in the world, I was a keen birdwatcher. The mynah birds here were so friendly they would land on my shoulder and eat cake from my hand.

One year later, I transferred to the biggest rig I had ever worked on. The Persons on Board (POB) numbered almost 500, and I was the only British person on board, yet I never felt out of place. The instructors, who I would help to gain their assessor qualifications, were from India, Pakistan and the Arabian Gulf. They were all ex-field senior technicians or supervisors.

On the platform, the installation manager called the work planner 'my travel agent' because he had to arrange so many trips by boat to other platforms for me. One time when I returned by boat, I was leaning against the safety rail enjoying the weather and daydreaming when I got knocked onto my backside. I looked around and saw a flying fish wriggling on the deck. I picked myself up, and the fish, and returned it to the sea. At dinner, I relayed the story to my friends who called it Andrew's 'fishy tale'. Deepak said, "Andrew, you sure it was not a flying shark?" That sent everyone into roars of laughter.

I liked the group I sat with at dinner. One time, in Abu Dhabi, I accompanied two of them for a night out. We ended up in a place called the Indian Club. There was only one light inside, and that shone on to the stage and spotlighted the two gorgeous performers. In the darkness, I couldn't see to pick up my beer. I learned a lot about India and its culture from my dinner companions. My friends were just like me, they liked to go out for a drink and entertainment and they would occasionally have a good moan at life just like me. I particularly liked Gopal, who acted as my guru, giving me advice about life and what food I should eat. He told me to visit Goa or Kerala because that is where you find the best Indian food, especially fish dishes. I enjoyed my job there and it didn't last long enough. My job was to train others and once they were trained, it was time for me to move on.

CHAPTER 22

TOO YOUNG TO RETIRE

The internet made it easier to get my CV to agencies and companies and after two weeks, I got an interview at a technical documentation company based in Hull. It did not bother me that the job was sixty miles away. I had never heard of the company, but I recognised Mike, the interviewer's name. As an expatriate, you met or talked on the telephone to many people and sometimes you knew them without having met them. It pleased me when he told me I could work from home.

My previous work involved the development of training programmes and this helped to make the task easier. Copies of the programmes were saved on floppy discs, which was the technology available to me during the nineties, and I referred to the discs from time to time. I spent four days at home writing the modules, and on Friday morning, drove to the office to discuss any corrections that might be needed. I met all the required deadlines for this project and informed Mike if I left the house during work time.

As a result, when I completed the contract, he immediately offered me another one. This time it was essential to do the work at the office and would mean I had to find a hotel to stay in during the week. The job was to review the operating and maintenance procedures for operations in the North Sea, and my task would be to review the training manuals. The job had started some weeks before, but I would get at least four months' work.

My first day in the office made me realise a skills gap existed in Britain. The reason I say this is that at sixty-four, except for Mike, I was the youngest on the project. Mike let us get on with the job, but insisted everyone took regular breaks from working on a computer. During a coffee break, I asked him, "Why does the company use so many people over sixty. Does this mean you cannot get younger people to take these jobs?"

"No, it doesn't mean that. We can get younger people, but they lack the broad range of skills older workers have. This group can finish a job in half the time that younger people would need."

"Do you mean people in their forties and fifties don't have the same skills as people in my age group?"

"Yes, that is exactly what I mean. During the sixties and seventies, British industry collapsed and funding for apprenticeships dried up. As a result, the emphasis shifted from practical to theory and shorter apprenticeships. This resulted in a skills gap."

"Does this mean I should be able to find work if I want it?"

"Believe me, Andrew, employers want to employ people over sixty."

For the first two weeks, I worked on Friday, then Mike suggested I start my workday earlier and stay later. The security guard opened the office at 6:30am and closed it at 6:30pm. As long as I worked for a minimum of forty hours, I could leave Thursday afternoon. It crossed my mind that this was a good job.

The cold winter days were upon us, so I welcomed the opportunity to work a four-day week. I was paid well so rather than travel home each day, I stayed in a decent hotel. It made life much better, and a bonus was the team were a friendly bunch and they were also staying at my hotel. The facilities at and near my workplace were good, especially the sandwich shop around the corner. When women from the drawing office delivered documentation to us, they drew the odd sexist comment from us 'old timers'. I asked one of them, "In this era of political correctness and equality, why don't you object to such comments?"

They giggled in amazement and one of them said, "We don't mind. We know you mean nothing bad, you're all gentlemen in this department."

Unfortunately, this perfect job ended. During the time I worked there, I learned a lot about operations in the North Sea. I had the knowledge and experience to apply for a job, but I knew I could not work on a rig in the North Sea because of the age limit. However, I knew I was a valuable asset because of my age and experience and I could find office work anytime.

Then a telephone call came from Bangkok. The caller was precise and direct. "My name is Doc. Chris, who worked with you in Abu Dhabi, recommended you. Are you interested in coming to Bangkok for three-months? The job is to write procedures and present them to supervisors and managers." I jumped at the opportunity. My experience and expertise were in demand. Being older was not so bad after all.

The timing was perfect. Two weeks later, after returning to Hull to get my visa from a Thai consulate, I boarded a flight to Bangkok to work for a manpower services company. Graham was the manager, with Doc as his second in command. They were ably assisted by the office assistants Kathy, Apple and Boy. Kathy took me to get my work permit and helped me to open a bank account.

My accommodation was in the Grand President, a German-owned hotel. It was in a perfect location because when I came out of the hotel and turned right into Soi eleven, it came out on Sukhumvit, one of the major roads in Bangkok, and a hundred metres from the Skytrain station. The quickest and easiest way to get around central Bangkok is to use this train. This would be the perfect venue for when Gilly flew out in her school holidays – a good central position and transport for when she went out to discover the tourist delights of Bangkok.

Doc introduced me to Dick, who would partner me for the presentations. He then introduced us to the people we needed to know and to Norman, a tall, lean American who would oversee the project. The subject of this project was about working practices and reducing costs. The programme included the basic operations of any big oil company, not unfamiliar stuff to me.

The first two weeks were spent familiarising myself with the work and meeting the people who prepared the programmes. A young Thai engineer developed the ideas and materials I would present. When I first met him, I concluded he would make it to the top when I saw what he had created.

The company hired facilities in the Tai-pan Hotel, away from the office and close to my hotel. In addition, a secretary was hired to do the arrangements and keep records. Nok had good organising skills and with her good nature, Dick and I found her easy to work with.

First, we did a mock-up session with the project team, who were very satisfied with our grasp of the materials. When we delivered the first two presentations, at least one team member stayed to support us and stayed for the free lunch.

The participants were mostly from senior positions in the company. Their reaction to the presentations was positive and the feedback was excellent. After we had delivered several presentations, I could tell the company strategy was working and the goal of becoming more efficient and reducing costs was being achieved.

I was enjoying my job and meeting new work colleagues, but what about my social life? What can I say about Bangkok? It is one of the most vibrant cities I encountered in my travels around our planet. It had everything a tourist could wish for, and they flock there in their thousands every year. If you wanted to see sex shows, they were there, but not everyone wanted to see this seedy side to the city. It had so many cultural and historical attractions to draw people here, beautiful buildings and monuments as well as some of the best shopping centres in the world.

On her first visit, I left Gilly to sleep to get over her jetlag and went to work. I had shown her around the area close to the hotel, and assumed she would stay in the hotel's vicinity to browse around the shops and familiarise herself with her surroundings and have lunch. I asked her to enquire at the hotel about weekend tours so we could relax together and maybe escape the city and explore the quieter side of Thailand.

When I got back from work, we met for a drink in the hotel bar and sat down where we could view the busy street outside. Relaxing with our cool drinks and telling her about my day, I asked her, "What's your day been like? I hope you don't want to return home just yet."

"No way, my day was brilliant."

"What did you do?"

"I did what you asked and enquired about tourist trips. They gave me loads of pamphlets. At breakfast, I browsed through them and planned my day."

"So what did you do?" My curiosity was aroused and I wanted to know what my wife got up to in my absence.

"I went to Jim Thompson's House. I had a map, and I took the Skytrain to the nearest stop to it, then used the map to find it. It was so simple."

"Who is Jim Thomson? I've never heard of him."

"I'm not surprised. He was an American who came to Bangkok with the military after Japan's surrender in the

Second World War. His father was a textile manufacturer. Jim was an architect himself, but he was still interested in textiles. He discovered an enclave of Thai silk weavers who lived in the heart of Bangkok. From this discovery, he set up a silk factory."

She paused for a drink and emptied her beer glass. I was amazed by my adventurous wife. First day in Bangkok and she was discovering more about the city than me! I ordered two more beers.

"The houses are amazing. His silks are there too and there was a student weaver in one house weaving a beautiful silk design. The houses were so cool. I sat on a patio area by a small river sipping iced tea and daydreaming about the people who had lived in this house. It was so quiet and relaxing, I forgot I was in the heart of a busy city."

"Wow! You must have been tired by then. Did you come back for a rest after your adventures?"

"No chance, I retraced my steps and took the Skytrain. One station was near a shopping centre, so I got off to look around the shops. I just arrived back five minutes before you." She smiled, and I gazed at her, speechless. What would she find to do tomorrow?

We showered and changed and set off for the night market. I prefer markets to museums. We never bought much, but we enjoyed the atmosphere as we mooched along the long narrow passages, admiring the tourist junk we didn't want to buy. We ate dinner, listening to some decent music played by a pop group up on a big stage.

The next day, when we met after I finished my work, I asked the same question. "What did you do today?"

"I attended an educational conference."

"An educational conference! I know you are a schoolteacher, but you are on holiday."

"I am, but I passed this building and saw a poster advertising a display of fashion by Thai students. It gave directions by Skytrain to the conference centre, so I went."

She smiled and sipped her drink as she showed me the identification tag she was given – 'Gillian Carruthers, representative from the UK'.

"I got there easily, but when I reached the entrance, I felt nervous, but I took a deep breath and went in."

"What happened after you went in?"

"I had a friendly reception and was the only European there, so my appearance generated interest. I was ushered to a booth where my educational details were recorded and then I was shown to the first exhibit."

"Did you enjoy it?"

"The fashion show was out of this world. There's a lot of talented designers here. I met several teachers and took part in two seminars. We exchanged ideas, and they were friendly so, yes, I enjoyed myself."

I looked at her and rolled my eyes. "Would you like a large vodka? I think you need it." I was constantly gobsmacked by her. What might she get up to next?

Some days, Gilly joined me for lunch at the Tai-pan Hotel, where she came into contact with people working in Bangkok. If she wanted to come to live in Bangkok with me, she would find employment easily. However, I would only be here a short time so we never discussed the prospect of her joining me permanently.

Soon after she returned home, we had a public holiday and I did not want to spend the time in bars in Bangkok. Spurred on by my wife's expeditions, I organised a tourist trip with Dick to the bridge on the River Kwai. We hired a taxi for the day and it worked out to be no more expensive than if we paid for an organised group tour.

The driver spoke good English and dropped us at some houses close to the river. It looked like he knew the people living there and arranged for one of them to take us to the bridge by boat. He told us to take our time, as the boatman would wait until we were ready to return. I enjoyed the boat ride, and the bridge looked magnificent as we approached it. I never expected to see many Japanese tourists there, but they outnumbered every other nationality. I visited several war memorials and cemeteries in the past, and this visit to the bridge had the same effect on me: sadness and nostalgia.

When we returned to the hamlet, the taxi driver drove us to Kanchanaburi. Our first stop was at the JEATH Museum, which was inside a temple compound beside the River Kwai. It's called that because they felt the use of the word 'death' was too horrible. The letters of JEATH represent the countries involved in building the bridge and railway, Japan, England, America, Thailand

and Holland. It was a simple and non-interactive museum, displaying artefacts, old weaponry, photos and other war remains. The museum displayed graphic images of the terrible conditions inflicted on the many young men who died and the ones who survived to tell their story. Letters written by prisoners touched my heart and made me very emotional.

The Second World War cemetery here served as a memorial place for the allied soldiers who sacrificed their lives as prisoners during the war. The total of identified casualties number 6842. The real total is probably much higher.

I served for over twelve years in the RAF, and I visited several war cemeteries. This visit made me think just how pointless and cruel war is. I asked myself, *will we ever learn?*

The answer is no.

We left our taxi at the railway station for a train ride along the 'Death Railway', which took us through magnificent scenery, rice paddies, a rock passage and over a wooden viaduct. There were no available seats on the train, so we stood talking to a couple who were missionaries. When the train stopped for us to get off, the lady fell and broke her leg. I whispered to Dick, "What can we do, we don't know where the nearest medical facilities are?"

The situation eased when some Thai people took over and carried the lady to a motorcycle that had a sidecar that looked like an attachment for carrying goods. The people were efficient and made her comfortable at a restaurant close by. I don't know where it came from, but in less than fifteen minutes an ambulance arrived to attend to her. Dick and I said goodbye and continued on the train tour.

When we headed back to Bangkok, I mentioned food and Dick immediately asked the driver to stop at a nice place. The driver pulled onto a side road and ten minutes later we arrived at a restaurant in the middle of a small lake and we walked over the bridge following the aroma of cooking food. My stomach rumbled in appreciation and anticipation. We invited the driver to order the meal and a magnificent array of dishes arrived. As usual, I enjoyed the fish and the delicate spices in Thai food. Our visit to the bridge and Kanchanaburi had been stressful, but worthwhile. Now I could relax and enjoy my surroundings.

Later, on the return journey, the driver stopped at a Buddhist temple and we went inside. I visited several temples in the past, but had met no western monks. I asked myself why would they choose this life and questioned if I should not become a monk. They were so happy and content and people gave them food for free and I had to work hard to pay for mine.

I was enjoying Bangkok, and it was great when Gilly came out to stay with me but it would end too soon. The penultimate presentation would be for a group of five Americans. They were all experienced operators in their forties or early fifties. I found Americans easy to work with, as they were experts in the field they work. I was unsure if they would accept being told how they could improve their procedures. In between sessions, I walked around the pool area and garden to clear my head. On my return to deliver the presentation, the group was standing outside, staring at the plate-glass window of the hotel gymnasium opposite. They were admiring Achara who was dressed in tight exercise gear and pounding the treadmill, as she did each morning. I waved to her and then greeted Rick, who had accompanied the group and was there to support me during the final sessions. I think he was there to get away from his desk and enjoy the free lunch. The participants were not in a hurry to get into the classroom and start the course. Rick introduced everyone and for one candidate named Austin, he added, "He's a hillbilly." I'm not sure if he meant this as a compliment, a criticism or a joke.

I had heard of the term, but didn't know the true meaning. I noticed Austin was chewing tobacco, so I guessed this was one aspect of the behaviour consistent with being a Hillbilly. Rick told me one of the group, Larry, was delayed and would join us possibly the next day. This didn't trouble me as this was a group with a lot of offshore experience.

Once we started, it surprised me how interested the participants were in what I presented. All of them supported the idea of saving money and being more efficient. Austin sat there listening intently while having a good chew on his stick of tobacco. I didn't like it when he placed a small spittoon at the foot of the table leg, but I ignored it. At least he was a good shot and washed the spittoon out and always left it behind when he came to lunch.

Larry turned up at lunch on the second day. His reason for arriving late shocked me to the core. New Orleans, where he lived, was underwater, up to twenty feet deep in places. Hurricane Katrina, the third-strongest hurricane to hit the United States in its history, had struck a week before he was due to return to work. When he and his family emerged from the safety of their cellar, they were almost drowned by the flood of water rushing through the door. When he finally got his wife up the stairs and through the open door, they were confronted by a tree that looked like it had grown in their living room and had grown so high it opened a gap in the roof. The roots of this tree that crashed into his home were swaying back and forth in three feet of water. Everyone sitting around him listened intently as he described the devastating scene he had left behind.

I said, "Larry, what were you thinking coming back here? Why aren't you back home with your wife? She must be distraught. She has so much to do. She has to get the tree removed and organise repairs."

"It's all right. The water subsided quickly and neighbours helped me cut the tree, remove it and then seal the roof."

"Yes, but few people would have left their home in such terrible conditions to return to work. I think I would have wanted more time at home."

"Andrew, my wife is a capable woman and tens of thousands of people now have no job. I still have a job, and we will recover from this." He was one of the lucky ones, his job was secure.

I recapped the course for him and continued the rest of the presentation. When we finished for the day, I joined the others at the outside bar. Everyone was there except Larry; he had gone to bed for a well-earned rest.

On the final day, Larry turned up for the presentation, but did not appear at lunch. He turned up soon after we started the final session. He explained he was late because it had taken longer to buy a present for his wife than he expected. He needed to buy it today because he would not have time later. We were all eager to see what he had bought; the box was too big for it to be perfume or jewellery. He gently removed the lid for us to see. Inside was a blue, flowered dress, not unlike the one Gilly was wearing when I first met her. Larry was so proud of his purchase. We all shook his hand and congratulated him on his choice. When we finished the presentation and went to the outside bar, Rick and I bought the beer.

After six months, I found out this oil company had saved over four hundred million dollars by implementing the project's recommendations. I felt good because I delivered the presentations to the people responsible for the savings. I had completed another contract.

CHAPTER 23

BOND AND BOMBS

When I reached sixty-six years of age, my family and friends told me I should retire, but with all this experience, why would I want to retire? I made a few telephone calls and got invited to do a few months' work at a Yorkshire college. Three days a week soon became five.

For most of my working life, I dealt with people with English as a second language. I always worked in situations where language could be a problem, but I never found the students I tried to help were a problem. They were mostly young people who enjoyed life and enjoyed having fun. I never minded what the task was, whatever I did would mean more experience and would look good on my CV. For one week, I taught practical work to a group of deaf-mute students. When I worked in China, a deaf-mute young man sold trinkets around the bars. A few of us took it upon ourselves to help him get a job. We canvased the tourist shops and one shop owner gave him a job. Within months, the owner's profits increased because of the young man's friendly nature. Tourists loved being served by him. I found this group just wanted to learn. When the lesson finished, I knew I had succeeded in this challenge. Everyone enjoyed the class and wanted to come back again.

My next task was to teach a group of people who were unemployed and were forced to attend college so they would receive their benefit payments. The register listed twelve students, and my task was to find a subject that would hold their interest and help get them into employment.

On the first day, two turned up on time, and two did not turn up at all. After a few more days, I got fed up because I could see only two people were keen to get a job. I refused to sign the attendance form for the others so they would not get paid, however, they just took the form to someone else and got it signed. I would have blown my top at this behaviour when I met them at the next session, but I received a call from Doc. "Andrew, I need you back in Thailand. One of our instructors at the training centre in Hat Yai has to leave at short notice. Can you renew your visa and get here in a week?"

I grasped this opportunity to explain my feelings about people who abused the benefits system. I told the ones who were not interested in me trying to help them a few home truths about life. The disinterested retaliated and blamed their upbringing, their parents and teachers: everyone and everything but themselves. One woman in her thirties burst into tears and apologised for her attitude. Not the best way to teach a class, I admit. Most people experience an awful week at work, this was mine. My philosophy is, and what I was trying to explain to this group, if someone is trying to help you, don't make your background an excuse. Grab every chance that will help to improve your job prospects and, ultimately, your life and relationship with the world. I enjoyed most of the challenges at the Yorkshire college, but not all.

I spent one night in Bangkok, then flew to Hat Yai where Chris waited at the airport for my arrival. Once more, I would be part of a small team, teaching young Thai people all about electrical and instrumentation systems used on offshore platforms. The training centre facilities were first-class, with classrooms on the upper floor and workshops on the ground floor. We were in the same grounds as the university, but we were separated from the general courses. Mr Choochart partnered me, and the students amazed me. When I passed one in the corridor, they always bowed their head. I had not been there long when I got an invitation to visit a class at the university. The students removed their shoes before they entered the classroom, bowed as they passed me on their way to their desks and treated me as an honoured guest. How could I not want to teach and help people who treated me like this?

Hat Yai did not suffer from the traffic problems you get in Bangkok. Restaurants served sumptuous, delicious dishes, both meat and seafood. My favourite choice, tiger prawns, were as big as lobsters. I never ate in the apartment because of the wide choice of good and cheap food.

Chris booked me into a downtown hotel until I could take over the apartment of the instructor I would replace. Prime ministers of several Asian countries were meeting in my hotel, as they did once a year, discussing the region's current affairs. I didn't see any of them but met a group of newspaper reporters who were there to cover the event. They took me in their minibus to one of the best restaurants in town, probably paid for on their expenses.

I moved into a well-furnished two bedroomed apartment on the top floor of a five-story block. I bought a television because one programme showed the news in English. From there, I could walk to work and, on the way, passed a 7-Eleven supermarket, so I never needed to shop in town. I only shopped at the big supermarkets when I needed to. A golden Buddha high on a hill near to the apartment overlooked the city. I felt it protected me from harm. On my way back from work, I would stop for a chat with Brian, an expat, who lived in a bungalow close by. His Thai wife, Sukon, regularly invited me to dinner, and she cooked a perfect curry. One time I was invited for dinner, but Sukon left before she had time to cook our meal. Brian told me she had gone to raise funds to give a homeless person, who had died in the street, a decent funeral. She was a very caring person, true to her Buddhist faith. She would arrange the cremation and the spirit of the person would rise in the clouds of smoke from the pyre, hoping to be reborn in a better form in the next reincarnation.

I often stopped and shared a beer with Brian after work, before I went on to my apartment. I never kept alcohol in my apartment because I was aware of the dangers being away from home and drinking too much. Besides, I liked a pub atmosphere and talking to people and watching, or not watching, television with a glass in my hand was better than being stuck brooding in an apartment. Most nights I crossed the 407 road to wait for a tuk-tuk to take me into town. I ate a lot of Thai food, but occasionally I headed for the Swan Restaurant or the Brown Sugar pub, which attracted expatriates, to eat western food. When we reached the clock tower, a landmark near my destination, I got out. As I passed the food stalls, the heat from the stoves made me thirsty and ready for my first beer and my dinner. I often stopped on the way home at my favourite seafood stall before taking a taxi home.

One Saturday night, September the sixteenth, I waited for transport to take me to town. I went out later because bars closed late on a Saturday, so I left my apartment just before 9pm. The tuk-tuk business was booming, all of them were full of passengers returning from town or going out for their Saturday night entertainment. Fifteen minutes passed, and I was still waiting for an empty vehicle to whisk me away to my night out when a motorcycle pulled in to give me a lift. Thai people were friendly and often stopped to give someone a lift. I recognised the driver from a previous occasion, so I got on the pillion behind him. The first time he stopped, I was dubious about travelling pillion, I had seen many cases of dangerous driving, but he was careful and drove responsibly. This was another person who followed the teachings of the Buddhist faith, good deeds help the person in their next reincarnation. Weaving through the traffic, we approached the roundabout just before the centre of town. I hopped off, thanked the driver and walked towards the Brown Sugar pub.

Even through the noise of the traffic and bustle of people's activity, I could hear crickets chirping… That was until the explosion! Smoke and debris billowed into the sky, accompanied by intense fire and the stench of sulphur mixed with petrol and other chemicals. It reminded me of bonfire night. I saw flames enveloping the front of the BC supermarket and several cars and motorcycles were on fire. A second loud bang came from the direction of the Brown Sugar!

A tangled, charred mess of cars and motorcycles burned and could explode at any moment. No one ran or panicked, so I stayed with the crowd. Safety in numbers. I did not consider the gas bottles or paraffin stoves used by the nearby street vendors could be affected by the heat and cause a secondary explosion.

Minutes later, I heard more explosions and became more nervous, but not afraid. Police officers and soldiers cordoned off the immediate danger zone. Police escorted us along a narrow street and away from the danger.

Once out of the immediate danger zone, people dispersed, and I wandered around, not sure which direction I should take. I needed to tell Chris what happened and I was safe. He knew my social habits, and I had mentioned my Saturday plan to him and invited him to join me, but, fortunately for him, he was busy. In those days, I did not own a mobile phone, few people did. I needed help, so I entered a restaurant to ask if I could use their phone. I hoped someone could speak English because I could not speak much Thai.

Within minutes, I was talking to Chris, who was in Bangkok for the weekend. I relayed the facts of the bombings as best as I could. "What are you going to do now?" he asked.

"I want to eat, but I am not sure where I am. I'm phoning from a restaurant so I could eat here."

"Hand the phone over to the proprietor, I'll sort this out."

Chris was fluent in the Thai language and talked to the manager. It wasn't long before they brought me a scrumptious Thai meal and a bottle of beer. He had also asked them to arrange some transport to take me back home.

The bombings were shown on Thai television, but I did not get all the facts until I arrived back at work and the gruesome events unfolded. Six bombs were detonated in strategic parts of town. Two exploded in front of the Brown Sugar pub and one inside the Big C shopping mall. The bombers placed the bombs on motorcycles and triggered them by mobile phone. No organisation claimed responsibility. Four people lost their lives and eighty-two were injured. Those killed were a Malaysian, a Canadian, and two Thai people.

Graham, one of our instructors, was one of the injured and was taken to hospital. Later, Chris and I visited him and we discovered all foreign casualties were being looked after, courtesy of the Thai government.

I could not let this disastrous event get me down and influence what I would do. I enjoyed my work, my friends and Thailand. I missed being at home and I missed Gilly, but I knew I just had to overcome my worries and get on with my life.

Gilly came to visit and my friends, particularly Sukon and Brian, took care of her and showed her around if I was working. She was taken to places I did not know about, places only Thais knew about and were well away from tourist areas. She was privileged to be given an insight into the everyday life of Thai people.

At the weekend, they invited us to go with them to visit the east coast. Sukon drove their big four-wheel drive to Songkhla and turned up the east coast towards Nakhon Si Thammarat. As we passed through the outskirts of the town, I saw buildings that looked like concrete apartment blocks with no windows. They had openings in the walls like those in medieval castles used for firing arrows or bullets at the enemy. I was puzzled by them and contemplated their use. Were they for breeding birds? Were they a modern version of dovecotes, where pigeons and doves nested to provide food for the inhabitants of a castle throughout the year and specifically during a siege? My ideas were neither serious nor silly and amused me. Soon, other sights grabbed my attention and my contemplation was forgotten as I relaxed into my seat to enjoy the rest of the journey.

We continued up the coast for a hundred miles, taking in the beautiful beaches and fishing villages. We pulled in at a restaurant on the beach, the setting could not have been better. As we approached the entrance, we were met by a lady and Sukon chatted to her in Thai. She led us towards a tall, wooden structure, similar to a place where a lifeguard would sit and observe bathers. However, there were no people on the beach, only us. I paused when I spotted a brahminy kite – a sea eagle – tethered with a piece of thin chain close by, gazing at us with its unblinking eyes. It was a beautiful, powerful creature, and I needed a photograph. Gilly had gone on ahead and was the first to clamber up the six-foot ladder, followed by Sukon, Brian and me. The eagle played up to the moment and opened its powerful wings. It was a perfect for a photo but I was too far away and too late. We sat around a square table with our legs dangling above the sand below. The same lady brought bottles of beer and placed them on the low table. This was a new experience for Gilly and me. The closest I could compare it to was probably a private booth at a Japanese restaurant.

The food took some time to come and to begin with the peaceful surroundings did not encourage talk. I listened to the shushing of the waves and felt the gentle, warm breeze on my face. I sighed with happiness. Eventually, after we had all soaked up the calm atmosphere, we chatted. I started the chat off by asking about the concrete buildings I saw on the way out of Songkhla. Brian explained, "They are homes for the swiftlets to make the bird nests we use for soup."

Gilly said, "But they live in caves. We saw them in the Niah caves when we lived in Sarawak, in Borneo."

"Not the farmed ones, Sukon knows about them, she will explain."

Sukon continued, "A birdhouse is a building where conditions are similar to a swiftlet cave. Birds live and breed in it. Birds' nests are profitable and with fewer people trained to gather them in their natural setting, the government acted and came up with a solution to this problem. The Gulf of Thailand has many fish farms, so the government decided it was possible to farm swiftlets. It has taken years, but now it is successful."

"I worked on a farm once, perhaps I should buy a swiftlet farm?"

"Andrew, if it was easy, everyone would do it. It takes many years to find the best places to locate the farms. You need to find out the swiftlets' flight path, the number of birds in the area, and the nearest source for food and water. The conditions must be right for them to survive."

"It sounds difficult."

"Yes, it is difficult, but the government has developed swiftlet training courses for farmers and protect the birds by law."

"Why do they nest here and not fly back to the caves?" Gilly asked.

"The birds are attracted to the birdhouse by using a recorded sound and by creating the right conditions to encourage them to stay. It's a bit like having a pet falcon or other bird of prey. They have to be trained."

The meal was amazing, the prawns were some of the biggest and tastiest I have ever eaten, the fish – just gorgeous. The day finished with me lying sprawled in the sand. I was convinced the eagle thought I had drunk too much Singha, but in reality, my foot slipped on the way down the ladder.

Halfway back to Hat Yai, Sukon turned off the road and onto a bumpy track that led to the beach and a traditional fishing village. We walked along a driftwood boardwalk to enter the village. I could tell right away the people here worked hard. A woman and two men sat repairing nets. A driftwood pier headed out into the sea where fish traps were located. As we approached, a group of five children ran over to greet us. I think they were more inquisitive than welcoming. Sukon spoke to the woman mending nets. I recognised the woman's reply, which was the Thai phrase for 'welcome'. Small houses built from materials that more affluent people had discarded were built on soft sand. They stood on stilts to prevent them from flooding during high tides. Fish were laid out on wooden stands to dry and an operating smokehouse was close by. I closed my eyes to take in the sounds and delicious aroma permeating my surroundings.

As Thai custom dictated, we were offered a drink, a plastic tumbler filled with warm water, and the woman happily chatted to Sukon. Four small fishing boats were tied at the water's edge, ready to depart for the next fishing trip. A vessel, capable of carrying around a dozen passengers, was propped up with round wooden poles and a man was painting its hull, and another man was checking its engine, which looked to be from a motor vehicle. I could see a metal fixture for swivelling the propeller in and out of the water when the driver needed to slow or stop the boat. Sukon negotiated with the woman to buy fish and prawns and thanked her for allowing us to visit. A long drive lay ahead, but I didn't mind.

Our next exploration would be to Phuket, the largest island in Thailand. I booked our visit to coincide with an important Thai celebration, the festival of light, where floating baskets and banana leaf boats were released into the water to symbolise renewal.

I booked through a travel agent and luckily got a hotel on Patong beach, near to shopping, entertainment and good restaurants.

Gilly decided the last few hours of daylight would be better spent around the pool so she could soak up some sun with an exotic cocktail in her hand. By the time we finished dinner, I was ready for my bed, I did not relish going out, but I knew that after walking off a good dinner, I would change my mind. The hotel concierge gave me instructions on the best places to go and those to stay away from. We set off at a gentle, easy pace to find some nightlife.

Conscious of Thailand's reputation for beautiful girls, transvestites and sex shows, we entered an outdoor area where there were twenty bars of oblong shape with tarpaulin roofs. Around each bar were high stools for customers to sit on. Inside each bar were around twenty young women serving customers, who were predominantly male, and hoping one of them would buy them a drink so they would get a commission. I guided Gilly to a seat at a corner of one bar. When we perched ourselves on bar stools, a beautiful, scantily clad girl took my order. As she put our drinks down, she asked, "Would you like to play Connect 4?" There was no hidden agenda in her request, no sexual hints. I knew she was referring to the board game and, by now, I was good at playing it.

"What's your name?"

"My name is Cassandra. What's your name and madam's name?"

"I am Andrew and this is my wife, Gilly," I said. "I will play, but, Cassandra, these are the rules. We play for beer, if you win I buy you a beer and if I win you buy me a beer. Do you agree?"

Gill gave me a disapproving look, but I knew if I had said a drink, I would get stung for several expensive peppermint cocktails, so beer would be cheaper. Bar girls are experts at Connect 4 and I expected to lose despite being a good player.

"Okay, I agree."

"Get yourself a beer before we start."

She took a bottle of Tsingtao from the fridge and the game from under the bar. Soon after we started, another girl approached Gilly and said, "I like your hairstyle, madam. Where are you from?"

I never heard the answer, I concentrated on the game. Cassandra won the first two, but when I won the next one, we attracted spectators. We played for three hours and stopped with the score at even. I bought Cassandra a few beers on the way and slipped her a hundred-baht note before we left. I felt good about my Connect 4 success.

When we returned to our hotel, a woman pianist was playing romantic music on the piano in the hotel lounge. This put me in a romantic mood, so we relaxed to enjoy these soft, contemporary tunes before retiring to bed.

I woke up needing coffee. We planned to wander around Phuket town in the morning and spend the afternoon on the beach. After dinner, we would return to the beach to join in with the celebration of the festival of light. We set off after breakfast and several cups of coffee.

There were no high-rise apartment blocks on Phuket and most buildings were wooden with upper terraces and arched ground-floor porches. There were plenty of shops with colourful fronts that had louvred windows. They were impressive, but nothing else interested me. I am not a fan of boutiques and artist studio galleries. I knew Gilly enjoyed these places, so I tried to be as patient as possible to allow her time to browse in the shops and look at the art displays. I was disgusted at one point when I noticed an unusual display in a window. There was a demijohn filled with some sort of preserving agent that held a human embryo. I know Southeast Asia has some odd customs, but I hoped that this was not one of them. Thankfully, Gilly had seen enough and wanted to go back to the hotel.

We changed and went to the beach where we ate a plate of noodles, drank a soft drink then soaked up the sunshine. Unlike Gilly, I am not a beach person or an avid reader. I soon fell asleep on the soft sand but for how long, I could not say. Someone disturbed me, and I turned onto my back. The sun had reached a high point, and the rays made me blink, but I could see a mature woman holding a box in her hand, standing close to me. I heard her say, "Massage?"

"Yes, please." I turned back onto my belly.

She kneeled over me to work her expert hands over my body to the soft background music from a transistor radio and I fell asleep again. When I woke up from a beautiful dream, the sun had dropped to a position that showed an hour must have passed. Gilly was engrossed in reading her book because she never moved her head as I took my wallet from her bag and removed a 200-baht note.

The lady smiled and thanked me. I must have paid the correct rate because she turned to leave. After taking a few steps, I called her back and removed another fifty baht and held it out for her to take. "For you, you give a very good massage."

She looked pleased. I also knew if we came to the beach tomorrow, she would look out for me as I was a good customer.

Loy Krathong translates to 'floating basket' and is part of Thailand's festival of lights. It is like the New Year celebrations in the UK and a way of saying goodbye to the old and welcoming in the new. The origins of Loy Krathong vary depending on who you ask. Popular legend says it relates to a beautiful lady of the court of the ancient city Sukhothai who was in love with the king. To get his attention, she constructed an eye-catching boat of lotus leaves and placed a lit candle inside. She floated it down the river and it did catch the attention of the king. He was intrigued by it and started a search to discover the whereabouts of the creator. He found her and they were married.

The Yee Peng Festival in Chiang Mai (also written as 'Yi Peng') is celebrated on the full moon of the twelfth lunar month every year. The belief here is that the rivers are filled to their fullest, and the moon is at its brightest. In Chiang Mai, Loy Krathong is preceded by Yee Peng (the lantern festival), during that festival, people release floating lanterns into the sky. The act of releasing the lantern, and Krathong, symbolises letting go of all the ills and misfortunes of the previous year. Buddhists also believe, if you make a wish when you set off the lantern, it will come true. Whatever the beliefs, the festivals are a time to celebrate with parades, beauty pageants and merriment. I wanted to be part of it.

Thanks to its accessible location, immigrants, mainly Chinese, had come to Phuket to seek their fortune during the tin mining boom of the 19th century. Because of this boom, the Baba (Peranakan) culture was born. The island's multicultural makeup means it has a diverse cuisine from super fresh seafood to some of the best curries outside the Indian subcontinent. After selecting our restaurant, we chose a dinner Phuket-style. I ordered a duck roll starter, spicy prawn and sour soup, red snapper, spicy green papaya salad, tom yum baked chicken and multi-coloured ice cream to finish. We listened to the piano music and downed a few cocktails before setting off to the beach.

The ceremony had already begun, I could see many lotus boats had been launched to drift on the ocean and lanterns filled the sky above us. The beach was quite crowded with people drinking and dancing on the sand to music blasting from several sources. When a street seller approached with the lotus boats, I said, "Sorry, I don't know what to do."

A woman sitting near us called out, "I will show you, and if you buy me a boat, I will get good luck."

She approached with another female reveller and I ended up getting three boats for the price of two. Gilly didn't want one, she wanted to sit and take in the spectacle. I followed the ladies to the water and watched them prepare their boats. Before they launched them, they lit the candles and put gifts into their boats. They made a wish or recited a prayer, before releasing them in the outgoing tide. Now it was my turn.

"Have you got some coins?" one asked. I took the change from my pocket and showed her the coins. She said, "Put them in your boat."

"What now?"

"Now you will be rich, is there anything else you want to put in the boat? Perhaps a gift from your girlfriend?"

"No, that will do."

"Okay, no problem, I will kiss you for good luck and love."

She put her arms around my neck and kissed me full on. She was an attractive woman but wore too much lipstick. I knew I would be in trouble if Gilly saw her kiss me. I staggered back across the sand with my arms around both women. I could tell by the look on Gilly's face and her silence she had seen everything.

We got back to the hotel just before 1am. The piano player was about to finish for the night but stayed to play a couple of numbers just for us. I went to the toilet and on the way back I saw the piano player conversing with Gilly. She saw me and moved away. Gilly turned to me with a scowl on her face.

"What's wrong?" I asked.

"Don't you dare leave me alone again!"

"Sorry, but I didn't know she would kiss me. It's not my fault."

"I'm not referring to the beach, I knew you were enjoying the festival and everything was innocent. I mean her."

"I don't understand what you mean?"

"The piano player fancies me!"

It took all my willpower not to laugh. I knew if I did I would get assassinated in my sleep, so I pleaded, "Sorry, darling, I didn't realise she fancied you. Let's go to bed."

"Yes, I want to go, don't you dare tell any of your work colleagues about this and don't make any funny remarks."

"Promise."

I was off the hook but kept on her good side when we got upstairs.

Having watched the film *The Man with the Golden Gun*, we were both eager to go to Phang Nga Bay and James Bond Island. This Bond movie was played non-stop in many of the bars. They were so proud that the movie had been filmed in this region of their beautiful country. The journey on a long-tail boat took us through the limestone pinnacles, a breathtaking experience. We were given cushions to sit on and a shade protected us from the sun. As the water was calm, the journey took no time at all. James Bond Island itself was very scenic and a fantastic place to take photographs. Gilly smiled all the time as I took her photograph from every vantage point on the small island.

We continued around the bay, stopping at some caves, and lastly at a pearl farm some distance from the shore. The wooden walkways and buildings were picturesque. We were led and seated at a table in one of the wooden buildings as a seafood lunch was included in the tour price. The souvenirs were fairly priced and Gilly wanted to look at the gift shop. I left her to it and I crossed over on a walkway to see the people working with the oysters and making jewellery from pearls. I enjoy a good barter, so I started. Fifteen minutes into my bartering, the lady seller took advice from a large, scar-faced man working with oysters. I was at the crucial point in my negotiations when Gilly came hurrying across, shouting, "Come on, the boat is about to leave."

"Just a minute," I yelled.

The scar-faced man eyed me up and down when I said to the woman, "Last chance, this is my final price."

She went over and spoke to the man. He cursed and came towards the table that displayed the three necklaces I wanted to buy. He bellowed what sounded like, "I'm going to kill you."

I felt like running as he brought the knife up, then stuck it into the table, inches from the necklaces. He grabbed a paper bag and stuck them inside. He sounded upset as he demanded payment. To be on the safe side, I gave him an extra fifty baht and ran for the boat. Still shaking, Gilly gave me a grim look, and I knew I had returned to not being her favourite person.

I got into the boat and sat down. I sat in silence to give her time to cool down. If there had been a backrest, I would have fallen asleep. A few minutes later, it got very dark. The other passengers were getting anxious as they looked up at the sky. I was used to Southeast Asia skies, but I had witnessed nothing as bad as this. I knew a terrible storm was coming when the birds flew past, heading for shelter. Gilly leaned over and put her hand in mine. "Are we going to be all right?" she asked as the rain pelted the boat. I glanced at the boat driver, who seemed unperturbed by the turn in the weather. It surprised me that the boat felt very stable. It must have been built with severe weather in mind and the other passengers were relieved when they saw the boat was coping in the storm. I tightened my grip on her hand, and she looked at me with a smile on her face. "At least it's warm rain."

I returned her smile. "It's been a brilliant outing, and the bonus was the pearls. They were a real bargain."

"You could have been killed getting them." I brushed off this comment by hugging her but agreed with her completely. The storm subsided, and we left the boat wet but happy.

I can't say that Phuket was my favourite island, but it was a memorable, enjoyable visit.

EPILOGUE

Have I lived a good life? Yes, most definitely. If I had my life over again, would I live it differently? Some aspects I would. A more important question to me is what did I learn from working and travelling in other countries, and can this be passed onto others?

My learning curve was long and difficult. It is easy to make mistakes if you think what you have been brought up to believe is true. I discovered that people in the world are not like what I was led to believe. I worked alongside Chinese, Japanese, Malaysian, South American, Arabs and Europeans. I had several Russian friends. None of these people wanted to harm me or my country.

Politicians and rich people are mostly blamed for what we don't like in our world and we think of dictators as evil people. If we close our eyes, ears and minds to the world, it will not change. I cannot make anyone support what I believe and don't want to do that. All I want to say is, after I opened my mind, I gained a more open view of countries and their inhabitants. Perhaps you, my reader, if you do the same, your views and opinions will change. However, it is not much use reading about it, you need to get out there, do it and experience it yourself. Meet the people you think are different to you. Listen to what they have to say and be prepared for surprises. They may be more like you than you imagined, with similar hopes and dreams.

Travelling, for me, has been a wonderful experience, but it can be dangerous. Plan well and expect the unexpected. I did some silly things and took risks I should never have taken. Thankfully, I am still around to tell the tale. Becoming an expatriate differs from just taking a job in another country to earn enough to pay off the mortgage, or just to have a good time. It is about involvement, helping others while helping yourself.

The number of expatriate jobs for westerners has diminished, but there are still plenty of opportunities out there. Teachers and medical staff are in demand. You should have a job lined up before you consider moving. If you don't have a job to go to, then you need funds for three months and an open return ticket. Don't forget to buy good insurance cover. Know the immigration and work permit regulations before you venture out. This would be the only advice I would give. The rest is common sense. Working in Kuwait was my first experience of being part of an international workforce. I broke the rules there and that is not a good thing to do. If I had been arrested and thrown into jail, I would have deserved it. My actions would not have been excused by my pleas from prison, saying I never meant to, and did not hurt anyone with my behaviour.

If you can't afford to travel, you can still meet people from other countries. Millions come to Britain to work and holiday, you only need to talk to them. If you have skills to offer and have proved yourself in previous employment, you could probably get a job in another country. If you are young and just want to take time out, you can still travel and meet people. You have your language to offer. People from all over the world want to learn English. You don't need to be a teacher to help them, just do it.

I look back and ask if I had the right attitude towards others and I can honestly say that for the first few years working in Kuwait, I did not. I was discriminatory and always right, and I didn't care enough about people's feelings. My attitude changed through talking and listening to others. I am not saying everyone else's views are wrong. I am saying if you take the time to meet people you may find that your views will be enhanced.

Looking back on the past forty-plus years, what has stuck in my memory is the comments that have made me think. If foreigners talk about Britain or the British, they normally use the term England or the English. When they generalise, they say 'the West' or 'Westerners'. After a sneaky smoke break during Ramadan, I had a conversation with two Arabs, one from Syria and the other from Jordan. The Jordanian said, "It was the West that created borders." This is certainly true with the division of countries that were made after the Second World War. This made me remember the shepherd boy in the Kuwait desert and the Bedouins.

I ask myself, have I got my facts and understanding wrong? Is what I hear and read in the media a true reflection of the facts? It would be wrong for me to say that torture and bad things didn't happen. I can say that I witnessed no one being mistreated or tortured. I ask, why is it that my students, my friends and colleagues talked to me about their culture, their beliefs, their laws and their government, yet they never mentioned the bad things? What I think was evil were the suffering refugees mourning their loved ones killed by bombs manufactured, delivered and supported by the West.

Working for long periods in different countries has allowed me to see them develop. On my first visit to Singapore in 1982, I saw a country on the brink of success. Today, it is the envy of the world. I watched China grow at a phenomenal pace. A few years after I finished working there, I returned to Shekou and found it hard to believe what had taken place. Booming businesses, world-class shopping and entertainment, low crime rates and few drug problems. People were proud of their success. Countries like China and Malaysia have got much to offer travellers who are adventurous and want to meet people.

I did not stop travelling once my expatriate status ended and have visited many countries since. I enjoyed Iceland, I was there the night they qualified for the 2016 European Nations Cup. A massive TV screen was set up in the main square and it felt like everyone in Reykjavik was there. There was no score, but a lot of noise. It's a magnificent country to visit, and if you visit at the start of the tourist season, it is not so expensive.

More recently, I visited Riga, the capital of Latvia, and loved it so much I had to have a second visit. I had never been to the opera and Gilly, being keen on the arts and the theatre, wanted to go, so I tagged along. The group of people sitting in front of us were friendly and welcomed us. I enjoyed watching *Madam Butterfly* in one of Eastern

Europe's famous opera houses. Another visit worth doing is to fly into Vilnius, the capital of Lithuania, and go by coach from there to Riga. It was easy to arrange through the internet and a very pleasing journey. I want to visit more Eastern European countries, there is so much in the world to see. If you are polite and ask about their country, meeting people is easy.

When I was a boy, the future was the twenty-first century. Now it is the twenty-second. My grandfather was born in the eighteenth century and he taught me much. I followed his principles, some of them I live by today. His advice to me was, "Never disrespect your mother, don't question your father, and follow the orders from your superiors." Except for showing disrespect to my mother, he got the rest wrong. I say to young people; the future is today. Ask questions, then make your mind up about the good and the bad of our world. If you don't, your descendants will suffer. I would like to compliment the young because I believe they will get it right. Most of them will live until they are one hundred, so they have more time than my generation, to meet, learn from, understand and appreciate other countries, their people and culture.

ACKNOWLEDGEMENTS

Wikipedia – For providing my research material.

Delton Training Services – Arnold Almond for providing me with the opportunities to travel.

Sikom Supplies – Jacinta, a fantastic person.

Wong Hee Jiong – For giving me the chance to return to Malaysia.

Tony Xiang – Guide and mentor.

Linda Poulter – A great neighbour.

My other friends and colleagues I have met and worked with for just being good people.

Gilly, for her patience.